The Fifth Impossibility

The Fifth Impossibility: Essays on Exile and Language

NORMAN MANEA

YALE UNIVERSITY PRESS ■ NEW HAVEN & LONDON

A MARGELLOS
WORLD REPUBLIC OF LETTERS BOOK

The Margellos World Republic of Letters is dedicated to making literary works from around the globe available in English through translation. It brings to the English-speaking world the work of leading poets, novelists, essayists, philosophers, and playwrights from Europe, Latin America, Africa, Asia, and the Middle East to stimulate international discourse and creative exchange.

Yale University Press books may be purchased in quantity for educational, business, or promotional use. For information, please e-mail sales.press@yale.edu (U.S. office) or sales@yaleup.co.uk (U.K. office).

Set in Electra and Nobel types by Keystone Typesetting, Inc. Printed in the United States of America.

ISBN: 978-0-300-17995-8 (paperback)
Library of Congress Control Number: 2011943139

A catalogue record for this book is available from the British Library.
This paper meets the requirements of ANSI/NISO Z39.48-1992 (Permanence of Paper).

10 9 8 7 6 5 4 3 2 1

CONTENTS

ACKNOWLEDGMENTS

"Exile," first published in *On Clowns* (New York: Grove Press, 1992).

"A Friend in Berlin," first published in *Chattahoochee Review*, winter/spring 2009.

"Empty Theaters?" first published in *World Policy Journal*, spring 1993.

"Writers and the Great Beast," first published in *Partisan Review*, 1 (1994).

"The Incompatibilities," first published in *New Republic*, April 20, 1998.

"On Clowns: The Dictator and the Artist," first published in *On Clowns* (New York: Grove Press, 1992).

"Happy Guilt," first published in *New Republic*, August 5, 1991.

"Blasphemy and Carnival," first published in *World Policy Journal*, Spring 1996.

"Cioran," first published in *Conjunctions*, 31 (1998).

"Through Romanian Eyes: A Half Century of the *NRF* in Bucharest," first published in *Salmagundi*, spring 2010.

"Berenger at Bard," first published in *Partisan Review*, 4 (2000).

"Made in Romania," first published in the *New York Review of Books*, February 10, 2000.

"An Exile on September 11 and After," fragment from an interview first published in *Partisan Review*, 2 (2002).

"The Walser Debate," first published in *Partisan Review*, 3 (1999).

"Some Thoughts on Saul Bellow," first published in *Salmagundi*, 148/149 (fall 2005–winter 2006).

"The Exiled Language," first published in *The Writer Uprooted: Contemporary Jewish Exile Literature*, ed. Alvin H. Rosenfeld (Bloomington, IN: Indiana University Press, 2008).

"Casa Minima," first published in *Abitare*, 479 (2007).

"Monuments of Shame: Twenty Years after the Berlin Wall," first published in the William Phillips Lecture Series (New York: The New School for Social Research, 2009).

"The Silence of the Eastern Bloc," first published in *Jerusalem Post*, May 5, 1989.

"A Lasting Poison," first published on *Project Syndicate*, November 20, 2008 (copyright © Project Syndicate/Institute for Human Sciences, 2008).

"Crime and Punishment, Refugee Style," first published on *Project Syndicate*, November 15, 2007 (copyright © Project Syndicate/Institute for Human Sciences, 2007).

"Revolutionary Shadows," first published on *Project Syndicate*, September 3, 2011 (copyright © Project Syndicate/Institute for Human Sciences, 2011).

"Against Simplification," first published on *Project Syndicate*, August 15, 2011 (copyright © Project Syndicate/Institute for Human Sciences, 2011).

"Another Genealogy," first published in *Adevarul* (adevarul.ro) in 2011.

"The Dada Capital of Exiles," first published on *Project Syndicate*, August 31, 2005 (copyright © Project Syndicate/Institute for Human Sciences, 2005).

Part I

EXILE

The increased nationalism and religious fundamentalism all around the world, the dangerous conflicts between minorities in Eastern Europe, and a growing xenophobia emphasize one of the main contradictions of our time: between centrifugal, cosmopolitan modernity and the centripetal need (or at least nostalgia) for belonging. We are reminded again and again of the ancient yet constant predicament of the *foreigner*, the *stranger*.

It seems that although he is taught to love his neighbor, man fails to love his neighbor as he loves himself, and fails also to love a stranger like a neighbor. The stranger has always been perceived as different, but often also as a challenge, even a downright threat which undermines the unifying traditional and conventional structures of society. The very premise of the stranger's existence presupposes re-evaluation and potential competition.

We find ourselves in a world in which the concepts of citizen and citizenship migrate far beyond any borders designated at birth—an instant global reality created through intense world air traffic and which, via satellite, invades everyone's home TV screen. And today's world of rapid migration and instantaneous communication is also a world on the threshold of a revolution which it still is, rightly, afraid to acknowledge. I refer to the *genetic revolution* which could create a new meaning for our human destiny. Stupendous means of genetic manipulation may force mankind to reconsider on a dramatic scale its morality and its laws, with unforeseeable consequences for the future of the human race. And if we add to this our conquest of outer space, we must ask ourselves again, what do they mean in this context: the event called *homeland*, the challenge called *foreigner*, the reality called *exile?* And how do we perceive from the vantage point of our unstable, transitory, and pathetic domicile called *human life* the tension between the particular and the general? The modern world faces its solitude and its responsibilities without the artifice of a protective dependency or of a fictive utopian coherence. Fundamentalist and separatist movements of all kinds, the return of a tribal mentality in so many human communities, are expressions of the need to re-establish a well-ordered cohesion which would protect the enclave against the assault of the unknown, of diversity, heterogeneity and alienation. A dismembered Soviet Union and a united Europe are only two obvious examples of the kinds of contradiction that convulse our present and, certainly, will convulse our future. There is, on the one hand, the need to do away with restrictive barriers and achieve a democratic, multinational, economically efficient system; on the other hand there is the desire to replace the totalitarian state, the center of tyrannical power, with a conglomerate of states, each with its own center of power, of uncertain democracy.

Recent debates about the canon in American universities are highly significant for the persistence in our post-industrial modern world of a tension harbored in all of us between centrifugal and what are centripetal, nostalgic tendencies.

When discussing the question of the *foreigner* one should not forget the phenomenons of colonialism and proselytism. Who, in these cases, is the stranger? The colonizer and the missionary, ruling and converting? Or the native, centered in his exotic refuge, historically marginal, for whom assimilation into a unifying civilization is an alienation, an incomprehensible mutilation?

One must ultimately search for substance and meaning in one's own experience, one's own limited biography. The present biography bears a European imprint in a century that has loaded its biography with terrible sufferings. Europe means not only the cradle of Western democracy but also the tragic totalitarian experiments of fascism and communism.

I was five years old when in 1941 I first left Romania, sent to death by a dictator and an ideology. In 1986, at 50, by an ironic symmetry, I left again, because of another dictator, another ideology. *Holocaust, totalitarianism, exile*—these fundamental experiences of our contemporaneity—are all intimately related by a definition of the stranger and of estrangement.

The National Socialist doctrine proposed a totalitarian centripetal model, centered on the idea of a pure race and the nationalist state as the embodiment of the will to power. It was an idea which found many advocates and adherents, since the Nazis came to power through free elections and ruled through a relative coherence of ideal and fact. The National Socialist state embodied the most violent negation of, and the most brutal aggression against, the *stranger*. A suspect citizen with "impure" roots and dangerous opinions, the stranger became the demonic embodiment of evil. The very premises of humanity were placed under a dark question mark. Not only has the Holocaust entirely reversed the terms of a debate about assimilation and the stranger, it has also reiterated, with gloomy precision, as Saul Bellow put it, the old question, with *what* should one be assimilated? With what should one be assimilated, when, in one of the most civilized European countries, the "final solution" could offer only one final and unique assimilation?

And with what could one assimilate oneself if, by a miracle, one survived what today is conventionally, and even commercially, called the Holocaust? To what can the stranger who has survived adapt after hell? The answer to this question is amazingly simple in its obviousness: to live, and nothing but. The survivor readapts to life; looks to live with that impertinence of banality which is life itself. The return, rebirth, and readaptation to the most elementary acts of life are at once pathetic and mysterious, both pitiable and grandiose.

I was destined to be reborn, to grow up, and mature in a society which in a byzantine way combined fascism with Stalinism.

Communism claimed a humanist vision of progress, came to power by revolution and was maintained in power by force. As the contrast between the ideal and the real sharpened, and as the prohibition on revealing and discussing this contrast was enforced, there developed a pathology of ambiguity in which apathy, hypocrisy, and duplicity became the ground rules of assimilation, that is, alienation. The centripetal communist system did not solve, as it had promised, the old contradictions, but supplemented them with new ones. The question of the stranger in a society that estranges everybody from it—while forcing everybody to assimilate their own alienation—takes cover under dubious and sinister masks. Today's nationalist and extremist explosions in the former communist states can surprise only those who have not directly experienced the atomization of a society in which the indoctrination of duplicity began in the cradle.

Bertolt Brecht considered exile "the best school of dialectics." Indeed, the exile, the refugee becomes a stranger as a result of change. By his very existence, the *stranger* is always forced to think about change.

In Berlin, during my first year in the West, I pondered daily the question of estrangement. I thought not only about the internal exile from which I had just escaped, but also about the concept of exile itself. I felt that once again history had spurned my aspirations and was forcing me into an adventure I had not desired. During my entire postwar life I had searched, thanks to reading and writing, for an inner resistance, against often unbearable external pressure. It is hard to believe that in a totalitarian society the "I" could survive, and yet interiority was a mode of resistance. It acted as a center for our moral being, a means of disinterring oneself from the corrupting aggression of the environment, as a hope, however uncertain, for the integrity of conscience. The "I" remains even in the totalitarian environment where external pressures are always dangerous, perhaps especially there, the site of a clash between the centripetal necessity to preserve the secret, codified identity and the centrifugal tendency towards liberation.

During my agonizing Berlin transition, I was overwhelmed by doubts and questions from the past. And precisely because that transition happened in Berlin, I *also* had to confront my ethnicity, as I had already confronted the invective "alien" in my own country. Precisely because the need for a homeland is more acute in those whose right to a homeland has been questioned, losing it also pains them more. On the threshold of a capital decision, facing a new and possibly final dislocation, I had to ask myself once more who I was.

During my stay in Berlin I was often advised to request from the German authorities the recognition of German ethnicity on the strength of my birth in Bukovina and my German linguistic roots. Many of my compatriots had done so and were already comfortably established in their new citizenship. I could have requested German citizenship, like many of my former neighbors and colleagues from Suceava, capital of the region called Buchenland, that is, country of beech trees (though Buchland, country of books, would have also been a fitting name. It is not by chance that the greatest German poet of the last half a century is the Bukovinian-born Paul Celan).

But it so happened that at that time I was told about Transylvanian Saxons and Swabians who proved their *Germannes* (German roots) "legally" through their or their families' belonging to the SS or to the National Socialist Party. I did not have any such proof to show the German authorities; such stories troubled me and all of a sudden notions of identity and ethnicity acquired a new dimension.

The homeland unveils its ambiguous meanings especially during the violence of rupture, which renders more intense the need for self-questioning. The world of estrangement also means alienation from self as well as from others: exile in the most humble quotidian sense as much as in the purest transcendental form. So we may ask why I, guinea pig of two totalitarian systems, fascist and communist, why I, still agonized and bewildered, stumbled along the Berlin Wall terrified by the inevitability of exile. Was it because of the fear of freedom?

For the mature adult, exile tardily reformulates the premise of initiation and becoming, reopens the gate to life's extreme risks and potential, calling into question all the steps of past experience. Moreover, for those prematurely traumatized, for those never truly free from the psychosis of the provisional, from the threat of being thrown once again into the chaos of the unknown, exile suddenly releases all the old fears.

One does not so much lose a precarious and dubious stability as discover oneself to be deeper in the abyss of never-ending instability. The writer, always a "suspect," as Thomas Mann said, an exile par excellence, conquers his homeland, his placenta through language. To be exiled from even this last refuge represents a multiple dispossession, the most brutal and irredeemable decentering of his being, a tragic end. As Primo Levi said about the camp, "to accept the eclipse of the word, signaled the approach of definitive indifference."

This is why, in the spring of 1988, at my first meeting with an American writer who later was to become a close friend, I pompously declared: "For me, another Holocaust has just begun." There was a burning that reached all the way to the center of being, the language, the fathomless depths of creativity.

Five years have passed since I felt that burning, and I must confess that I now feel not only the curse, but also the privilege, of being an exile. I have finally accepted this *honor*, doing so in the name of all that is suffering and epiphany, in the name of loneliness and challenge, of all the doubts and never-ending apprenticeship it implies, for its emptiness and richness, for the unfettering of myself and clash within myself. And also for the wounds of liberty. If I have the strength to repeat Dante, *"L'esilio, che m'e dato, onor mi tegno"* (I hold in honor the exile I was given), I am probably in sympathy with our centrifugal century.

Camus' stranger, Meursault, is estranged not only from his country, religion, and family, but also from the world and himself. He is not part of an ethnic, political or erotic persecuted minority: his loneliness is a way of bringing the absurdity of the human condition to the level of consciousness. The shot that consecrates the expulsion of the stranger called man is nothing but the indifferent explosion of an impersonal sun gone crazy in the absolute banality of an ordinary summer afternoon. The accused K., Kafka's double, forever ready to justify the absurdity of an invisible and implacable justice, is the precursor of the alienation which pervades and defines the modern world.

The stranger consciously or unconsciously is always in potential or partial exile, and all real writers are perpetual exiles of this world even when, like Proust, they hardly leave their room. Their relation to their country of origin is complex and dramatic in ways other than those of simple exile. Thomas Bernhard without leaving his country disavowed it, forbidding the publication of his books in an Austria that refused to analyze and acknowledge its wounds.

The artist is, no matter how paradoxical it may seem, a secret laborer of love. Against all odds, love continues to tempt the artist in exile as well, no matter how sarcastic, or evanescent his work. He daily reinvents the premises of the difficult search; he honors his virtual reader, a stranger similar and dissimilar, with the gift of an exacting love. Thus he can continue his never-ending adventure and humanize his shipwreck wherever he may be.

Translated by Ilinca Zarifopol-Johnston, April 1992

Part II

FROM ONE SHORE TO ANOTHER

A FRIEND IN BERLIN

In the morning, when my gaze meets a new day, I am welcomed by the tree's crown of leaves. Its harmonious connection with time. I watch it, I remember the lesson it offers me. Stability, the everlasting harmony emanated by nature's inner nature.

I look at my watch, I wait. An annoying dependency, maybe, a subterfuge. One should probably depend only on oneself. Never wait for anything, be self-sufficient. Or else, be content with each morning's silent message, the sky, the sparrows, the tree in the courtyard. ... In front of the window, a solid tree with many rich branches keeps vigil. I understand the lesson it offers me. Yet, I look at the watch, I wait for the postman to arrive.

One could ask me whether, in a foreign country, human relations end up acquiring an unnatural sense of drama as a consequence of travel and long-distance correspondence. But I've been familiar with this tense situation for years, since I lived at home. I find it now away from home. I could say that I find myself again, thus, in this unpacified tension.

Partir, c'est mourir un peu (To leave is to die a little) ... Today, for many people, the famous quotation no longer has a melancholy touch.

To travel has become, at least for a part of the planet, a constant possibility and even a fashion. *Partir, c'est changer un peu* (To leave is to change a little) ... A natural need to get away from the familiar, a need for regeneration, for contact with the new. Nostalgia for the exotic and the unknown. A sort of self-deceiving therapy. *Partir, c'est tricher un peu* (To leave is to cheat a little) ... Western standards aren't, however, valid everywhere. One shouldn't forget the contrasts and contradictions of today's world. The geographical areas where the economic and political reality is an impediment to this need for circulation, for emotional and informational exchange, are still numerous.

I left Bucharest on a cold, crisp Sunday. The hours I shared with friends before my departure had taken on the weight of a painful uncertainty. Not only the uncertainty of the departure that could have been stopped at any moment. Another uncertainty, which resulted from the departure itself.

We couldn't or didn't dare give it a name. Long, ashen silences, interrupted at lengthly intervals by the glasses' clinking. In wartime, separation must have been like this. Now there was war only between Iran and Iraq, or in Nicaragua, or who knows in what faraway places, inscribed only on a map, not in memory. We promised each other a happy reunion, with everyone in a better mood.

By comparison with my fellow citizens, my travels began rather early. At five years old, my first expulsion. A journey, from one place to another, in cattle trucks, in carts or on foot; the camp where I was sent. The unknown, death's mark. The second journey sealed another unknown: fifty years old! . . . Another sound of the gong before the curtain rises, another speed of time. Another destination.

The Saturday before departure I canceled all dates. Except one, which I couldn't give up. I waited for my guest in the hall on the first floor, by the elevator. He showed up at twenty past eleven. A short, skinny man with thinning blond hair, a shy smile. Pale face, blue eyes, always moist. His blue uniform was crumpled as always, his hands trembled slightly.

He was staggering under the weight of his bag. He began to take out the piles, he set them down on the radiator. I let him sort his stuff, finish his business. When he was about to leave, I came out of the dark. I greeted him, shook his hand. I asked him to come for a few seconds up to the little apartment on the fourth floor. He seemed surprised, but didn't say anything. He just nodded his small, pointy head. In the elevator, next to one another, I could smell the mixture of sweat, alcohol, and soap that he usually gave off. He was freshly shaven—that didn't happen every day.

I went in, invited him to sit down. On the table were set the bottle and the glasses. I poured. I gave him a glass. We toasted. He didn't ask anything. He just took his heavy bag off his shoulder. Put it down by the leg of the chair. Sat down. Watched me and waited. I didn't know how to start.

For years I had been preoccupied with a text. It kept moving inside me in shifting versions, but I could never just sit down at the desk and begin. Maybe because it would have been finished in several impatient, grandiloquent sentences. It needed a narrative structure fit for a longer, coded text, in order gradually to develop the true complicity between character and theme, between subject and object. The object was more than just an object. Something virtual, an obsession. Every day, the character ran down the stairs from the fourth floor all the way to the first to open, at a certain morning hour, the gray box. The unwritten narration had a title, "Defining the Object." I knew the premise it needed in order to function, how the relation between man and object would gradually have come to life until their nebulous merging—a man who someday, after his death, becomes destiny, and an object that gives him daily servings and messages about this destiny, at the time still a work in progress.

The man before me couldn't have understood such idiocies. I had once asked him how he'd become a "mail carrier." He explained it to me: he'd been a carpenter, he'd gotten ill with a lung ailment. Stayed a long time in hospitals, then changed his job.

It wasn't easy to carry day after day, morning and afternoon, rain or shine, in cold weather and through muddy streets, that heavy bag full of newspapers and envelopes. Quite different to carpentry, which he couldn't continue. Money wasn't too bad. The addressees to whom you bring a letter or money or a notice for a package give you something or other. When you have a certain relationship with people, you "carry on" their lives.

Talking to him about the magic box would have frightened him. Telling him that he stored the messages from the Big Unknown whom we strive to find a name for, babbling absurd, codified pseudonyms, I would destroy any hope of congeniality. I filled the glasses again; we toasted. I confessed I would be gone for several months. I asked him to give the mail, as always when I was absent, to my old neighbor living next door. He downed the glass in one gulp. He liked to drink, I knew it. Then he took a piece of pound cake. He watched me cunningly, smiling. I filled his glass once more. He wiped his lips with his palm. "Far away?" "Not that far away. Now the world is small, everything is close." "Yes, I understand. I meant, beyond?" "Yes, I'm going to the West." "I see . . . . Only several months? Several months, you say? Well, now!". . . "Well, sure! How long should I stay? I have to come back home." "Now, it's none of my business. I'm just talking, no offense. I'll leave the mail with the neighbor, the teacher. Not to worry. Don't you give it a thought. Just look after yourself. I mean, see how things are going over there, think about it. The mail will be taken care of, it's no big deal. That should be the least of your problems . . ."

He bowed, thanking me clumsily. Took his bag, edging toward the door. He had no idea how important his presence had been each and every day.

BERLIN! The horror-name of my childhood. It was from Berlin that what had happened to me and my family had come. And wasn't what we lived through after the war also a consequence of it? The journey could be a pilgrimage to the place that was a crossing for one's existence and that of so many others.

I arrived at noon. Snowstorm, cold. The city rose amid arrows and ribbons of neon. Well-lit, warm apartment. I went out to orient myself. Rathenauplatz. I recalled Musil's character in his great novel . . . First contact with the city. *Partir, c'est brûler un peu?* (To leave is to burn a little?)

I'm more interested in people than in houses, in streets rather than in monuments, in the atmosphere of a small, picturesque pub, rather than in contemplating statues or public events. I've probably lost interest in, and respect for, history. Have I ever truly had it? In childhood, no one told me the stories one usually tells children, I had no chance to like them. They bore me, I didn't learn this kind of escapism early on. I would be content if I meant nothing to it too, if it let me alone, after bothering me for so long.

And yet, one evening I went to see the Reichstag. Then I arrived at Checkpoint Charlie. History embodied? Two eras were in dialogue within me, through me. A dialogue I would rather have forgotten. At least for a while, even for a very short while. The need to forget, its impossibility.

After several weeks of isolation, I looked for the people. Berlin gradually came to life, unveiling its rhythm, its diversity. I was stimulated by the city's contrasts, not only by its heterogeneous population and by its political and administrative division. The peacefulness of the neighborhoods spread amidst woods and lakes, pastoral enclaves with a look of imposing solidity and the comfort of civilization bestowed upon them by well-being. In contrast, there was the bohemian vibration of the city's vivacious downtown.

But I fell in love with Berlin's population as a whole the night I watched them at a circus show. They instantly became ideal partners of gags and mime. The wonderful Roncali evening conquered even the most skeptical of spectators. I'd heard so many times: "Berlin is not Germany," "Hitler conquered this city only after heavy fighting," "What is livelier today in Germany one discovers in Berlin, in its tension, complications and ferment. . .".

They often talk here of the dark Nazi period, but also of the ambiguities of the postwar political situation. I listen in silence. "At a certain human level, individuals understand each other instantaneously, you know. No matter what language, color or experience," the German teacher who works with the foreign guests says. My librarian friend adds: "Don't idealize. If you had to work, live the daily grind, you'd soon run into cunning, meanness, and envy."

Berlin puts me in an advantageous position: I don't have to discover the routine; I can simply look for possibilities.

"We hope you are over the pre-departure turmoil and that this year will be therapeutic," my friend writes from Italy.

"The situation has worsened. Mother can no longer see at all. She often has angina attacks. To take her from her bed to the bathroom takes a quarter of an hour. The mail arrives with great difficulty. We received the postcard you sent forty days ago only yesterday," Father writes from sweet Bukovina.

"First of all, we'd like to send you our warm greetings and to wish you the best on the occasion of your visit to Berlin and for the New Year. I can't understand it that you didn't know that we signed a contract for your book," my new friend from Zürich writes.

Yes, the letters have begun to arrive. They are different from what they used to be. Less tense, it seems, less codified.

He who arrives with a fellowship from Eastern Europe isn't the same as his French, English, Swiss, or Brazilian colleague. No, it isn't just the letters that have a different vibration. The everyday tension comes from the successive, alternating shocks of normal life. The powerfully lit streets, the heated houses, the buses arriving as scheduled, the numerous stores full of merchandise. That is to say, the very attractive packaging. A friend told me: "The most important industry here is that of packaging."

Yet, aside from the great ease and comfort, is man still alone and vulnerable? How does he deal here, in his freedom, with uncertainty, illness, demagoguery, greed—so many of reality's sad aspects? The similarities between systems, as well as their differences, are being worked out in a dialogue that is far from reassuring for the future of today's world.

The comings and goings at night on the Ku'damm, the burlesque joy around Württemberger Plaza or on Europa-Center. The charm of the little square of Savigny Platz. The Parisian street corner with its little garden in front of the Kurbe theater. The picturesque Kreuzberg oriental ghetto. The distant quiet reigning around the mansions of Grünewald. The train and the little pleasure boats crisscrossing the city. The natural frame of daily life. In the end, an inner landscape. A sign that I am adapting, maybe. Or maybe the beginning of a real relationship with the surroundings? Discussions about Nazism and prewar Berlin, about protecting the environment, and the student movements of 1968, about glasnost and Reagan, and the modernist monuments on Ku'damm. About literature and Boris Becker's latest tennis game, about the marriage crisis and the Queen of England's visit. I watched the Berliners on the street and at the theater, at outings and in offices and buildings, but also in parks, joyful and naked under the stingy sun of a crippled summer.

I won't declare theatrically, like so many officials: "I am a Berliner." If I were, I would probably see its difficulties and contradictions more clearly, I would find a less superficial, more critical and articulated, reason for my attachment to it. The city's spirit would attract me not only with its lights and movement, but also with its opposite face of shadows and failures, wounds and howls.

One beautiful July afternoon, in the Rathaus-Schönberg bus station, a young woman answered my question with unusual graciousness. She took a map from her purse to show me the place where I wanted to go. In the bus we sat next to each other. I understood that literature meant something to her. I waited until she got off to accompany her . . . I lost her, like a slender apparition, as always happens to me with promises I don't know how to keep, how to appropriate. She had told me, however, that she lived in Wilmersdorf, but there was no way I could send her a copy of my book, coming out here this fall. Was this brief encounter a sign of acceptance by the city?

One morning, my friend paid me a visit. He rang the doorbell. I looked at my watch. It was barely past ten. I rapidly brushed my hair with my fingers, I straightened my collar. I rarely received visits, and the time was not convenient.

I opened the door. An elegant gentleman. Gray pants, dark blue coat. Thin-framed glasses, matching his delicate, open face.

"My name is . . ."

The name didn't seem familiar.

"I am your postman."

"Oh yes! Yes, of course, yes, yes." I understood, suddenly.

He asked me what country I came from, for how long, whether I was enjoying Berlin. Oh, very nice, yes, yes, very nice of this gentleman to inquire about me! I thanked him. He smiled, as if wanting to add something. He asked me how I pronounced my name. If the accent fell on the first a or the second a. Then he smiled again.

"I've noticed you receive a lot of mail. From many places."

Indeed, I received many letters, and waited for them all impatiently. Yes, the day began with my reading my correspondence. I can't help it, every day I watch for the mail. It makes me glad, all the more so that I now know the one who opens the doors to my new day.

"I'd like, if possible, to ask you to save the stamps from your letters for me. I'm a collector, you know . . ."

I keep a vigil by my window, watching for the little yellow car. It always arrives around ten o'clock. It stops right in front of the house where I live. A slender gentleman, always wearing the same clothes, gets out. Gray pants, navy blue coat, blue shirt, blue tie. Thick hair with a nice trim, glasses. His controlled gestures have a certain elegance and cheerfulness. I see him stop to answer some old lady or young man, whose questions are very likely always the same. He's never in a hurry, chatting with them, even if they take more of his time than necessary.

On his shoulder he carries a bag that's always full, and in his hand a pile of envelopes. He always begins his round with the house where I live. Maybe because several foreign guests live here, so there are more letters. The day begins around ten o'clock.

The little yellow car, parked right in front of the house, under my window. "Schreib mal wieder" ("Write again") says the car door. The polite, refined gentleman gets out, cheerful, but in no hurry. He could be anything: a professor, an engineer, *Steuerberater,** a cello player, anything.

He takes out the pile of envelopes, puts the bag on his shoulder. Looks once again inside the car to see if he left anything. Closes the car door. Now he's in the courtyard. I'm waiting to see him get out. I go down, open the mailbox. The urn with the ashes of the days. The lottery box from the Devil or God, from the police or a lover. A sentence for life or a death threat. A connection to others or to the

*A tax consultant.

earth or the sky. To chance and destiny. To myself. To myself, of course. Am I writing these letters to myself to keep the rules of the game going? Could it be that the beings inside me are in dialogue via the unlikely addressee that I am, thus fueling daily life for their own fun? A dark, childish game. Or maybe a naïve author's cruel script, with tears, hugs, laughs and pratfalls.

A foreigner, here? A foreigner or estranged anywhere, in the end. I have found here all my old habits. I carry them with me anywhere. *Partir, c'est rester en même temps* (To leave is to stay at the same time) . . .

He just went out. He never shuts the gate. He goes out, cheerful, the way he comes in. He never takes the trouble to push the gate shut behind him, not even lightly, with his shoulder. A bizarre carelessness for such a careful, proper man. I watched him every day, anxious to see if I was wrong. No, I wasn't. He would cheerfully open the gate, enter the courtyard, slowly cross the paved alley, enter the building, come out. The gate always stayed wide open behind him. I wonder who this gentleman is, whether the mission given him by chance reaches its goal too easily, in such trivial disguise.

I see him get out of the car again, take out his bag, heading for the gate. I go down, eager to welcome him in the lobby. He is already at the door, facing me, near the labels indicating the names to which he dispenses a daily serving of chance.

He greets me, I answer. I smile, he smiles. I show him the red coupon: the notice to pick up a package.

"When did you receive it?"

"I found it yesterday in the mailbox."

"That means you weren't home, that you were supposed to go to the post office to pick up your package."

"I was home all day."

"Well, my lazy colleague doesn't want to bother to go all the way up to the fourth floor. It's easier to throw a notice in the mailbox! Then it's up to the resident to go to the post office and pick up his package . . . I'll take care of it. I'll send the notice to the post office and they will send you your package here."

He fills in the form for me. What can he think about someone who is addicted to his mailbox? A home, a minuscule home we are still permitted. The urn with the days' ashes. A coffin of hope . . . A box full of lottery tickets.

He would probably answer me that as a foreigner it's normal to be dependent. But I was the same back home! I feel like shouting.

Should I tell him about the text I've never managed to write? I kept looking for a title. "84"? 1984. The number of my destiny, my mailbox number, there, in the apartment building where I used to live. Or the title of a famous book? In the end . . . yes, in the end I kept Defining the Object . . . Just a title, nothing more, not a line.

The text, I never wrote it, though I had found the formula: the repetition, slightly modified, of a half-a-page text, the character at different ages simultaneously hiding and unveiling the object in question.

"How would you define such an object?"

I never asked him. He was filling out the form, with a very preoccupied air. Then he began to distribute the envelopes into the mouths above the names inscribed on each box. He moved from one to the other, throwing in the bait. He moved to another one, still watching me. When he finished, he thanked me for the stamps. Each Saturday I hang on my mailbox an envelope with the stamps I cut out during the previous week.

He was about to leave when, I don't know why, I extended my

hand to shake his. He seemed surprised, smiled. We shook hands. When he was by the door, he turned back. He seemed to remember something.

"Have you been to the Wall?"

I didn't answer.

"Have you been to the Wall?" he repeated, with his hand still on the doorknob.

"Oh, of course . . . Right after I got here. For us, in Eastern Europe, it's a special moment. We've seen it from the other side. For Eastern Europe, you know, it's more than a simple . . . I mean, it has a special . . . It isn't simply emotional, it's . . ."

I'd spoken fast, I couldn't find my words. He made a gesture, as if he knew already or as if this story had no interest for him, he'd heard it too many times.

"No, I wasn't speaking of our Wall. I was thinking of something else, another wall. I was asking about the Wailing Wall . . ."

Of course, the Berlin Wall. The Wailing Wall, of course. As if someone had guessed behind my words some other words I hadn't uttered. As if our friendly conversation was a code for another one, tangled, old, unending . . .

He noticed my bewilderment and hurriedly explained:

"I saw, from the stamps you've given me, that you receive letters from Israel too. I thought that maybe . . . I wouldn't have wanted to . . . I was just wondering if . . . I would have liked . . ."

This time, it was he who couldn't find his words. I answered briefly: "Yes, of course. I have. I have been there too."

He seemed satisfied with the short answer, didn't insist. I watched him as he left. Then I watched the sky, the sparrows in the tree in front of the house. The tree, its quiet faithfulness.

Translated by Daniela Hurezanu, winter 2009

EMPTY THEATERS?

Following a lengthy decomposition, the communist system in Eastern Europe collapsed, but the collapse failed to bring about an equally sudden democratic and prosperous normality. After the decades-long confinement by totalitarianism, why can't people, and East Europeans in particular, grasp the true dimension of freedom, why can't their actions reflect the demands of this great moment? Why are honesty, courage, tolerance, and cooperation stifled by demagogy, cynicism, and brutality? The simplest answer, as Thomas Mann put it, is that freedom is something more complex and delicate than force.

After their flight from Egypt, the ancient Jews needed to wander through the desert for forty years in order to rid themselves of the habits of slavery and give birth to a truly free generation capable of making their dreams habitable. The perplexity shown by many at the uncertain, often explosive, situation in Eastern Europe seems a form of naïvety, if not arrogance. Similar historical events should allow us to understand the burden of guilt, compromise, and revenge; the confusion, the identity crisis, the displacement, the void that liberation from a repressive authority somehow has to fill. Indeed, it is preposterous to expect democratic manners from those who are deprived of their daily bread.

We are not talking here only about the consequences of the perverse decades of communism. First and foremost, we are talking about human nature. Let us recall what happened in France in 1946, 1947, and 1948; that is, in the years after a relatively brief period of occupation. Paraphrased below are the entries for the period taken from the Jean Gilder-Boissière diary, which, when published in 1950, provoked a scandal. A bottle of wine that costs 42 francs wholesale is sold for 568 francs in a good restaurant. More and more people are nostalgically referring to the time of the occupation, when life was better and even the theaters were offering shows of a higher quality. A famous publisher who brought out a pro-Nazi magazine during the war has founded a publishing series under the aegis of Maurice Thorez, the General Secretary of the French Communist Party. Albert Camus has resigned from the newspaper *Combat,* enraged that only the tabloids and party newspapers can surmount the economic squeeze. Three hundred armed communists attack the printing offices of their own newspaper, *L'Humanité,* where workers, protesting about their meager wages, barricaded themselves in. An underground SS organization that was falsifying papers to prove that the leaders of the French Resistance were actually active accomplices of the Germans is uncovered. Groups of former accomplices are demanding the rehabilitation of Pierre Laval on the ground that the former collaborationist prime minister was executed under circumstances unworthy of a civilized justice. And many of the collaborationists consider themselves not only victims, but also the new prosecutors, moral sternness proving to be much more widespread among those with guilty consciences.

A quote from December 28, 1946: "During the occupation, 29,000 people were shot in France. Of them, 75,000 [*sic*] were communists. After the liberation, the most profitable business was to sell Resistance certificates to . . . former collaborationists." Or, as a Surrealist Romanian poet who had been a communist in the underground stated after the war, "There were so few of us; yet we turned out to have been so many."

There is a difference between a wartime occupation of four years and the decades-long siege of Eastern Europe, but there are also some similarities. Today, we are witnessing two simultaneous, familiar, and opposite trends: a laborious regeneration and a powerful reassertion of past conditioning. Clearly there are still many obstacles to the East's integration into the system of Western democracy. A certain sense of discouragement is understandable.

But the East European stage is not empty. Though free of the official masquerade and lacking the fervor of the socialist underground, today the stage is noisier and more contradictory than ever. It is crowded by new actors, scenarios, and a new play of masks—a dramatic, frenzied, and striking enactment of the whole human tragicomedy.

Fragmentation, dispersion, all-too-rapid conversions, and annihilating excesses can produce a misleading sensation of emptiness and motionlessness. The one-party system provided its subjects with a shared obsession with survival—sought through opportunism—and the avoidance of confrontation.

The communist East also provided the West with a common obsession with survival, whether through compromise and even complicity with the East or in opposition to it.

Eviction from Utopia

A decisive interdiction in Paradise was the Creator's, the Censor's forbidden fruit. The Bible calls this first taboo "the tree of knowledge." Contemplative and submissive, if not downright apathetic, man could have remained forever in the slumbering kingdom of apparent perfection, but this would have annihilated him. It would have meant death, or, even worse, the monstrosity of ignorance. The voyage into the unknown and the contradictory, the imperative to know the world and oneself—the beginning of consciousness—meant individuality, the individual expression of liberty and responsibility. Defying the unique and supreme authority meant eviction from heaven, from utopia. Becoming free, taking the risk, was naturally followed by a crisis of identity, of affiliation; a crisis of self-definition that was supposed to include, but also to go beyond, the very act of taking the risk. Left alone with the world and with himself, mortal, hence real, man was forced to earn his daily bread "by the sweat of his brow." In order to overcome the crisis, which also was the first economic crisis, he had to become active, rational, and pragmatic. But before long, moral guidance was needed to save mankind from a Hobbesian struggle for survival.

In this respect, the Ten Commandments are more than the reflection of moral urgings; they are social rules as well. Compared to the first and unique interdiction, these rules brought diversification and differentiation, since they referred to relationships among humans and not to the relationship with a sole supreme and exterior authority. As the basis of relationships among all people, irrespective of rank and origin, they were the expression of an incipient democratic evolution.

Who Am I?"

The biblical narrative offers us man's first vision of himself and of Divinity, each reflected in the image of the other. Thus, history is the history of human risk. It tells us about the *risk beings* who define themselves and acquire their identity by each of their undertakings. It is not accidental that in Eastern Europe—where a move away from the apathy of submission is taking place—we are witnessing not only an identity crisis, but also, and all too often, a need to identify with new myths. This need for new myths means a need for exterior spiritual protection from the existing confusion, from loneliness and the ever more feverish competition for survival or power.

This is also true in the West. Free of its outside enemy, the West finally has a chance to analyze its own crisis; the crisis of the code of coexistence among people and between people and nature. We are living in a world in which liberty and responsibility have to be redefined and regained at every moment. A world of secular relativity in which mass uniformity and depersonalization often appear as the outcome of "democratization," of a mass-media culture. A global, post-industrial, perhaps already postmodern, society. More then ever before, the question "Who am I?", as the Czech writer Bohumil Hrabal recently reminded us, becomes essential to understand the immediate past and also to divine the future.

"Who am I?" is also a prerequisite to understanding what has happened in this diseased century, threatened on the one hand by totalitarianism and on the other by the growing violence of aliena- tion; threatened by the sharp conflicts between the traditional need to belong and the estrangement of our modern world. This is a question we need to ask in order to understand both the world of lies that "true socialism" turned out to be and the world of money (as consumption-oriented capitalism, in its present, late phase, has often been defined).

This question "Who am I?" is inevitably linked to the question "Who are we?" What is this New World toward which the eyes of those liberated from the oppression of utopia turn, a utopia that kept promising them a New World again and again? The Western world is not the paradise imagined by those who understand democracy only as well-being, comfort, and free will; it is a *human* world, both imperfect and perfectible, much as the inferno of tyranny was just another *human* product, imagined, built, endured, and challenged by human beings. The benefits and dangers, the chances and de- privations of our fast-changing world cannot be understood without observing those human beings who populate it with their wishes, myths, and confusion. And maybe there is no one who knows the differences between those two worlds better than the exile. In this respect, the exile from the East is a precursor in the experiment in which the countries in that part of Europe are just now em- barking upon.

Like Adam, the exile has gone through the exhilaration and anxiety of liberation, the nostalgia of belonging, and the shock of estrangement. He has been reborn, by the "sweat of his brow," from anonymity and the trauma of the unknown. Step by step, neurosis after neurosis, he has regained a broader meaning of the world and of otherness, a stricter sense of responsibility, a more acute awareness of death, hence of reality. He has gained a more active and lucid understanding of the ephemeral, of limitation and unlimited aspirations. He is the *risk being* par excellence, who has finally accepted the suffering, honor, and privileges of exile. Exile permanently instructs one in change, in transition. The exile becomes, one might say, a kind of expert in transition.

Taking the Risk

Not so long ago, I was asked what is the most important theme for the East European writer today. I responded by saying that the most challenging literary task seems to be scrutinizing the distance between the core of the victim and the core of the oppressor. The essential theme, not only for art at the end of this century, but also for understanding a present that defines its uncertainties by recycling the past, could be the study of this distance. More precisely, the study of the dynamic, and frequently ambiguous, relationship between the center of the victim, if such a center does exist, and the center of the oppressor.

This is a burning topic for the East European writer now, when, burdened by unhappy decades of illusions, suffering, and frustration, East Europe seeks to revive its withered hopes. It is a pressing topic for the Western writer as well, in a time when competition becomes synonymous with selfishness, computerization with depersonalization, profit with idealism, vulgarity with power, and oppression with success. This is a theme that especially appeals to the exiled writer, who has broken connections with both worlds and is aware of the differences and similarities between them, the tension of their dialogue, the dangers that threaten them both.

The *risk-being* was expelled from the inertia of Paradise because of his knowledge and conscience. A human being defined by the risk of individualization—and art is the very exponential function of risk, of creative freedom—remains essentially vulnerable. Vulnerable and contradictory, the human being is, however, defined by an ever-present instinct for self-preservation. Self-preservation on the one hand, and the need for risk on the other, have always determined our tense existence. Pushing the artificial, the product of human creation, to its very limits, modern society has also increased to unimaginable proportions the likelihood of risk and, paradoxically, the means of self-preservation as well.

The tension between the inborn instinct for self-preservation and the irrepressible need to risk is more obvious than anywhere else in the present transition to a new millennium. The writer in exile understands these conflicts because he has experienced them. To him, the New World has become the whole world, the stage for all his fellow humans from all corners of the earth.

In this era of globalization, exile itself has become an emblem, no matter whether it is experienced by someone in his own country, his own room, and in his own language, or outside and far removed from them. The moment we are all experiencing is convulsive. The theater of the world is convulsive, as is the time in which we live, no matter where we live. We are all exiles.

Freedom and beauty are what each of us manages to draw from the vast realm of the possible and turn into a palpable accomplishment. As André Breton said, "Beauty will either be convulsive or it will not be at all."

Spring 1993

WRITERS AND THE GREAT BEAST

As it rushes to an end, this century, more than any other, could be called the century of the intellectuals. When its beginning and end are compared, whether on a mundane or a fundamental level, pivotal developments are immediately obvious; the mind's achievements in science and technology; the deep schism in art; and the radical upheaval that has shaken the individual and society.

Spectacular accomplishments and extreme dangers have accompanied the dramatic worldwide expansion of uncertainty in this new era. The year 2000 approaches replete with all the manmade means of planetary catastrophe. Although the macabre play of man's imagination has anticipated this catastrophe, his conscience is inclined to relegate it to an uncomfortable side road.

The fear at the threshold of this new millennium differs from its tenth-century counterpart in which an end-of-the-world psychosis was linked to the gods and fate. In a desacralized world, as Heisenberg said, "man stands on this earth only in relation to himself." It seems as if mankind is being herded onto an enormous ship, or, more exactly, into a large metal hull with a compass that does not point north but towards the mass of the ship itself. . . . And the genetic revolution could well result in a horrible apotheosis through its creative artifices and manipulations.

Given the widespread crises jeopardizing our transition to a completely different world, the "crisis of the ideal" is no longer a problem simply for intellectuals—whom dictionaries usually define as more interested in thinking and understanding than in feeling or acting. It is a problem for us all. Moreover, this crisis is not merely a question of overpopulation and the arms race, of under- and over-development, of fanaticism, environmental destruction, and the arrogance of power, but of the deep imbalance in human existence that unleashes all of those. When he suggested that the banality and chaotic absurdity of daily existence cannot be overcome without a transcendent goal, Einstein was referring to the centripetal force of the idea. The collapse of the totalitarian communist system and the threat of new forms of totalitarianism—whether of a religious nature (incited by Islamic fundamentalism, for example) or a nationalist one—again raise the question of transcendent "ideals" with heightened urgency. Without such ideals, man falls prey to emptiness or self-destructiveness. And yet, he apparently does not know how to defend himself effectively against the cynical and catastrophic manipulations of these ideals. This is not only a question for philosophers, who were once called the functionaries of mankind; it is a question for every conscious inhabitant of the present in which the past parodies its tragedies as farces.

When Marx called us to take leave of the past with a laugh, he surely did not suspect what "real socialism" would look like, or that its citizens would feverishly come to desire its complete destruction. The world's first socialist state—which was to be the Soviet Union and not Germany, as many socialists believed at the beginning of the century—dissolved before the new millennium could herald its surprises. Foolish history once again aimed its sarcasm at the dreams of perfection and the rationalized schemata of its imperfect guinea pigs. The abandonment of socialism was not brought about by a "leap forward" into communism, where laughter would probably have been rationed and collectivized; rather, it occurred as a "regression" to capitalism, the first phases of which Marx himself had analyzed and chastised with unparalleled acuity.

The euphoria of this abandonment followed hard on the heels of a punishing transition. Perhaps abandoning socialism requires a painful step back before it can promise two steps forward. The transition, with its misery, confusion, and humiliation, has provoked pity rather than laughter. But above all it has inspired well-founded concern—as much in those who must endure the hardship of the transition as in outside observers. After the utopia, the masquerade, and the terror or totalitarianism, a post-communist kitsch has sardonically perfected the tragicomedy of our tormented century. Whether they are artists, scientists, or even farmers, intellectuals are confronting the parody that predestined them to be heroes, aware now of their roles in the farce.

Poverty. Profiteering. Demagogy. Diversionary tactics. Rebirth. Renewal. Hope. The burden of the past: mistrust, guilt, vengefulness. The confusion of the present: new hierarchies and new truths, and, with them, the uncertainty of the future. The isolation and instability of freedom threaten the ease which succeeded the routine of subjection, a routine which also brought the comfort of fatalistic apathy. Freedom is what each of us is able to realize out of our fleeting assumptions. Supporters of democracy are more often motivated by the prospect of wealth than by the complicated rules of respecting individuality or fostering pluralism. Now, an astonishing number of "heroes" have already replaced an enormous number of opportunists under the dictatorship. Former activists or political functionaries—now unscrupulous businessmen—hold in contempt their old comrades who insist on dreaming of restoration. Former dissidents have blossomed into shrewd politicians or remain relicts of a reverse Stalinism. Impassioned politicians creep off into introspection and silence; timid loners are promoted as the champions of the hour. Impromptu liberals are confronted with old and new conservatives, extremists, idealists, ideologues. Old and new profiteers, the formerly and the newly naïve, stir up the great and by no means innocent masses, who in turn regenerate their own adaption instincts.

Those who for years were forced to suffer through tedious lessons in Marxism and political economics discover that capitalism, not socialism, teaches that "existence determines consciousness" and that the workers of the world never did unite, precisely because they were interested primarily in their own material lives, which differed enormously from one country to the next. Should we still be surprised by the recent threats of extremism under different banners or by the potential explosiveness of discontent that could pave the way for new forms of dictatorship? After the failed experiment in "abolishing man's exploitation of man," its survivors will be subjected to another painful experiment: the transition from state ownership of evil to individual and corporate ownership of good and evil.

However fantastic its stagings may often have seemed, totalitarian society was not an unearthly or demonic deviation, as many believe, but a human reality. The pulse of totalitarianism beats in man (and can be detected in the family, in schools, at work, and so on); otherwise, it could not have (and cannot) become an ideology and a system of government. "Social engineering" grew out of dissatisfaction with, and criticism of, democracy's imperfections and was claiming to be a transcendent ideal. We should keep in mind that Hitler was elected to power in Germany at a time of acute industrial and political crises; that the Russian Revolution of October 1917 did not erupt in the most gruesome period of tsarism, but under Kerensky's brief democratic government. As Lenin said, every revolution needs five minutes of freedom.

The fact that the first free elections in Algeria in 1992 gave fuel to the fundamentalists reminds us that the Ayatollah Khomeini first came to power when the Shah began to "liberalize" his rule. Are we allowed to see Nazism as a trivialized and diseased "Romanticism"? Or only as racist nihilism that led to the Holocaust? Should we consider communism a demagogic "humanism," or only a simplistic rationalism that is subservient to tyranny, culminating in the Gulag? When Stalin called writers the "engineers of the human soul," he styled, condensed, and revealed an entire pedagogy of terror, justifying its horror with a utopian vision.

It is no coincidence that intellectuals have experienced with particular intensity the contradiction between the "ideal" and the critical intelligence that reveals the ideal's weaknesses. While many intellectuals from the East can be reproached with opportunism (one hardly needs an especially keen eye to recognize the perverted ideal in profane socialist reality), many intellectuals from the West simultaneously served as their accomplices in the free world by preserving, in a corrupt fashion, an already compromised communist ideal. They transferred their dissatisfaction with the imperfections of the democracy in which they lived and whose privileges they enjoyed to a specious ideal. Yet it would be as false once again to hold intellectuals entirely responsible for the "totalitarian compromise," as it would be to credit them with all anti-totalitarian heroism. There were enough blue-collar, as well as more or less influential white-collar, workers in the East and in the West, who played the same double-dealing game. Situations must be judged within their historical contexts, for only thus do they gain the complexity and clarity that justify analysis. Those rushing to condemn or glorify today should be reminded that, for the totalitarian regime, an intellectual was, at best, a fellow traveler, and for democratic society he remains an odd, marginal figure.

Lorca and Mandelstam symbolize the martyrdom of thousands of artists and intellectuals. This does not excuse those who collaborated with power out of naïvety, fear, or greed. And many did—from all social strata. The totalitarian system sadistically manipulated basic preconditions of humanity and relied on the apathy, confusion, egoism, and enslavement of the masses. For intellectuals, the pitfalls of intimidation, temptation, and remuneration were also constructed upon basic human preconditions. It is hardly surprising that nonetheless intellectuals stood up before those who opposed tyranny, either in secret or in open confrontation. They simply followed their vocation. Freedom is in fact the main precondition for intellectual works in which the ideal and critical intelligence reinforce each other. They are ultimately inseparable.

Politics is obsessed with power. Creativity is synonymous with freedom. The totalitarian state represents absolute power; under a totalitarian system, art is not only a provocation, as it is for any form of authority; it is, purely and simply, the *enemy*. Remaining honest and maintaining one's moral and artistic integrity, under continual surveillance and censorship, under the pressure of constant risk and growing taboos, requires a silent, lonely heroism. There were many clear instances of defiant courage, however: some artists and scientists rebelled against the terror, boldly opposed the opportunism of their surroundings, and overcame their own mistrust of rhetoric by explicitly opposing tyranny.

In a political system that considers culture one of its greatest weapons and honors its artists with astonishing privileges and punishments, the writer is beset with traps, intended in the long run to compromise and destroy his identity. So he learns to protect himself even from the pitfalls of his own thought. While "bourgeois" governments had considered them with relative indifference, in the first years of the so-called "people's regime," many intellectuals were surprised and flattered with unexpected attention, and many fell victim to their seduced vanity. Only after a long time and much bitter experience did they realize that the respect they had been granted represented merely another form of surveillance and that their privileges were the reward for their complicity. The nightmarish first decade after the war, with its militant Stalinist motto, "With us or against us" (which potential prisoners translated as "Everyone who is not with us is against us—and so will be destroyed"), has been engraved, to prolonged and inhibiting effect, on people's memory in the East. The number of those in league with power was not small. The natural instinct of self-preservation also functioned in borderline cases—especially in borderline cases. When Kádár's slogan was recast in the 1980s as "Everyone who is not against us is with us," the entire metabolism of survival had changed. Yet the essence of totalitarian pedagogy remained just as false. "Real socialism" was, in the end, an endless education in deceit.

The extensive pathology of the system, expanded and refined over four decades, both supported and gradually undermined it. The unfathomable extent of the system's structural decay became apparent only after the edifice collapsed, exposing the rubble behind its façade of jargon and freeing the prisoners held captive by its duplicity. The chronic deformation of existence requires a meticulous diagnosis. If those who observed this process firsthand have truly seen through it, seen how it insinuates itself within one and takes root, they should be the first to reject the cheap, shabby rhetoric of oversimplified verdicts with which totalitarianism has indoctrinated its subordinates and often its opponents. Yet as Nietzsche said, those who look too long into the abyss are themselves invaded by it.

Unfortunately, polarities often prove complementary. Intellectuals know this as well as, if not better than, anyone. Many antifascists were communists, and not a few opponents of totalitarianism are conscious or unconscious pioneers of another form of despotism. It would be tragic if the collapse of "real socialism" were to inflame fanaticism of an opposite extreme and reinforce the proponents of an antiquated conservatism or even kindle an outbreak of religious, nationalist, or political extremism.

The liberal spirit of democracy, discussed today in an atmosphere of growing conservatism as if one were discussing the *dernier cri*, is not merely opposed to totalitarianism but is completely foreign to it, beyond any polarities. Many can justify from personal experience their fierce skepticism of contemporary political kitsch and their distrust of its many forms of manipulation—even now that the so-called communist mask has fallen from the tired, disfigured faces of millions of captives in the East. The narcissistic celebration of the free-market, consumer society on the other shore, which now claims divine legitimation as well as victory, does not lack in unintended irony.

With the Holocaust, totalitarianism, and exile, our century has extended the limits of *formation through deformation*. For a boy in love with books, such as myself, the difficult years of Stalinism brought not only a mind-numbing avalanche of shoddy, substandard "socialist realist" tracts, but also the discovery of the great Russian classics, which had been translated as part of the ideological program to cement the friendship with our "great neighbor to the east." It was a superb schooling in the transcendent and the critical spirit that examines such ideals. Yet it was also a therapeutic schooling in beauty, goodness, and truth, and in their subversive force, which those in power could not begin to understand.

Indispensable for prolonged inner exile, my education surely also led, in the end, to actual exile. The long, harrowing years as an engineer, during which I had hoped to evade more easily the pressure of indoctrination, were only the first stage of this unfinished adventure in alienation, in foreignness. I had many opportunities in adolescence and in later years—and still have today—to reflect on the process of *formation through deformation*, on the conflict between the individual's struggle toward openness and freedom and the oppressive, restrictive pressure of the Great Beast, as Simone Weil called society.

The repressive function of restricting and reducing individuality in a totalitarian regime equates not only with prison—the regime's symbol and quintessence—but also with its countless intrigues, ruses, and tricks of control, by spreading distrust and denunciation through the fear of one's neighbors, colleagues, or family—that hysterical mixture of complicity, guilty conscience, and disgust through which tyranny functions without functioning. A worldwide dungeon, divided up into numerous private and state cages watched over by both the penal colony's inmates and its guards. A fierce, progressive poisoning of the social conflicts which relatively open systems meet with pragmatic strategies and democratic compromise.

I began publishing during the period of so-called "liberalization," when the dogmatists were searching for alibis, but the Party still demanded a steadfast "engagement" from its artists. "Pressing Love," my first story published in an avant-garde journal in 1966, tried to oppose the prevailing canon precisely through its lack of political content. This timid, erotic story sought to re-establish a natural subject and a normal language. Little wonder, then, that the official literary press immediately tore the story to shreds and that the journal in which it appeared was suspended a few issues later. It is no less significant that when my novel, *The Black Envelope*, my last book published in Romania—a description of the everyday hell of the Ceauşescu regime—appeared in 1986, it was mutilated beyond recognition by the censor's interventions, at a time when writers interested in "aesthetic" rather than political questions were given preference.

"Censorship is the mother of metaphor," wrote Borges. One of the communist censor's most perplexing taboos was the Holocaust. I was, because of personal experience, preoccupied with this topic. Skeptical of melodramatic public displays of suffering, mortified at the ease with which the Holocaust is trivialized through the cheap marketing of extreme suffering in other parts of the world, and outraged by the hypocrisy, dishonesty, and cynicism with which it was made suspect, manipulated, and avoided in my own country, I have always been interested in the literary potential of this topic—a topic that ought to have caused an overpowering, traumatic, and crippling silence. Horror refuses to aestheticize, drastically restricting creative freedom. The greater the difficulties, the more I felt they deserved to be mastered. Faced with painful and dangerous consequences, encoding this tragic subject seemed both unavoidable and one way to "protect" it from the grip of manipulation. My story, "Weddings," sought to transfigure such a dilemma. I thought the image of a boy who, after his return from a concentration camp, was trained to give anti-fascist speeches at assemblies and family celebrations such as weddings, birthdays, and christenings, summed up both the situation of a persecuted minority and the general state of postwar Eastern Europe: the perversion of truth in the realm of the official lie and in the herdlike world of private life.

The illusion that censorship inspires creativity, as is sometimes claimed in the West and as many writers and readers in the East resignedly believe, may sometimes seem a frivolous sophistry. When describing firsthand experiences of reality, erotic life, religious feeling, and especially concrete political problems, Aesopian language doesn't always work to aesthetic advantage and often results in a lack of honesty. Truth seeks to preserve itself in obscurity and ingenious artifice and survives only in fragments, in ambiguous, often cryptic, forms. Readers in Eastern Europe looked to literature for what they could not find in the newspaper or in history and sociology textbooks. They chased truth between the lines, while the author accepted the distortion of his artistic work as the necessary price of solidarity with his audience.

In those difficult times, culture stimulated underground life and exerted a counter-force to state power by restoring trust in creativity, ideas, beauty, and intellectual dialogue, at a time when actual dialogue was strangled and corrupted. But culture did not destroy the totalitarian system; the system collapsed under its own weight because of the lack of breathing space and freedom, and because of catastrophic economic bankruptcy. Today, art's balance sheet is disheartening. Mountains of discarded texts are the era's sad remains. The entire epoch's devaluation includes the books it gave birth to: those that served the system but also many that sought to resist it or appeased its arrogance in order to avoid being devoured completely.

I can picture everyone's social apprenticeship as the adventures of an "Augustus the Fool," stumbling from one false trophy to another—and all the more so for the artists, those ambitious creators of chimeras. And yet, the totalitarian experience remains unique because it reflects in an extreme situation not only the sinister potential of the mundane, but also the social pathology totalitarianism cultivated in such absurd contortions. This was not a monolithic society, as communists hoped and many anti-communists claimed. Instead, it distinguished itself by equivocation, deception, ceaseless hypocrisy, and mystification. Only the Chief Buffoon and his retinue of tormentors still believed, in the last years of the circus, in the absolute magic of terror and in the hypnotic power of empty promises. If the tragedy of totalitarianism is unforgettable, its grotesque comedy also cannot be forgotten. Like so many extremes throughout history, they are inseparable. In this context of society's dead ends, the place of the artist—an extreme protagonist in extreme circumstances—acquires great importance.

The honest survivor cannot indulge in frivolous illusions or exaggerated lamentations about the fate of mankind. Paradoxically, the writer who has had to defend his integrity (with that ambitious and vulnerable mix of ethics and aesthetics I once called *estetica* in a Romanian pun for "East-ethics") understands that the game of art will always defy, but can never tame, the Great Beast. This applies even more to exiles, outsiders of all systems, if not of the whole world. A writer who has undergone the most extreme experiences does not consider Flaubert's vision of himself as a *saltimbanque* extravagant. Parodic fiction's ironic revenge on the Great Beast, despite its limitations, does not necessarily exclude greatness.

More than ever, we desperately need a "transcendent ideal" in our centrifugal, materialistic, artificial world, from which the concept of the ideal seems to have been banished—a world in which atomic, ecological, and demographic dangers exacerbate a general sense of panic and confusion. On the other hand, in the disastrous aftermath of totalitarian systems of all persuasions, a clearsighted approach to the manipulations unleashed by every ideal is all the more essential.

We cannot afford to neglect any element of this dilemma—especially today, when it is heightened by the global crisis of a mass-produced and entangled world. The isolation caused by the daily routine's "horrible brutality" and "hopeless banality" is no longer a strictly intellectual stance but a societal condition. Einstein, called a "logical empiricist artist" by one of his students, claimed that man "in his search for harmony" creates scientific and artistic works with which to balance the stifling limitations of daily life. This consolation apparently remains hidden deep within our crisis. Overwhelmed by "the strange adventure of being human," the Romanian author Max Blecher (1909–38), a soulmate of Franz Kafka and Bruno Schulz, wrote more than fifty years ago: "I pray to be awakened to another life, to my true life. It is certainly broad daylight; I know exactly where I am and that I am alive. And yet, something is missing." Today millions of people would probably echo these thoughts. As "functionaries of mankind," intellectuals are reclaiming Blecher's words as a reminder of the extreme experiences with which they have identified themselves in this incomparable, ruined century and as a motto for their growing uncertainty and future responsibility.

Translated by Tess Lewis, January 1994

THE INCOMPATIBILITIES

In the rough transition to democracy, the countries of Eastern Europe are going simultaneously forward and backward. The "forward" movement concerns their contract with the future: their adaptation to the social and economic requirements of the capitalist world, and the international accreditation that this will bring them. The "backward" movement is owing to their fragmented and incomplete evaluation of their history before and during the era of communism, a history that was manipulated and falsified by the ideology and the interests of the single Party of the totalitarian state.

Since 1989, this tension has often made itself felt in the everyday life of Eastern Europe. In Romania, the question of NATO membership for ex-communist countries found almost the entire political spectrum of the country taking a pro-NATO position. Suddenly the promise of a stable, integrated future within the European Community appeared to offer a cure for the country's traumatic past, which was seen as resulting more from the aggressiveness of the neighbor to the East (and from betrayal by the West) than from any shortcomings in the public life of the country itself. And then, at the same euphoric moment, a book appeared to complicate matters. A glimpse of a new Romanian future coincided with a glimpse of its past, with the publication, in 1996, of *Jurnal, 1935–1944* (Journal, 1935–1944), by the Romanian-Jewish writer Mihail Sebastian.[1]

This chronicle of the dark years of Nazism reignited the great debate about anti-Semitism and the Holocaust in Romania. These are subjects that some would have preferred to ignore. Sebastian's important book—it is appearing in a number of European coun-

tries, and it deserves to be published in the United States as well*—
exposes the deformities of a decade in which "everyone was a little
wheel in the huge anti-Semitic factory of the Romanian State." In
the writer's journals of those days, the banal regularity of his daily
life—with its book reading, its love affairs, its poverty, its meetings
with friends—sets the brutality and the fear in sharp relief. In Sebastian's world, however, the quotidian is ready at any moment to
kindle to vast reserves of ferocity.

In this respect, Sebastian's *Journal* resembles Victor Klemperer's
massive journal of the years 1933 to 1945, *Ich will Zeugnis ablegen bis
zum letzten* (I will Testify to the Bitter End), whose publication in
Germany in 1995 also had a powerful impact. The much-delayed
publication of these books in Eastern Europe, where the Nazi period was frozen in the clichés of the communist period, is witness to
the everyday lives of "assimilated" Jews awaiting death from the
world to which they thought they belonged. But Sebastian was an
elegant stylist, who moved from theme to theme with admirable
ease, and this book is a greater literary achievement than Klemperer's. It offers a lucid and finely shaded analysis of erotic and social
life, a Jew's journal, a reader's notebook, a music-lover's diary. Above
all, it is an account of the "rhinocerization" of certain major Romanian intellectuals whom Sebastian counted among his friends, including Mircea Eliade, E.M. Cioran and Constantin Noica, writers
and thinkers who were mesmerized by the nationalism of the extreme right and the Nazi-fascist delirium of Europe's "reactionary
revolution."

Rhinocerization? The odd term derives from Eugen Ionescu's play
Rhinoceros, a farcical allegory of the incubation and birth of fanaticism, or "the birth of a totalitarianism that grows, propagates, conquers, transforms a whole world and, naturally, being totalitarian,

---

*Now published as *Journal, 1935–1944* (2000), trans. Patrick Camiller, with
an introduction by Radu Ioanid.

transforms it totally." The playwright described his play as the story of "an ideological contagion." Ionescu is one of the few admirable characters to emerge from Sebastian's journal, a friend with whom Sebastian saw eye to eye in rejecting the totalitarian temptations of the left and the right. Ionescu has himself given a memorable description of the atmosphere in Bucharest at that time. "University professors, students, intellectuals were turning Nazi, Iron Guard, one after another," he wrote. "From time to time, one of our friends would say: 'Of course I don't agree with them at all, but on certain points, for example the Jews, I must admit. . . .' And this was symptomatic. Three weeks later, the same man would become a Nazi. He was caught up in the machinery, he accepted everything, he became a rhinoceros."

In poignant sequences that are not easily forgotten, Sebastian dwells on the gradations of this "machinery" of brutalization, and on the historical context in which it developed. Today, more than half a century after it was written, this journal stands as one of the most important human and literary documents of the pre-Holocaust climate in Romania and Eastern Europe, of the conditions in which the Judeocide could be unleashed.

Mihail Sebastian (this was the pen name of Joseph Hechter) was born in 1907, to a middle-class Jewish family, in the Danube port of Bráila, a town that he always loved; and he died in an accident in the spring of 1945, less than a year after Soviet troops entered Romania. (He was rushing to give the opening lecture on Balzac at the newly opened Popular (Free) University in Bucharest, and was run over by a truck. Recently, some people have tried to connect the accident to Sebastian's resignation from the communist paper *România Liberá*, for which he wrote briefly in 1944.) During the interwar period, Sebastian was well known for his lyrical and ironic plays (*Star without a Name, Let's Play Vacation,* and *The Last Hour*), as well as for urbane psychological novels tinged with melancholy (*Women,*

The Town with Acacia Trees, The Accident), and his extraordinary literary essays.

Sebastian's activity as a journalist centered on the conservative paper *Cuvîntul,* which was edited by Nae Ionescu (no relation of the playwright), and this often set him at loggerheads with both the left-wing press and the Jewish press. Nae Ionescu was a lively minor thinker preoccupied with metaphysics, logic, and religion. He never wrote an important work. He was, rather, a charismatic figure—a kind of guru—for young Romanian intellectuals between 1922 and 1940. He ended up as a supporter of the extremely right-wing, extremely nationalistic "Christian-orthodox" Iron Guard movement. Many years later, in 1967, Mircea Eliade bizarrely included Nae Ionescu in the *Encyclopedia of Philosophy,* and wrote this about his mentor: "God, for Nae Ionescu, is present in history through the Incarnation . . . man's mode of being is completely fulfilled only through death, death is above all transcendent." A Romanian reader will recognize in Eliade's words more than a strictly academic evaluation.

Sebastian's *Journal* begins in 1935, when Nazi Germany was flexing its muscles, and anti-Semitism was rife; the danger of war was growing more acute. Indeed, a year earlier Sebastian had provoked a hue and cry with his novel *De douá mii de ani* (For Two Thousand Years). Written in the form of a pseudo-diary, and somewhat in the style of André Gide, the novel portrays the identity crisis of its protagonist, a young Jewish intellectual in Romania, in a period when the country itself is undergoing the crisis of modernity. The first-person, nameless narrator, an architect by profession, records his apprenticeship years of friendship, love, and culture, but also the shock of his encounter with Romanian anti-Semitism.

Sebastian's characters include the mesmerizing professor Ghita Blidaru, a sharp and passionate critic of modern values (modeled on Nae Ionescu), the nihilist Párlea (modeled on Cioran), the "Europeanist" architect Vieru, the Zionist Sami Winkler, the Jewish

Marxist S.T. Haim (modeled on Bellu Zilber, a peculiar member of the then-illegal Romanian Communist Party), the Yiddishist Abraham Sulitzer, and the British businessman Ralph T. Rice. The last lines of the novel express the protagonist's breakthrough into a feeling of resignation. Is he a Romanian? Is he a Jew? Who, precisely, is he? As he gazes at the villa that he designed and built for his "native Romanian" mentor Blidaru, he no longer seems to care about the search for roots. He experiences a moment of serene separation. He accepts with equanimity the two-thousand-year-old heritage of the outsider. A house where its wanderer-builder always wished himself to be: "simple, clean, and calm, with an even heart, opened to all seasons."

Sebastian's novel is set against the background of an anti-Semitism that had not yet taken the extreme form of the "Final Solution." But the catastrophe was rooted in what preceded it, as is suggested by Ionescu's preface to Sebastian's novel. Sebastian had asked Nae Ionescu to write the preface in 1931, when he started work on the book. Ionescu had guided Sebastian's early steps in journalism. As a professor of philosophy of religion and a scholar of the Old Testament, he had a good knowledge of Judaism. Though Ionescu was politically committed to the right, he had a few years earlier rejected "the theory of the national state" with all its "police-type absurdities."

By the time Sebastian finished his novel, however, Europe had already lurched violently to the right. In Romania it was not just an "anti-Semitic" year, it was, as Sebastian put it, a "hooligan year." And in keeping with the political weather, Nae Ionescu had become one of the ideologues of the Iron Guard, also known as the Legion, the right-wing extremist organization that deployed anti-Semitism as a major political weapon within a kind of terroristic Orthodox Christian fundamentalism.

In 1934, still believing in his old friend's loyalty of "conscience," Sebastian gallantly repeated his request for Ionescu's endorsement of his book, and his former mentor, now a "Legionary Socrates," respected the promise he had made. He wrote the preface. And the words with which Sebastian expressed his shock on reading the preface have been conveyed by Eliade in his memoirs: "Nae gave me the preface. A tragedy, a real death sentence!" This was no exaggeration.

Nae Ionescu's preface argued that Jewish and Christian values are essentially irreconcilable. The really virulent language comes at the end, when the Jewish-Christian conflict is seen as soluble only through the disappearance of its cause, the Jews. The Iron Guard ideologue provided a definition of Romanian identity: "We are Orthodox Christian because we are Romanian, and Romanian because we are Orthodox." This was not a new definition; prestigious intellectuals had already espoused it. What was especially dramatic, and especially dangerous, was the historical context in which these inflammatory pronouncements now appeared.

Especially hard to forget was the part of Nae Ionescu's preface in which "Judah," having "refused to recognize Christ the Messiah," was declared an essential, irreducible enemy, a "dissolver of Christian values." The indictment was total, unconditional:

> It suffers because it gave birth to Christ, beheld him and did not believe. . . . Judah suffers because it is Judah. . . . Iosif Hechter, you are sick. You are sick to the core because all you can do is suffer. . . . The Messiah has come, Iosif Hechter, and you have had no knowledge of him. . . . Or you have not seen, because pride put scales over your eyes. . . . Iosif Hechter, do you not feel that cold and darkness are enfolding you?

The writer of the novel that was being introduced was not referred to as Sebastian, but as Hechter, as "Judah."

Thus the hooligan year 1934 was given a hooligan scandal. At the time, it seemed to some commentators that Sebastian's willingness to allow this incitement to genocide to appear at the front of his

"Jewish" novel was perverse and cowardly. Assailed by fascists and Marxists, Christians and Jews, liberals and extremists, Sebastian replied with an essay, "How I Became a Hooligan," which appeared in 1935, the year in which his *Journal* begins. He wrote that anti-Semitism, which "channels toward Jews the hate-filled distractions of organisms in crisis," was nonetheless "on the periphery of Jewish suffering." In 1935, he still had a certain condescension toward external adversity, seeing it as minor or rudimentary in comparison with the ardent "internal adversity" that besets the Jews.

Despite the dangers closing in from all sides, Sebastian continued to dwell romantically on the "spiritual autonomy" that Jewish suffering conferred upon the Jews. Judaism was a strict and tragic position in the face of existence. "No people has more ruthlessly confessed to its real or imagined sins; no one has kept stricter watch on himself or punished himself more severely. The biblical prophets are the fieriest voices ever to have sounded on earth." Sebastian locates the "open wound" of Judaism, its "tragic nerve," in the tension between "a tumultuous sensitivity and a ruthlessly critical sense," between "intelligence in its coldest forms and passion in its most untrammeled forms."

Sebastian liked to refer to himself as a "Danube Jew," and defined his identity as follows: "I am not a partisan, but always a dissident. I have confidence only in the single individual, but in him I have a great deal of confidence." He was adamantly opposed to the idea (it was all around him) that the collective has priority. "The death of the individual is the death of the critical spirit," and ultimately "the death of man." Sebastian's enemy is man in uniform: "Is it religion you want? Here's a membership card. Or a metaphysic? Here's an anthem. Or a commitment? Here's a leader." He thirsts for dialogue and friendship, but he clings to his faith in solitude: "We can never pay too high a price for the right to be alone, without half-memories, without half-loves, without half-truths."

As for the country that he never ceased to love for its paradoxes, its contradictions, and its eccentricities, Sebastian was not inclined to flatter it. "Nothing is serious, nothing is grave, nothing is true in this culture of smiling lampooners. Above all, nothing is incompatible. . . . Compromise is the blossom of violence. We therefore have a culture of brutality and horse-trading." The formulation profoundly describes a time when collusion and compromise were preparing a future of violence. Sebastian recalls the surprise that a Frenchman visiting Bucharest in 1933 felt at the intellectual "cohabitation" prevalent in the country. A notorious Iron Guardist, "caught in the act of intellectual tenderness" with a notorious Marxist, explained that "we are just friends—which doesn't involve commitment." *Just friends:* this, for Sebastian, is a "summing up of Bucharest psychology," a psychology of stupefying mélanges and metamorphoses. "Incompatibility: a concept completely lacking at every level of our public life." The formulation recurs in the *Journal:* "Incompatibility is something unknown on the Danube."

This and other statements appeared even more prophetic as the situation in Romania became more and more extreme. In 1937 the Iron Guard (supported by Sebastian's friend Eliade) scored a major success at the polls. Finally there were no illusions. "All is lost," Sebastian noted on February 21. The anti-Semitic government led by the poet Octavian Goga introduced into official discourse the evil "energy" of a language attuned to new imperatives: *jidan* (kike), *jidánime* (a horde of kikes). The official review of Jewish citizenship, and the elimination of Jews from the bar and the press, was followed by further restrictions and humiliations.

The danger grew. Officially inspired anti-Semitism gradually became a cheap entertainment within the reach of more and more people. The Iron Guard "rebellion" in January 1941 unleashed the predictable horrors in a city terrorized by armed street clashes and murderers chanting religious hymns. "A large number of Jews have been killed in Báneasa Forest and thrown there (most of them naked)." Sebastian noted on January 29. "But it seems that another lot have been executed at the slaughterhouse, at Stráulesti." A few days later, when he was reading about anti-Semitic persecutions in the Middle Ages in Simon Dubnow's *History of the Jews*, he turned again to what had happened. "What stuns you most about the Bucharest massacre is the absolutely bestial ferocity with which things were done . . . the Jews slaughtered at Stráulesti were hung up on abattoir hooks, in the place of split-open cattle. Stuck to each corpse was a piece of paper with the words: 'kosher meat'. . . . I cannot find more terrible events in Dubnow."

The worst fears were coming true. Even before the horrors, Sebastian had recorded premonitions. "An uneasy evening—without my realizing why. I feel obscure threats: as if the door isn't shut properly, as if the window shutters are transparent, as if the walls themselves are becoming translucent. Everywhere, at any moment, it is possible that some unspecified dangers will pounce from outside—dangers I know to have always been there. . . . You feel like shouting for help—but to whom?" This was written, as if in a state of siege, on January 14, 1941.

Many of Sebastian's friends were now in the enemy camp. The failure of the Iron Guard revolt infuriated and embittered them. "The Legion wipes its ass with this country," said Cioran immediately after the Iron Guard was defeated. Eliade expressed the same reaction more professorially: "Romania doesn't deserve a legionary movement." In 1941, General Ion Antonescu, a former ally of the Legion who was obsessed with "law and order," established a military dictatorship with the support of the Führer. This did not put a stop to anti-Semitic murders. The summer of 1941 brought not only Romania's entry into the war, but also a fresh round of atrocities. Massacres took place at Iaşi; and long before the Nazi gas chambers were established—also in Iaşi—the sinister experiment of a "death train" killed hundred and thousands of Jews by asphyxiation in sealed wagons on a journey heading nowhere.

"A simple account of what is reported about the Jews killed in Iaşi or transported by train . . . is beyond any words, feelings or attitudes. A bleak, pitch-black, crazy nightmare." Thus Sebastian in his diary on July 12, 1941. A few months earlier, in April 1941, the military dictator Antonescu told his ministers: "I'll retreat into my fortress and let the crowd massacre the Jews. After the massacre, I'll make order." And in September 1941, after the Iaşi massacre, and after Romania entered the war on Germany's side, Antonescu explained that the fight was not against the Slavs, it was against the Jews. "It's a mortal combat. Either we win and the world will be purified, or they win and we become their slaves."

In the autumn of 1941, the Jewish population of Bukovina began to be deported to Transnistria. On October 20, Sebastian writes: "An anti-Semitic dementia that nobody can stop. Nowhere are there any restraints, any reason. . . . I see pallor and fear on Jewish faces. Their smile, their atavistic optimism freeze up. Their old consoling irony dwindles away." The *Journal* goes on to record the census of residents with "Jewish blood," the "carnage in Bukovina and Bessarabia," the obligation of Jews to give clothing to the state and of the Jewish community to pay a huge sum of money to the authorities, the ban on Jews selling goods in markets, the confiscation of skis and bicycles from Jews. "There is something diabolical in anti-Semitism," we read in the entry on November 12, 1941. "When we are not drowning in blood, we are wading through muck." For a rationalist such as Sebastian to use the word "diabolical" is a measure of the bestiality provoked by the "vulgar" anti-Semitism of his time.

As Sebastian's journal proceeds between the blood and the filth, the "atavistic optimism" and the "consoling irony" grow dim. And the "internal adversity" of the Jews, with its self-criticism and its "spiritual autonomy"? The *Journal* itself illustrates the awful truth that those are the natural assumptions, the necessary assumptions, of the human condition, and in no way the self-consuming aberration of a particular people. Even when external hostility is everywhere, and internal adversity appears to be a forbidden or trifling luxury, critical introspection survives, and it becomes the instrument of the spirit's survival.

As the individual becomes just an anonymous member of a threatened community, the solitude by which Sebastian defined himself changes, even if its substance does not alter. "We can never pay too high a price for the right to be alone": for a besieged man, surely, this sounds like a frivolous understatement. For what is the "price" of the solitude of a whole community, a whole people? It defies any normal parameter of suffering. For this reason, the tone of the *Journal* is really remarkable. The intimate exchange between solitude and solidarity slowly gives way to a mournful compassion. The "old" private solitude allows itself to be welcomed by the new isolation of the persecuted group, in a wounded, coerced joining.

Under the pressure of hatred and horror, Sebastian's writing maintains the "grace" of its intelligence, which evil does not succeed in destroying. Marked now by the star of the captive minority to which he has been returned, the writer attempts to enliven the emptiness of waiting. He listens to music; he reads; he writes; he sees friends. A large and moving part of the *Journal* focuses on friendship, especially on his friendship with Mircea Eliade, the "first and last friend."

After the "death sentence" handed down to him by Nae Ionescu, the "hooligan" Hechter-Sebastian no longer claimed anything but the right to perfect solitude, "without half-memories, without half-loves, without half-truths." In the sharply worse conditions of the following years, however, he proved to be still in the painful grip of Eliade, persisting in a friendship of halves of memory, love, and truth. The crisis of Sebastian's friendship with Eliade grew steadily worse. As early as 1936, it was no longer possible for Sebastian to ignore Eliade's political affiliations. "I would like to remove any political references from our discussion. But is that possible?" The answer is not long in coming: "The street reaches up to us whether we like it or not, and in the most trivial reflection I can feel the ever wider gulf between us. . . . There are awkward silences between us . . . the disappointments keep piling up—one of them being his involvement with the anti-Semitic *Vremea*." (*Vremea* was a rather liberal weekly until the mid-1930s, when it started to "evolve" according to the spirit of the time.)

Sebastian is already grasping the character of Eliade's politics, though his lucidity is distorted by sentimentality, and by his essentially apolitical vision. In 1937, however, a "long political discussion with Mircea" leads to a sad realization: "He was lyrical, nebulous, full of exclamations, interjections, apostrophes. . . . From all that I'll just choose his (finally honest) statement that he loves the Guard, has hope in it, and awaits its victory." In the same year, Eliade's famous declaration of faith, "Why I Believe in the Triumph of the Legionary Movement," was published in the movement's paper *Buna Vestire*. It included the following question: "Can the Romanian nation end its life . . . ravaged by poverty and syphilis, overrun by Jews and torn apart by foreigners?"

It was not long before Eliade's question found an answer in the humiliations and the threats that his former friend, the alien Sebastian, born Hechter, had to endure, as he faced being overrun at any moment by the local "patriots." And further dialogue with Eliade only confirmed this. "I told him I was thinking of leaving the country," Sebastian writes on January 16, 1938. "He agreed, as if it did indeed go without saying." That is how it was: the "cleansing" of the country of its Jews was a self-evident ideal, for which the Legionary movement never ceased to agitate.

"I have only to walk in the door and suddenly there is silence." People speak about their Jewish acquaintance in one way when he is in the room and in another way when he leaves the room. On December 7,

1937, Sebastian finds Eliade's concealment of the truth "even more sad" than the terrible truth itself, which was that Eliade had traveled from village to village campaigning for the Iron Guard as a "propagandist" and also, it seemed, as a potential candidate of the Legion in the elections. Astounding reports reach Sebastian about what Eliade says in his absence. In March 1937, Eliade is disgusted by the "Jewish spirit" of a ballet. In 1939, at the time of the German invasion of Poland, Eliade says this: "The Poles' resistance in Warsaw is Jewish resistance. Only yids are capable of blackmail by putting women and children in the front line, so as to take advantage of German scruples." And the example of Poland, with Jewish "blackmail" and German "scruples," inspires in Eliade equally profound considerations about Romania: "Only a pro-German policy can save us. . . . Rather than a Romania again invaded by kikes, it would be better to have a German protectorate."

Sebastian's link with Eliade continued intermittently, until the latter left Bucharest in 1940 for the Romanian embassy in London, where eyewitnesses described him as a propagandist for the Iron Guard. Later Eliade was sent as a diplomat to Lisbon, where his fascist convictions were given more or less disguised forms of expression. About Eliade's time in Lisbon, Sebastian notes on May 27, 1942: "Now he is more of a Legionary than ever." (After the war Eliade referred only equivocally and in passing to his guilt.*)

So why did Sebastian cling to this friendship with a man with whom he should have been "incompatible"? Why did he himself become an example of the ambiguities that he denounced? Surely Sebastian did not delude himself that the friendship would protect him from the danger all around him? No, there was a different reason. For a rational and gentle man such as Sebastian, the illusion of friendship provided the encouragement of a normal past. Memories are "the only paradise from which we cannot be expelled," as

*See pp. 92–118 below.

the German poet Jean Paul observed. Moreover, Sebastian had a calm, resigned disdain for everything ideological and tribal. He had also a writer's curiosity about the surprises and the ambiguities he observed in himself and those around him, and this, too, perhaps, made him tolerant of his fascist friend. As early as 1936, when the ever wider "gulf" between him and his "first and last" friend could be felt in "the most trivial reflection," he asked in his journal: "Will I lose Mircea for *so little?*"

For so little! Sebastian's extraordinary words express his contempt for the mediocrity of politics, and his irritation at Eliade's deplorable "error." The innocent will show the world—will show himself, against the world—that he can save the guilty, as a friend and an interlocutor. He cannot admit that mediocrity has won the day even in the case of his brilliant and beloved Eliade, just as he cannot admit that there is not merely "incompatibility" between the intellectual and the man in uniform, but also a deeper, more subtle, relationship of attraction and repulsion, a relationship eager for the thrills and the compensations of vitality, mystification, martyrdom, and all manner of excess.

Perfectly aware of the abyss between himself and Eliade (an ideological abyss that was already filling with corpses), Sebastian nevertheless records the surprising moments of affection that linger in their moribund friendship. He cannot help being concerned by the risks that his friend faced in his ugly adventure, though he himself every day feels the cold and the darkness of the threat from the uniforms of Eliade's "comrades." Sebastian's portraits of Eliade, Cioran, Nae Ionescu, and other Romanian intellectuals in the grip of the nationalist delirium are devastating precisely because of their calm, patient, affectionate tone, their mingling of horror and candor.

In its historical context, the Sebastian–Eliade friendship stands as a symbol of everything that signified terror and hope, ambiguity and fear, cowardice and chance, in the Jewish-Christian relationship in

Europe in the obscene decade between 1935 and 1945. These staggering and shocking Romanian "compatibilities," their double-dealing
and triple-dealing with complicity and compromise, played a role in
the dissipation of moral (and not only moral) certainties, offering
terrible, or generous, surprises. This might explain both the horrific
persecution and the eventual salvation of a large part of the Jewish
population of Romania. Sebastian's *Journal* records, with growing
weariness and bitterness, the precise forms of disguise and fakery.

After the Legionary revolt was defeated in 1941, Sebastian watches
some of its ex-fanatics hurry to accommodate themselves to the new
situation: "From one day to the next they renege, modify, attenuate,
explain, agree on a line, justify themselves, forget what displeases and
remember what suits them." He discovers in horror how his friend
Eliade—who had presented himself at the Romanian embassy in
London as a future dignitary of the Legion—sums up this year in
which the most dreadful anti-Jewish massacres were carried out in
Iaşi and Bucharest. "There have been two extraordinary things for me
this year," Eliade wrote from London to a mutual friend: "the astonishing weakness of the Soviet air force, and my reading of Camoëns."

And yet, even in this nightmarish atmosphere, a few figures
brighten the pages of the *Journal.* First and foremost among them is
Eugen Ionescu. In Cişmigiu Park in Bucharest, as one of Hitler's
speeches was being broadcast on the radio, Ionescu stood up choking
at what he heard. "He was pale, white in the face. 'I can't take it. I
can't.' He said this with a kind of physical desperation. . . ." Sebastian
records on October 3, 1941. "I felt like hugging him." He also notes a
message from another friend: "You make me feel ashamed, Mihai—
ashamed that you suffer and I do not." And after the anti-Semitic
massacres in Iaşi, he recalls the reaction of two university professors
in the Moldovan capital. One covered his face with "a gesture of
impotence, fear and disgust": the other uttered just a few words: "The
most bestial day in the history of mankind."

Finally, in 1944, when the Red Army entered Bucharest, not a few people changed sides in a flash. "Everyone is rushing to fill posts," Sebastian records, "to make use of titles, to establish rights. . . . A taste for lampooning alternates in me with a kind of helpless loathing [for] all the imposture, all the effrontery, all the sinister play-acting."

This, then, was Sebastian's odyssey, which he experienced all in the same place. In 1934, declaring himself to be a "Danube Jew," the hero of Sebastian's novel *For Two Thousand Years* movingly states on the author's behalf: "I should like to know what anti-Semitic laws could cancel the irrevocable fact that I was born on the Danube and love this land. . . . Against my Jewish taste for inner catastrophe, the river raised the example of its regal indifference." In 1943, he was asking, "Shall I go back to those people? Will the war have passed without breaking anything—without anything irrevocable, anything irreducible, between my life 'before' and my life 'tomorrow'?" In 1944, he was preparing to leave "the eternal Romania in which nothing ever changes." His description of an encounter with a Jewish captain from the U.S. Army suggests which destination he had in mind for his adventure: "an unaffected young man full of vitality, concerned about us as Jews, concerned about democracy and its reality. A human being. A new figure. Really somebody." But Sebastian's hope of leaving "the land of the Danube" was cut short by his accidental death on May 29, 1943. He was 38 years old. Death spared him any postwar experiment with "compulsory happiness" in communist captivity in his own country.

The publication of Sebastian's *Journal* sparked a powerful reaction in Romania. Several editions have already sold out, and the discussion continues in the press. The book provoked a catharsis in a society that seems afraid to scrutinize its past and hesitates to admit its own contribution to the Holocaust, in a country in which criticism of the nationalist tradition in culture is sometimes considered an unpatriotic act, if not actual blasphemy. "In reading it," writes Vasile Popovici, a writer from Timisoara, where the anti-Ceauşescu revolt began in 1989, "you cannot possibly remain the same. The Jewish problem becomes your problem. A huge sense of shame spreads over a whole period of the national culture and history, and its shadow covers you too."

Still, the number of those who are willing to make the Jewish problem their problem is not very large. For a significant number of public voices in Romania, the Holocaust seems to be (as Jean-Marie Le Pen once put it) a "detail" of the war. Even those who recognize the scale of the catastrophe do not always seem prepared to accept what it reveals. This is especially evident in the debate about Marshal Antonescu, the military dictator during the period of Romania's alliance with Nazi Germany, to whom the Romanian Parliament paid homage in 1991, and who has been honored in many public places in today's Romania. When a distinguished Romanian intellectual with democratic leanings intervened a few years ago in the controversy about the rehabilitation of Antonescu, he argued that an "exclusive, overwhelming" emphasis on the dictator's anti-Jewish policy "would prevent science—in this case, history—from honestly and objectively performing its duty." Similarly, in the polemics surrounding the publication of Sebastian's *Journal*, there have been voices "annoyed" at this new and weighty testimony in what some see as an overly protracted discussion of the Holocaust. Not surprisingly, doubts have been cast on the authenticity of the text. Critics have ruminated on the subjectivity of private journals generally. All this, so as not to face the evidence of what Sebastian wrote.

It is little wonder that even the infrequent empathy with the suffering of the Jews is peculiarly expressed. In 1997, the director of the publishing house *Humanitas*, the very house that published Sebastian's *Journal*, gave a talk affectingly entitled "Sebastian, mon frère" at the Jewish Community Center in Bucharest. He explained his solidarity with Jewish suffering in terms of his own hardship under the communists and the post-communists. It is an analogy that leaves no room to evoke anti-Semitism and the Holocaust properly, or to analyze honestly the "happy guilt" of such intellectuals as Eliade, Cioran, Nae Ionescu, and Noica.

Also, in an editorial statement entitled *"Vintoarea de vrájitoare,"* or "The Witch Hunt," the director of the important magazine *România literará* complained that the condemnation of Céline and Hamsun was lasting too long. He deplored the "Israeli" campaign against Eliade, the recent debate in France about Cioran's Legionary past, and the "exaggerations" in Sebastian's *Journal.* Never mind that the (far from unanimous) condemnation of Céline and Hamsun has not precluded the recognition of their literary distinction, or that their guilt was owed not necessarily to their writings, but to their actual collaboration with the Nazis. By describing criticism in an open society as a "witch hunt," and comparing it with the communist repression of intellectual life, the editorial in *România literará* was promoting a shocking confusion of terms.

In contrast with such slips and ambiguities, we may cite a statement by another prominent Romanian intellectual. Writing in 1997, Petru Cretia observed that "the most monstrous thing after the Holocaust is the persistence of even a minimal anti-Semitism." In this context, he mentioned Sebastian's *Journal,* and the old-new compatibilities:

> I know public figures who, while parading flawless morality, impeccable democratic conduct, wise level-headedness, and perhaps a pompous solemnity, are capable in private—and in some cases elsewhere—of foaming at the mouth against Jews; here and now. I have seen irrefutable proof of the fury aroused by Sebastian's *Journal,* and of the feeling that lofty national values are besmirched by such calm, sad, and forgiving revelations on the part of that fair-minded (often angelic) witness.

This statement appeared just a few days before the death of this distinguished man of letters and good Christian. It was published not in a mass-circulation magazine, but in *Realitatea evreiască*, the newspaper of the Jewish community in Romania.

What, then, are we to conclude from Mihail Sebastian and his posthumous career? At least this: that the "forward" movement of Eastern Europe should be evaluated not only for its ability to modernize political and economic structures, but also for its ability to clarify the recent history of these scarred societies, and to direct them toward the full truth. This is not an easy task, and it is first and foremost the task of intellectuals, not politicians. But our future is premised on the quality, on the probity, of our understanding of the past.

Translated by Patrick Camiller, April 20, 1998

Note

1. *Jurnal, 1935–1944.* (Bucharest: Humanitas, 1996).

ON CLOWNS: THE DICTATOR AND THE ARTIST

Notes to a Text by Fellini

The year 1989 marked not only the bicentennial of the French Revolution, but also the centennials of two figures who—each in his own way—knew how to exploit the hunger of the masses and their vulnerability and gullibility.

> He was a tramp in the big city, using a park bench for a bed. He wore a weathered black derby and a frock coat askew on his shoulders—both tragicomic attempts at respectability. He drifted along the sidewalks, without family. He had no friends. Acquaintances saw him go into strange fits and thought him a clown. But he was a charismatic clown—the center of a show that he perfected and in which he functioned not just as the leading man but as writer, director, producer, and set designer. When his little black mustache had become emblematic, when he had grown into the idol of millions, a great Hollywood star called him 'the greatest actor of us all.' His name was Adolf Hitler, born just over a hundred years ago, on April 20, 1889.[1]

The Hollywood star who was so fascinated by Hitler's histrionic gifts was, of course, Charlie Chaplin, likewise born a hundred years ago, a hundred hours before Hitler. He too was a marginal figure, one of society's outcasts: his father was an alcoholic, his mother was shunted from one charity hospital to another, and the son slept in campgrounds and railroad stations. He was incapable of forming friendships, had difficulty communicating, but would prove to have an irresistible effect on the masses.

Chaplin plays the part of the Dictator in the movie of that name, with its famous scene in which the hero, in a frenzy of triumph, juggles a balloon that represents the globe. The actor emphasizes the grotesque elements in the tyrant's infantile schizophrenia. In its empathy with madness, his acting becomes ambiguously complicit. The character, initially conceived in a naïve, artistic fashion, flips over into a convulsive grimace of demonic ugliness. "Hitler may have been history's most murderous genius, yet his formula shared elements with Chaplin's. Both men tapped the need of the outsider to be let in."[2]

"Do you still collect humorous clippings from the contemporary press similar to those you published in *Augustus the Fool's Apprenticeship Years?*" a writer asked me in an interview that scandalized the official press for months on end. I had said that:

> the artist cannot dignify officialdom by opposing it in a solemn fashion, because that would mean taking it too seriously and inadvertently reinforcing its authority, thus acknowledging that authority. He pushes the ridiculous to grotesque proportions, but artistically he creates . . . a surfeit of meanings. . . . In today's rushed, confusing society in which everything mixes and is mixed up and destroyed, the ridiculous does run the risk of "swallowing up" art too. But the artist, even if he has been relegated to the position of a buffoon, tries to assume—albeit at the price of an apparent, momentary abnegation of the self— an ambiguous stance, to place himself on a shaky seesaw, to transform the loss into a later gain.

For me, the artist was an Augustus the Fool; mine was a deep solidarity rather than a superficial empathy with his game and with his destiny.

Where did the proud, romantic image of art with a capital *A* go? The artist's situation in the world is that of "Augustus the Fool," *der arme August*, as Hans Hartung's father nicknamed his son, clearly intuiting the inner nature of the artist that neither the painter's work nor his later life ever overtly disclosed. Aging Thomas Mann, the epitome of a rigorous, serious, and ethical author, saw artists as "eccentric spirits of the ridiculous," "brilliant monks of the absurd," "suspect," and "acrobatic": for him the artist was "neither female nor male, hence not human"; he called him "a grave angel of foolhardiness . . . under the roof of the tent, high above the crowd," performing an aerial balancing act in the great circus of the world.

In the world circus the poet looks like a Knight of the Sad Countenance, an Augustus the Fool ill-equipped for everyday life in which his fellow men offer and receive—according to their efforts, opportunities, and wiles—their share of edible reality. He is a bizarre bungler who dreams of other rules, other evaluations and rewards, and looks for solitary compensations for the role he has been saddled with, whether he likes it or not.

Nevertheless, he often demonstrates a deep and hence surprising knowledge of his fellow citizens, with whom he seems to communicate only superficially, and from whom he takes and to whom he returns a magic that is as calculated as it is spontaneous; there are sequences the citizens can recognize even when they appear mysterious and, on the surface, difficult—not always understood, even by himself. His weakness suddenly may be seen as an unconventional and devious strength, his solitude as a deeper kind of solidarity; his imagination becomes a shortcut to reality. One might say that his face is reflected in all the images of the circus that surrounds him, and the mirror turns fast, faster. It is a gift of a moment, a brief shock—a moment of amazement that stuns the entire audience for a fraction of a second.

But what do we see here—the tyrant, part of the troupe of buffoons? Can the frail vagabond (and cultivated man of letters) recognize himself even in this new face, in this disfigured mask in which no one can see the good, the true, the beautiful, but only the opposite? A tyrant is someone who manipulates, gives orders, enforces discipline, punishes and rewards according to the sovereign and sadistic laws of evil, ugliness, and mendacity. The tyrant: innumerable perfidious travesties, a smug rictus, fastidious and ridiculous uniforms, attacks of hysteria marked by sharp and bestial cries, plaintive infantile whispers, the stamps and roars of boars in rut—or the icy immobility of the vampire.

It isn't hard to believe that the poet–clown has already recognized that fact in his nightmares or in the course of his wanderings; it even seems that sometimes, somewhere, he has already borne tyrannical caprice and hatred. No doubt about it, this too is a human face, even when overlaid by wrinkled layers of fat and thick makeup. Yes, yes, the poor man—a vain fanatic, enthralled by the chimera of power, just a poor man, a solitary sufferer who turns his weakness into authority, his fear into assurance, his diseases into violence and farce.

And so, in the bright arena, Augustus the Fool faces the Clown of Power. Their eyes meet. Is all of human tragicomedy concentrated in that brief exchange? Is it attraction by repulsion, a powerful reaction catalyzed by the meeting of opposites? Can they be compared to one another, these actors playing different parts in the coded scenario called *Life on Earth?* Only if one watches the spectacle from the moon, or from so close up that one is blinded and can no longer see the contrasts in this global and rapidly changing masquerade.

An artist who has lived under tyranny (and even one who hasn't) cannot ignore the insurmountable moral barrier that separates the two roles. He can watch the spectacle from a cosmic distance—and yet he is ready to play the part of his opposite to the point of identification with him; he will cross that distance in order to scrutinize the counterpart with all the curiosity, imagination, and precision required by his task. The history of the circus as History? With its strange couple: the Artist–Fool and the Clown of Power?

Is the artist Augustus the Fool, is the tyrant the White Clown? Is Hitler a White Clown, and is Chaplin, who has mimed him with childlike irony, a traditional Augustus the Fool? Is this moment of juncture in the human dynamic the moment of truth in the great circus of the world?

While I am to this day painfully aware of the sinister radiation with which Hitler and Stalin ravaged my childhood and youth, I would never have understood the true nature of this radiation if I hadn't been compelled, in my adult years, to endure—to the point of suffocation—the paranoia of a small provincial tyrant who managed to expand, step by step, the small arena of his macabre circus to cover an entire country: "Antonioni is a silent Augustus the Fool, mute and melancholic. . . . Picasso? A triumphant Augustus the Fool, proud, confident, a jack-of-all-trades; he emerges victorious in his battle with the White Clown."[3]

In *The Europeans*, Luigi Barzini wrote about his impressions on first meeting Hitler: "To me, then, he looked like an improbable funny burlesque character, a sinister clown. . . . He was, I concluded, too improbable to last; there was nothing to worry about. . . . [He had] no more of a chance than Mussolini's operatic attempt to reconstruct the Roman Empire."

Hitler, a White Clown! And Chaplin, his imitator (or interpreter), is an Augustus the Fool. A buffoon, with a little black hat cocked over his ear, the oversized pants, and the elegant cane of a dandy.

The mask of the White Clown corresponds to the antinomy of good and evil we know from fairy tales and find so satisfying: "The face is white and spectral, with circumflexes above arrogantly raised brows; the mouth a narrow line, hard and unpleasant, distant, cold," says Fellini, "icily authoritarian like certain nuns in charge of kindergartens," but also, above all, "like those spiffy Fascists in shiny black silk and gold braid, riding crop in hand (typical clown gear), giving martial orders."

Is it hard to define the dividing line between Augustus and the White Clown? "There are White Clowns who began as Augustuses, but no Augustus the Fool who started out as a White Clown. This is probably the case because it is easier for a tolerant nature to imitate authority than for an authoritarian one to slip into a tolerant character."[4]

Our pitiful local clown: his ridiculous, self-awarded, ever more pompous titles, his endless speeches full of vast platitudes with their perennial hoarse bathos, their monotonous invective, their grammatical mistakes. The fear fueling his fanaticism, and the clever camouflage of that fanaticism; his stutter and puppetlike gestures, his manic insistence and schizophrenic industry, and his perplexity when confronted with anything still alive and spontaneous.

Many have started out as Augustuses—mediocre housepainters, humble provincial seminarists, apprentices in a cobbler's workshop. "The fascination of the moonstruck, the nocturnal, ghostly elegance" of the White Clown? "To children, the White Clown is a bogeyman because he embodies responsibility or—to use a fashionable term—repression," says Fellini. Repression—a fashionable term? There was a time when I would have responded to that statement with a superior smile, or else with the anguished howl of a sick beast: repression was our tangible present, the air we breathed every day, the atmosphere in every office and restaurant. The children laughed at the tyrant and couldn't understand why all the adults around them let him gain so much power over them. This too is a paradox, characteristic of this little clown who differs from Hitler or Stalin in that children find him merely ridiculous.

Ridicule has its own secret power, that of amusement, and it is vengeful. Repeatedly, Fellini refers to the anonymous citizen, "the child who is forced to play the part of Augustus" in his relationship to Mother (the state, the police, the authorities) and her constant prohibitions: "Don't touch that!" "Don't do that!"

By decree, our clown has changed the whole country into a huge kindergarten populated by militarized and industrious children; but he can't stand his own "children," or "subjects." If they obey, he spits on them and beats them up; if they act up, he cuts off an ear; if they disobey, he sews their lips shut; if they get sick, he presents them with a coffin and a bill for funeral expenses. "Order and discipline" are the only virtues he permits the anonymous throng. He communicates with the humble ones—from whose ranks he, the "most beloved, the most honored, the most revolutionary son of the people," has risen—but only through his guards. Anyone who dares intercept the presidential limousine with a petition invariably disappears, never to be seen again. The cape, the scepter, the palace, the anthem, the decorations. . . .

And his hunting parties!

The bears tranquilized, foaming at the mouth, bound, prevented from eating and drinking for many days before the hunt begins. The aerial surveillance of the hunting area. The red presidential helicopter landing in front of the castle. The guests from the Party circus, from the circus press, from the foreign embassies. Bit players from the secret police dressed as waiters, and the clown's bodyguards waiting in ditches, camouflaged in the underbrush. The portable fence deployed like a funnel with the opening exactly in front of the president's stand. The tranquilized bears gradually awaken and appear in the arena, unsteady and bellowing. The First Hunter of the Circus taking aim, closing his right eye, then his left. The moment the comrade places his finger on the trigger the Securitate snipers camouflaged in the underbrush also fire, with silencers, picking off the game. To the rhythm of the national anthem, the Supreme Clown thrusts out his chest for the gold medal; he is the best marksman of the time.

And what about his favored black Labrador? Born in England as Sir Gladstone and renamed, for the circus, Comrade Corbul (Raven), eating royally, nourished with British dog biscuits sent weekly by the circus ambassador in London—whose main diplomatic task, in fact, this is. The dog enjoys the rank of the highest officer in the circus hierarchy, but his importance is much greater than that of any general, admiral, or spymaster in the circus army and police.[5]

"White Clowns have always competed amongst themselves in the magnificence of their costumes," says Fellini. There was a very famous clown, Theodore, who "appeared in a new costume every day." So does our national clown, but vanity alone does not explain the tremendous effort this takes: fear plays a part in it. The outfit for dinner, the outfit for a working visit to the provinces, the one for important meetings, and the one for secret negotiations—each and every one of the clown's costumes is a matter of national importance. A special detachment of the Securitate is responsible for the clown's daily sartorial and nutritional needs, for a complete daily change of clothes, from socks and handkerchief to shoes and headgear. Daily, all this is delivered from a special outfitter's; every day, a special laboratory analyzes food ingredients and compiles the perfect menu, while also examining the excretions of the most beloved's alimentary tract. Special commandos check his office, his bedroom, his fountain pen, and his toilet for radiation, just in case some subversive agent, bent on saving the tyrant's subjects, has managed to contaminate a suit, a dish, a chair. At the end of the day, the articles of clothing are stamped with red and green ink (the colors of the Romanian extreme left and right) and taken to be incinerated in the presidential crematorium, which, like the special outfitter and the special laboratory for nutrition and excretion analysis, is part of the gigantic, multifaceted security organization of the great circus.

"The White Clown," says Fellini, "likes to slap people in the face." Our sadistic national clown has proscribed food, light, heat, and travel. He has destroyed churches and archives.

Father, mother, schoolmaster? The White Clown as an embodiment of the Ideal, a Knight of Utopia? An implacable visionary of the future, indifferent to the horrors of the transient present, focused only on what *must be done?* "Icily authoritarian, like certain nuns in charge of kindergartens"?

Some fifteen years ago I made the acquaintance of a doctor who had, in the days when the Communist Party was outlawed (1923–44), shared a prison cell with our great clown. I was curious to hear an opinion of him from a man who had been in a position to observe him close up, and daily, as just another cog in the isolated and doom-laden machinery of prison. This was it: "I judged *these people* according to the simplest possible criterion: I tried to imagine what tasks I would give them in my clinic. There was one I might use as an administrator, another who'd do as a driver, cashier, or night watchman. A few could have acquired the skills of a laboratory technician or equipment monitor. But *this one* . . . no, he couldn't have managed any practical task. He had never done any real work, did not have a craft, would never be able to learn anything. All he could do was make speeches. And boss others around. I couldn't have used him, not even as a night watchman." What the doctor could not explain was why *these people,* as he called his former comrades, now the "new class," were once his soulmates, and why he allowed *this one* to be his political instructor with such crass disregard of the criterion of normality one would have expected from an intelligent, honest, and courageous physician.

Elementary school children in uniforms with lapel pins. The Pioneer salute. The anthem. The Leader. . . . Families crammed into block housing under the control of a "block guard" installed by the "organs of order and surveillance." Entire city blocks of magnificent villas and one-family houses bulldozed to make room for standardized boxes in which the inhabitants can more efficiently be ordered about and watched. A gigantic program designed to destroy villages in order to transform agriculture into "agro-industrial complexes" and to "eliminate the distinctions between city and country" to turn farmers into wage slaves, their families boxed into human hives, above, below, and next to each other.

And all women, in both city and country, obliged to submit to regular gynecological examinations to make sure no pregnant woman dares try to deprive the all-owning state of a future subject. And the old ones sent to special reservations where they have to grow vegetables and clean out stables. And the extermination of dogs and cats, to ensure the uninterrupted sleep of the "working population." And in the earpiece of every telephone a tiny electronic cockroach, to enable the state to document and scientifically "care for" its victims.

Order, as much as possible, and the greatest possible degree of discipline. Maximal surveillance (a genuine world record: one fully employed police officer for every fifteen citizens and, for every police officer, fifteen "volunteer" informers). All this to make sure no undeserving member of the remainder of the populace can fall through the mesh of this gigantic net and divulge some secret of the state: the name of his factory, the measurement of pickle jars, the formula for the atomic bomb, the number of public urinals per city district, the clown's nickname, the holding capacity of the loony bins, the map of the country, the technology for the manufacture of sewing thread. And to make sure that no foreigner can discover the secrets of our paradisiacal circus: it is one's honorable duty to avoid all contact with them.

Everything has to do with *him*, and his favorite word is *everything*. We shall do everything, everything, *everything*, he barks in a hoarse monotone. To ensure the continuous growth of the leading role . . . the uninterrupted growth of the leading role . . . ever more highly developed discipline . . . and relentless continuous growth of the leading role of the Leader.

Years ago, a friend of mine who'd been living on the outskirts of the city wanted to move to the center. She had found a small apartment for sale on the Calea Victoriei. When it was time to do the paperwork, she found she needed a special permit because her windows faced the street and the Calea Victoriei was one of the main arteries the nation's clown chose for the morning drive to his office in the Central Committee Building, where he would work hard at governing from eight sharp in the morning until eight sharp at night, then return via another artery to the presidential villa. These were sacred streets.

Order, as much order as possible, and vigilance, uninterrupted vigilance, so that nothing could spoil his mood, cause him to become ill, or, above all, bring about the long-anticipated, fatal, liberating accident.

The most valuable resource is the human being, that is: *he*. A specimen like *him*, according to the calculations of the presidential astrologers, occurs only once in five hundred years. This justifies the pains taken over his nutrition, his excretions, his weaponry, the 365 pairs of pants and underpants, socks, pajamas, and nightcaps, the 365 pairs of shoes and slippers.

Then there is the photographer, the barber, the masseur, the cosmetician. There are the bodyguards and the stand-ins, and the interpreters for the 364 languages of the globe, of which he doesn't know a single one. The information and disinformation, radiation and counter-radiation. The portable toilet, the invisible shower. The noiseless pistol. All in the service of the country's only productive institution: the cult of the clown. And there is, of course, his Pussycat.

"The only female clown to achieve lasting fame is Miss Lulu. Gelsomina and Cabiria in my movies belong to the genus Augustus the

Fool. They aren't women, they are sexless," says Fellini. "Charlot, an Augustus, is equally devoid of human gender, just a happy cat that cleans its fur and walks where it pleases." Laurel and Hardy, "two more of the same type, they even sleep together like innocent children, as if sex did not exist. Exactly that was what made the world laugh."

And the Pussycat? The lover with poor teeth, the erudite illiterate, the commissar in skirts, the witch, the hysterical one, Auntie Porno? The spouse of the White Clown: is she, too, a White Clown?

People snicker, not only in secret, about the first couple of the land, forever locked in the presentation of the same routine: *the first couple.* In full regalia, the parvenus stage an imperial intoxication of bliss not seen anywhere outside the circus. He wears a sash and carries a scepter; she dresses in the toga of an empress, conscious of her fame as a scientist, confident in her vaccination certificates. He holds his secret councils with Kojak, Abdullah Jasser, Santiago Carlos, Kim Kung Kang or Benito Mafioso—to discuss the next worldwide measures to be taken for the liquidation of his adversaries and for the conditioning of the survivors to an existence in the catacombs.

Prudish and shy, he airs his obsessions in endless, repetitive, stammering tirades of invective, both at home and at the office. His little Lulu, on the other hand, takes in several sex movies every night, instead of sleeping pills, and falls asleep in a similarly pornographic position, mouth and robe wide open.

Miss Lulu, Lulette, Lena, Leanţa—a vicious White Clown who dominates her partner and terrorizes his entourage. Out of perversity? Insecurity? Frustration? All of the above, in mutual fidelity; compared to *him*, Hitler was just a waif. "The hermaphrodite" is what they call Hitler, and it is possible to remain a hermaphrodite even though one's spouse has used one to produce children. Hard to imagine our clown in that position, much easier to see her in it— uninhibited, grinning, urging him on, screaming. The most elevated couple: a hermaphrodite and a stale matron . . . Miss Lulena, who walks like a duck, baring her gums above small yellow teeth, mouth open, threads of saliva dripping: and the engorged hermaphrodite, stammering in his red jammies decorated with braid and medals, advancing upon her. Miss Honorary Doctorate, the shameless hussy.

A supreme commander who has never seen combat, a supreme scholar who never finished school. In a golden frame on her ostentatious desk stands *his* portrait, retouched by the best experts of Interpol. On *his* desk, framed in platinum, we see the precious smile of *her* ugliness, decorated with flowerlets and little stars: Miss Lulena, decked out in jewelry and medals and false diplomas, still nothing but a fraudulent Pussycat.

She always spreads her legs, even in the most festive presidential photographs, and always holds her little purse right in front of her pussy, the demotic designation of that unnameable primal spot.

I have taken an infantile, vengeful pleasure in Fellini's text, reading it only from one perspective, reading and rereading it, always with this subtext in mind—to align our ridiculous national clown with all those other White Clowns. Yes, indeed: "the mouth a thin line, cold, full of antipathy, remote" in an ugly face whose homeliness becomes monstrous with its liver spots and its wrinkles born of so much cursing. "Icily authoritarian, like certain nuns in charge of kindergartens"—yes! "Like those spiffy Fascists in shiny black silk and gold braid, riding crop in hand"—yes! A Clown in White in his "striving for higher goals," in his hilarious honky-tonk small-town improvisations, lacking in style and definition, in his sterile, cartoonlike animation à la Duvalier and Idi Amin.

I have exhausted Fellini's text in my secret enjoyment of it; I was incapable of reading it impartially. In a totalitarian state, every detail of everyday life, every word and gesture acquires a distorted and hidden meaning that reveals itself only to the indigenous dwellers.

Only those who live in more or less normal societies can find this code lunar and fascinating. That poor, ridiculous creature! An illiterate upstart! Stammerer! Chimpanzee! Monster! Vermin! Leech!

A White Clown? That's too great an honor. . . . He was too small, too unfinished, too stupid for that. Yet it is much harder to see him as belonging to the seemingly more modest, in reality far more distinguished, category of Augustus the Fool. That's unthinkable. Augustus is much too dear to me; I have always seen the artist as an Augustus, a loser.

In my last year *there*, I read Montale's great poem "The Poet" countless times.[6] In a time of increasing deterioration and degradation of everyday life, the sovereign sarcasm of his verses helped me at times to endure the ubiquity of the dictator. I knew the poem by heart and repeated it to myself with sadistic determination, carefully measuring out the poison the poet had distilled so masterfully.

"Only a short thread is left me / but I hope I'll be able to dedicate / my humble songs to the next tyrant." Thus Montale begins the confession he ascribes to "a poet." I wasn't alone in sensing that only a short thread was left me: over the years, the tyrant had worn us down, insinuating himself into our daily nightmares, and I knew that even if I managed to save myself, I would be scarred forever by the toxins of this macabre period of my life.

"He will want / spontaneous praise gushing from my grateful / heart and will have it in abundance," I repeated, making faces, thinking of the ghost possessed by this very desire for "spontaneous praise," who lorded it over not only a crowd of poets but also the thousands and again thousands of anonymous frightened people squeezed into his circus prison.

"All the same I shall be able to leave / a lasting trace," I consoled myself, thinking about my famous and not-so-famous predecessors and contemporaries who felt that their only responsibility was to posterity.

The final lines, however, I would whisper, since that was the only way I could enjoy the exaltation with which art proclaims its fundamental truth, parodying it at the same time: "In poetry / what matters is not the content / but the form."

That gave me satisfaction. I had already succeeded several times in finding the right form for the encoding of my antipathy for the tyrant; what's more, in my novella "Robot Biography" the aggressive "content" took on a high-risk form when I made January 26 the sinister main character's birthday—the day of tremendous festivities in honor of the tyrant's birth.* The horrified reaction of my friends to this impertinent frivolity both delighted and terrified me, but it also gave me hope that other readers would notice how spontaneous aversion had made me demonstrate that form and content are indeed united in works of art.

"Better to be a free human being, never mind all the problems with which one may be burdened, than to be the buffoon of a lamentable buffoon," a friend wrote to me in a letter around the time of the buffoon's birthday. The friend enclosed a big bundle of newspapers that sang the praises of the event. Every year, huge festivities are organized in his honor, with pomp as solemn as it is provincial, making even the policemen laugh as they form the thousand-long human chains to restrain the merriment and pressure of the masses.

For me, this sinister carnival was already a thing of the past; I was on the other side of the wall and had landed in West Berlin, a city that brought to mind similar caricatures and a similar collective brutalization.

I looked at the pile of papers. They seemed to have been printed on toilet paper and tore as soon as you turned a page. The ink left red, green, and black smudges on my fingers. I was barely able to read a few sentences: dementedly repetitive, the clichés chased one

---

*January 26, Ceaușescu's official birthday.

another and promptly induced lethal boredom. All the years endured in that empire of horror and perverted language, all the neuroses and nightmares, stirred up the old, indissoluble poison in me.

In those same weeks of painful, intermittent recovery, I came across a repulsive but useful potboiler, a godsend to the Western media's appetite for sensation. Repulsive because of its subject (our little dictator with the speech impediment) and also its author (a former general who had been in charge of the dictator's secret police and now had entered the service of "freedom" and new masters), but useful because of the revelations this connoisseur was offering the public in his depiction of a clan of upstarts, a gang of circus clowns made up of philistines, crooks, and cynics who had gained power and used it to develop their mediocrity and meanness to the fullest degree. There was the trade in Jews and Germans for convertible currencies, euphemistically called "reuniting families"; there was the espionage and disinformation, the hobnobbing with Arab terrorists, fire-eaters, hypnotists, animal tamers from the KGB. There were the situations that made our "Leader" throw up—when, for instance, American authorities wouldn't comply with his demand for an "official" ban on protest demonstrations during his visit to New York, or when he heard that he'd been betrayed by one of his most faithful servants; the attack of hysteria when he first met the new US ambassador, who was black (an insufferable insult to an old internationalist). I read about the tantrums of his spouse, the one with many honorary degrees, directed against their circus house managers when they had forgotten to place orders for special toilet bowls from Paris or London. I found out about her piquant "hobby" of watching movies of adultery committed by some of the highest figures of the state, clandestinely filmed by Securitate specialists for this express purpose.

It was probably no accident that during this same period between Inferno and Purgatory (tyranny and exile) I found, in a Parisian journal, these sentences addressed to Julien Hervier by Ernst

Jünger: "The artist has to focus on his painting, his poetry, his sculpture, the rest is ridiculous. That is why I could never criticize an artist who benefits from the favors of a tyrant. He can't say: 'I'll wait until the tyrant is overthrown!' because that might take ten years, and in the meantime his creative power would wane."

I agreed that "the rest is ridiculous." It is, however, not just a question of the ridiculous but also, first and foremost, of the horror, the destruction of the last enclaves of quotidian normality, the daily risk of physical and spiritual death. It was impossible to escape from that "rest," which had become the all-encompassing, aggressive, absurd, and suffocating *whole.*

The buffoon of a lamentable buffoon? To the best of my ability, I managed to sidestep the monster's masks and traps. I never vied for the tyrant's favors, I wouldn't have granted him a syllable of praise. Dead-eyed, I stared at the dead pages of the dead newspapers. Suddenly, Fellini's "impertinent loudspeaker" came to mind: "A loudspeaker, an Augustus, simply refuses to transmit the program given by a White Clown."

All the dishonest newspapers that poisoned our days with their unchanging refrain, all the loudspeakers playing the same tune: what if, one day, they provoked a revolt, what if they found a method of revenge, of mockery, by changing, reversing the code? A warped sentence, a missing letter that simply escapes from one of his great honorary titles, an impertinent blot on the idyllic retouched photograph. . . . At the right moment, the "impertinent loudspeaker" manages to pull off a gag that serves to demean the tyrant: "It surrounds him, ridicules him, mocks everything the White Clown utters," says Fellini. "It is the revolt of the means of communication —altered news to counter the insulting nonsense loudspeakers were forced to disseminate during the Fascist years." And not only during those: our generation had its own White Clowns and everyone was his Augustus.

I refused to serve our tyrannical clown not because I disdained his favors but because I tried to ignore him as best I could. I wasn't even interested in that realm of the "ridiculous" that can only be called "the rest" of the very first shaky and confused days of terror that later mounted rapidly and murderously, like an avalanche that collects, devours, annihilates everything in its path. I took good care not to hate him, because that would have meant granting him too much importance—even though like a huge, tireless octopus he had already discharged so much shit that we were almost suffocating under it. Now that everybody hated him and hoped for his death, there was no longer anything one could do against him.

Only when a disaster has become obvious and irreversible does hatred become irreversible: against Hitler, only in the final months of the war, when disaster overwhelmed the entire German people; against Stalin only after his death, when the monster was no longer dangerous and the myth had turned rancid.

All the heads of state of both East and West received our ridiculous national monster with highest honors. Even during his first period in power, while he was still exploiting misconceptions and presented himself as a champion of the good, he disgusted me just as much as in his final decade. I was instinctively appalled by him even before he started baring his teeth in the horrendous Grand Guignol performance. It would not have been possible for me to dismiss the entire masquerade only as the "ridiculous rest." With increasing frequency, he unsheathed his claws, and his bark grew ever louder. His demonic, murderous ridiculousness was no negligible "rest," it was the *whole*, and no one was able to escape.

Not long after the tyrant came to power, a writer who moved in medical circles showed me a "psychiatric profile" of the tyrant prepared by a group of respected specialists. Even then there was reason to fear the worst: even then, this leader, this best-beloved son of the people, should have been taken into custody without delay, on grounds provided by these documents.

Soon his paranoia became evident: in labor legislation that tied every wage earner to his place of employment, to force obedience and facilitate surveillance; in family legislation that made divorce difficult to obtain, banned abortion, and discriminated against unmarried couples; in school legislation aimed at the politicization and militarization of children. It was obvious in his tirades, delivered in a state of trance for hours on end to starving audiences, about the future of the circus to be built by happy slaves whipped ever onward by stern kindergarten teachers. The clown kept in his circus troupe only the hypnotized dwarves whose job it was to applaud him, and the brawny armored giants who made up his national security system.

Even back then, I was cautiously preparing my departure from the "labor zone," as it was called in the language of the menagerie, a zone that was to become, in less than a decade, a swamp for rhinos to wallow in, those who like to bathe in ordure and denounce others.

One needn't exert one's imagination too much to visualize the state of revulsion and fear, exhaustion and depression, that drives a person to the psychiatrist. The latter knows, of course, that the illness in question is affecting all of society, but each patient is an individual case whose "self-denunciation" has to be taken seriously and treated.

It is a razor-edge situation in which Augustus the Fool no longer mimes ambiguity but is possessed by it, and in which the boundary between hallucination and reality begins to dissolve. A minute dose of "simulation"—for example, the assignment of excessive importance to certain real symptoms (or others derived from one's reading)—can ultimately lead to a genuine disturbance.

In the totalitarian circus, where faking is not immediately obvious either to the physician or to the less aware patient, the waiting rooms of psychiatrists' offices become sanctuaries of refuge, prayer, simulation. They become "legal" hiding places where one can withdraw from the marshy arena and its lies, punishments, and daily moans.

Since psychiatric repression has been used against so many "undesirables," it may seem unconscionable to hand the state the simplest weapon it can use to destroy you. And I didn't belong to the "desirable" ones, then or later. And yet . . . My patient waiting in front of physicians' offices did finally lead to "liberation" and "victory": I was declared unfit to work. The annual humiliation of a medical examination protected me from a multitude of other daily humiliations. Had the truly diseased one (who'd made the entire nation ill) decided to retire, be it for obvious "reasons of health" or for reasons of age—equally obvious for a long time—I would have "recovered." As things were, I was the afflicted one, and the portrait of the buffoon that stared at me from every street corner compelled me to increase the dosage of my medication daily. Thus, at last, a connection had been established between us. The curious role reversal was just a pale reflection of the schizophrenia the true madman had imposed on his entire domain.

In such borderline situations, what becomes quite evident is the fundamental difference between the interpretation of a role—with its subtle symptoms common to all professional diseases, including the play called life and the play called death—and the actual role a human being has been assigned on the great stage of the world.

Does the White Clown represent only ridiculous authority, and Augustus contrariness, laughter, and suffering? "The appearance of a White Clown (the Fascist) transforms us into similar clowns as soon as we surrender and return the Roman salute in a disciplined fashion," says Fellini.

"You are much too serious. You are too ethical, and you are not playful enough. The image of Augustus the Fool doesn't fit you at all," said a friend years ago after I published *Augustus the Fool's Apprenticeship Years*. Suffering to the point of grimaces, I was forced to accept Augustus the Fool as an autobiographical reality. This identification was not only the result of a withdrawal from my surroundings, of loneliness and its burden of vulnerability, and it was more than a simple refusal to obey; it was in fact a consequence of my deep solidarity with people's unhappiness.

The bad actor gradually polarized the hatred of a whole shackled nation into lethargy. In this state of tragic, general despair, Augustus's laughter and tears gain a great resonance among his fellow sufferers.

Existence under terror distorts your perceptions and frequently tempts you to make risky and far-fetched associations. No matter how far you have removed yourself from that existence in both time and space, it is impossible to rid yourself of your dark obsessions.

In the summer of 1988, in Washington, I watched the circus of the presidential elections and was reminded of the clown "back there." The presidency of the Actor was over, and now it was time for the new actors of the new presidency. The childish and vulgar theater of competition for acclamation gave rise, in the exiled Augustus, to rather pessimistic thoughts about the human species. Anyone coming from the so-called socialist East needs some time to rid himself of illusions about the "reverse" utopia. But even if these disappointments were irritating and if the new vice president Coturnix reminded me—surprisingly enough—less of telegenic Robert Redford than of a minor Stalinist Party secretary in a provincial town of the 1950s, my terror still remained *over there*.

Only over there could my reading of Fellini's essay evoke that childlike *Schadenfreude* in me. Even if one watches the American election circus on the tube through Fellini's telescopic lens, one is still *over there* in one's mind. This may be so because Jünger's statement applies *only* to old or young democracies in which one still has the option to ignore the political brouhaha, or at least to put it in parentheses. That, however, becomes impossible when the ridiculous reigns supreme over all of human life, tortures everyone without respite, and slowly but surely cripples them: then it is not only *the rest* that is ridiculous, but the whole, and it can't be ignored because it won't ignore you, won't let you go.

The circus of free, freely manipulated elections in a democratic society does not give cause for optimism. While watching it I was spontaneously reminded of the FBI file on Charlie Chaplin, discovered years after his death. It was 1,900 pages long, covering the period between 1922 and 1978 (thus extending one whole year beyond his demise), and contained so many absurdities that no satirical cabaret could do them justice. And yet, while witnessing all the shallow gags that accompanied the spectacle of the US presidential elections, all I could think about was the incomparable face of our tiny national clown.

Are the tyrant and the suppressed masses truly irreconcilable in every respect, or is it a matter of unconscious reciprocal stimulation? Do labor camps and totalitarianism arise only when a society's energy is perverted and suffocated? Is the dictator only the enemy or also the creation of the masses?

"It is said that Antonet, a famous White Clown, never spoke a word to Beby, his Augustus, outside the arena," Fellini writes. The clown takes revenge on the anonymous masses when he comes and throws tantrums when his superiority is not admired. How did our national clown react to his daughter's love affairs? Or (how shameful!) to the marriage of his son—to a Jewish woman! No one even bothered to explain the national importance of the new divorce laws to that imprudent boy; they simply mailed the divorce decree to him.

Could it be that the dictator too is an artist, obsessed with the impossible? Could we consider the diseased, fanatical boy who called himself Caligula a poet just because he appointed his favorite horse to a ministerial post? Does the gigantically morbid ever achieve the ineffable distant horizon all poetry strives toward? Is the despot a knight of utopia?

Duality inheres in every human being, certainly in poets and also in leaders, even though the latter like to forget it. "The station-master in my movie was a White Clown, and thus all of us become Augustuses. When you stand in front of a White Clown, you can't help but assume the role of Augustus," confesses Fellini, who then adds: "But only the appearance of an even more sinister clown, the Fascist, transformed us into White Clowns when he forced us to return the Roman salute in a disciplined fashion."

Finally, the author attempts to define his own location in the fabulous circus of the world. "If I try to imagine myself as a clown, I end up seeing myself as Augustus the Fool." In the real world it seems risky to venture between the uncertain and diffuse bound-aries that define human experience. "Yes, I consider myself an Augustus the Fool, but I am also a White Clown," Fellini continues. Then he concludes with a meditative sentence: "But perhaps I am the director of the circus, the physician of the mad who has himself become mad." An outsider, a pariah, a melancholy dreamer and an unwavering researcher, an undecided mime, a man obsessed by irresolvable questions.

Does the chimera of reality become more real than reality itself? Among the characters whose passions and follies the artist lives through, whose disasters he "appropriates" and whose abysses he illuminates, he must not forget that of the tyrant. We encounter the tyrant among children, as well as among despotic kindergarten teachers, among married couples and lovers, parents, grandparents, co-workers, and recruits. Only too often, he sits on the highest throne and terrorizes a whole nation, a whole world. He lives his part without being aware of it; he is simply an aberration of nature. Paradoxically or not, only art can render this horrifying, real, cyclical natural catastrophe credible and mysterious. (Alfred Jarry's words on his deathbed reveal the identification that can exist between an author and his creation: "Daddy Ubu will now try to sleep.")

The minor comedian, the paranoid hero, who has fulfilled his ambition to take over the world's great stage for a while with his attacks of arrogance, devastating masquerades, absurd rituals—it is possible that even he, the tyrant, is granted moments of fanatical insight, but he will never be blessed with the clarity and talent of the artist who interprets him for a while. Chaplin plays Hitler with the same degree of genius that he applied to so many other, different, even diametrically opposed, roles, whereas Hitler only "played" himself.

Does unwavering observation of the grotesqueness and vanity of Power finally lead one to a kind of compassion tinged with fear, or to an arrogant feeling of purity and superiority?

During my final year *over there* I saw him at close range. Not on television, greeted with somersaults and magic tricks by some presidential colleague at some foreign circus, or on a trip within the country on the occasion of one of those "working visits" that begin with the howling and twitching of the masses, continue with his advice bestowed on trained slaves in factories, stables, colleges, crematoria, schools for parrots, and end with an endless speech on hairraising visions of the future, the same speech delivered a thousand times before, always in front of the same horrified captive audience.

No, this time I experienced him in tangible proximity. I had just returned from the police precinct where I had submitted my typewriter to its obligatory annual examination: in the national clown's opinion, only those worthy of a special permit were entitled to the possession of such an instrument. To obtain this special permit, one had to fill out a form and pass an annual test that involved a personal appearance, dangerous machine in hand, at the police precinct of one's residence, to have the form checked and also to type a control text just in case a letter had changed, an exclamation point or a comma had worn out, or—even worse—in case the owner and hence the machine had been stricken with some contagious disease that could be transmitted through typed pages, causing a collective epidemic. As everyone knows, the viruses of our time are such sly and stubborn creatures, well camouflaged, almost invisible, but aggressive, terribly aggressive, and simply unstoppable once they get going.

I had to wait my turn for over an hour, but everything went without a hitch. There were a lot of people waiting in front of room 23, the number indicated on my form. Particularly impressive were the old folk struggling in with their heavy old models. The three young officials in civilian garb, probably members of the Securitate, were polite and bored, possibly even mildly skeptical about the value of this new circus routine; in any case, the procedure was performed with dispatch.

First came the routine questions. Do you own an automobile? If so, what make? Do you own your apartment or do you live in a state-owned apartment? Who shares it with you? Employment of spouse? Relatives abroad? Trips abroad? Relatives in this country? Any members of the Party Central Committee or employees of the Ministry of the Interior? I knew that the questions had to be answered in writing in one's own hand. They no longer shocked me as they had the first time, when their absurdity and utter irrelevance to the subject of this test still had an intimidating effect. I filled out the form in a quick scrawl, then typed two copies of the assigned text, as well as two sets of the impressions made by every key, and, once again, received my permit. Feeling quite good about it all, I headed back home with my magical toy.

While still in the elevator, I heard the piercing, paralyzing howl of a police siren. The militia! I hurried to unlock the door to my small apartment and ran to the balcony. The siren didn't stop, it was announcing an event: a small motorcade consisting of his limousine, then the limousine of his favorite dog, the ever-present huge black Labrador, the emergency physician's car, three police cars, and finally three less conspicuous vehicles carrying "technical" personnel. A modest convoy indeed, compared with his entourage on other working visits. This was obviously one of those unannounced blitz visits that the nation's clown decided upon as if struck by lightning, to the dismay of his unprepared subjects. Undoubtedly a surprise visit, because otherwise the sidewalks would have been packed with a dense crowd of applauding citizens, women, children, soldiers, employees, transported here for that express purpose.

The national clown wished to inspect the progress of construction of the White Palace. He had ordered the razing of some of the prettiest quarters of the city to make room for the palace and the Circus Boulevard that cut the city in two—or nine, or however many—segments, so that the Great Presidential Circus would finally dominate the skyline.

The convoy came to a halt next to the small bridge across the stinking waters of the city canal. He wanted to view the Perspectives of the Future. Around him swirled a gaggle of subordinates waving and carrying plans, maps, and portfolios, anxiously eager to anticipate the direction of his next step and to decipher the meaning of his every gesture with due alacrity. These were elegantly attired gentlemen, construction engineers, sculptors, decorators with crazed purple faces, jerking about in a frenetic St Vitus' dance, stumbling and stammering.

The surrounding balconies filled with gawkers: office workers, housewives, children. This was not the command audience that would obey police instructions to congregate at predestined points along the clown's route. For a moment one couldn't know what to expect from this mass of people; then some began to . . . applaud.

Not to yell, not to complain or curse; no, applause it was, even though sporadic, a sleepy reflex, an automatic reaction to a ritual that had entered their bloodstreams ever since the first circus routines to which they had been driven under the lash of severe kindergarten teachers. It was conventional applause but nevertheless spontaneous, independent of the usual pressure exerted by the police, perhaps triggered by fear of colleagues and neighbors.

I saw him plainly: from the 365 sets of his annual wardrobe, the special outfitters had chosen the appropriate one—overalls tailored from buff-colored silk. A rumpled cockney cap had been planted on his head, pulled down close to his eyebrows. His movements were deliberate, he did not raise his voice but seemed calm and sensible, not unlike a modest shopkeeper, and took notes of what people told him on a small pad. Everyone in his entourage took notes as well. The little boss seemed to pay special attention to everything the spiffy specialists managed to tell him, paralyzed by fear as they were. According to the day's predetermined program, he listened to them in silence. Among all these confused people he looked like the only normal person, the only one who could afford the mask of normality. The hysterically obsequious behavior of the cast of eminent authorities and the clown's slightly weary jester's calm established the beat of this touching and horrifying contredance.

The observer's confusion lasts only a moment: then he becomes aware of the fact that this comedian has destroyed his life, poisoned his days, his and everybody else's—this pitiful windblown vagabond, this gutter demagogue! His white mask—white as his skull. It is a feeling of humiliation to have lived so many years terrorized by a caricature—or is it grief for the human species in general?

For a moment, the observer feels unapproachably superior to this wild charade, suddenly transfigured by such crystalline incongruity—thus, an aristocrat: he, the outcast, the "artist," already knows that he'll have to pitch his tent elsewhere, as far as possible from this blood-drenched arena. ("He can't say: 'I'll wait until the tyrant is overthrown!' because that might take ten years, and in the meantime his creative power would wane.")

This last confrontation lasts only a second. Then he shakes the weariness off his shoulders, out of his head and his entire body, as if wanting to rid himself of the poison that has invaded every fiber of his being.

Irreversible time, time that gives nothing back: neither the house nor the books, neither the abandoned projects nor the lost friends.

Is it possible for evil really to be embodied in such pitiful and ridiculous envoys? Does the grandiose imprint of hell manifest itself in these laughable (even if terrible) stammered pantomimes?

He isn't even worth a curse. Nothing and No One and Nowhere —this is the summation of this catastrophe, concrete and terrible as it was.

His caricature grins from every wall of the country, the country that once embodied hope. A hope of a life, for better or worse, but a life: in the light of youth, at the time of decline, in the intoxication of love, in rebellious dreams as well as bitter disappointment. For better or worse? It was never free in any case, but it became hell only after the skeleton of this plague rose up against the firelit sky, in this carnival that glorified the future and celebrated death. He is tiny and white, the clown, a little white mouse, a carrier of the plague: a death's-head of nothingness.

Life *back there* consisted of waiting, of permanent preparation for something uncertain and continually postponed. That was the life this Augustus the Fool led until yesterday. A life in permanent suspension. Now it lies behind him, ever farther behind him, and yet it has stayed with him like a wound that won't heal; it partakes of every step he takes. A quote from the teachings of Rabbi Moshe Loeb: "The road through this life is like a razor's edge: hell on one side, hell on the other. Between those two runs the road through life."

What awaits this wanderer: a somersault into the void? The sense-lessness of new masquerades? the vulnerable post-adolescence of the aimless stranger among strangers? And what about big words, dear to children and old people and cherished by poets: freedom, conscience, dignity, bravery, sacrifice? They will do for the embellishment of gravestones.

"The loneliness of the poet—what is the loneliness of the poet?" This was a question in a questionnaire that a group of writers fond of aphorisms and wordplay amused themselves with in the first postwar years.

"A circus routine that hasn't been announced." That was the answer given by the young poet Paul Celan before he went into exile in the West, forty years ago.

Bard College, summer 1989
Translated by Anselm Hollo

Notes

1. Frederic Morton, "Chaplin, Hitler: Outsiders as Actors," *New York Times,* April 24, 1989.

2. Ibid.

3. F. Fellini, *I Clowni,* Bologna: Cappeli, 1970.

4. Ornella Volta, *Small Encyclopedia of the Clown.*

5. Although much of the material in the preceding paragraphs was common knowledge in Romania in the later years of Ceauşescu's regime, the stories did not begin to be published (as far as I can tell) until after 1989 or 1990. See especially John Sweeney's *The Life and Evil Times of Nicolae Ceauşescu* (London: Hutchinson, 1991) and István Várhegyi's article in *Die Zeit* (May 1990).

6. Eugenio Montale, "Una poeta," in *Quaderno di Quattro anni,* Mondadori, Milan, 1977.

HAPPY GUILT

I

When he died in 1986, in Chicago, at the age of 79, Mircea Eliade was a famous scholar of religion, the Sewell L. Avery Distinguished Service Professor in the Divinity School and professor in the Committee on Social Thought at the University of Chicago, and a well-known writer. He was the author of some fifty books, including short stories, novels, plays, essays, studies on philosophy and religion, and of countless articles. A *History of Religious Ideas*, in four volumes, is probably his most famous work.

Eliade's rate of intellectual production was, from his youth, extraordinary. His work is extensive and varied, from articles on popular science to erudite, scholarly books, from cheap novels to important works of fiction, from casual comments on casual subjects to sophisticated research. A man of enormous learning, he was also a restless, "wandering" reader and writer. In his fiction, as in his scholarship, we find the same themes: the myth of the eternal return, the *coincidentia oppositorum*, the crisis of Western man, the sacred and the profane, the archaic roots and the cosmic feeling of the human condition, the role of ritual and myth, of magic and archetypes. The most important theme of all, probably, is the theme of initiation, and his books were stages of his own endless initiation into what he believed to be the inexhaustible mystery of the human being and the world.

Eliade's passion for knowledge, for reading and writing, dated back to his high school years in Bucharest, where he published his first article ("How I Found the Philosopher's Stone") in 1921, at the age of 14. After receiving his master's degree in philosophy in 1928 at the University of Bucharest, he went to India for three years, to study Indian culture and philosophy at the University of Calcutta. He considered it his greatest spiritual experience. "In India I discovered what I later came to refer to as 'cosmic religious feeling,'" he wrote in 1978, in *Ordeal by Labyrinth*.

Eliade received his doctorate at the University of Bucharest in 1933, with a dissertation on Yoga. (It became a standard work on the subject.) He was appointed assistant to Nae Ionescu, famous professor of logic and metaphysics, and began his teaching with a course on "The Problem of Evil in Indian Philosophy." Eliade was fascinated by his mentor and friend, even when Ionescu became a propagandist for Italian fascism and German Nazism, and a passionate supporter of the Iron Guard, the Romanian extreme-right and ultra-nationalist movement, a kind of Christian orthodox fundamentalism.

When some of the leaders of the Iron Guard, including Ionescu, were imprisoned, Eliade—himself a supporter of the Iron Guard— ran into trouble with the authorities, even though he was already an important figure in Romanian culture. Still, he was appointed cultural attaché to the Romanian legation in London in 1940. A year later, when Romania entered the war on the side of Germany, Eliade had to leave London, and was sent to the Romanian legation in Lisbon. When the war ended, he remained abroad, in Paris, where he taught at the Ecole des Hautes Etudes, and later at various European universities, before settling, in 1956, at the University of Chicago.

Eliade's *Journals* and *Autobiography* cast an interesting light on his life and his work, which partook of the troubled culture of this troubled century.[1] Unfortunately, they do not in any way excuse or demystify Eliade's ideological and political history during the fascist period. Eliade once wrote, in another context, that "a [demystifying] attitude is altogether too facile," that he preferred "the camouflage adopted by the sacred in a desacralized world." "I made the decision long ago," he confessed in *Ordeal by Labyrinth*, "to maintain a kind of discreet silence as to what I personally believe or don't believe."

In 1936, however, he had written that "to me, it is a matter of complete indifference whether Mussolini is or is not a tyrant. Only one thing interests me: that this man has transformed Italy in fifteen years, turning a third-rate country into one of the world powers of today." That was five years before Paul de Man, a young and addled intellectual on the make in Belgium, penned the anti-Semitic, pro-fascist newspaper articles that recently provoked such a furor. But Eliade was older and wiser; and not least for that reason, his views of the time, when he believed sincerely in Mussolini and in Corneliu Zelea Codreanu (the "Captain" of the Iron Guard), deserve the same scrutiny. Of course, Eliade could not predict the terrible consequences of his views; he had been obsessed since his youth with the relation between the sacred and the profane. And it is difficult to know whether his views evolved in the many years that he lived in the West. What we do know, through his own writings, is that his skepticism of the Western model of democracy never left him.

Eliade's brilliant scholarly work concerned myths and archetypes, and so it is not surprising that, despite his persistent anti-communism, the scholar admitted to an interviewer that Mao could be seen as "the last emperor," "the guardian and interpreter of the right doctrine and, in everyday life, the person responsible for his people's peace and well-being"; or that "the myth of Stalin reveals a nostalgia for the archetype"; or that Lenin's tomb, though it is not at all religious in essence, became symbolic of a "lost, or confusedly desired, higher state." It would have been a welcome surprise if Eliade, in his later autobiographical writing, had come to contradict his earlier positions, to reassess his involvement with totalitarian ideology. Surely his *Journals* were his last chance, but he did not take it.

Perhaps some exoneration will be found in Eliade's unpublished writings. In any event, in the context of the recent political changes in Eastern Europe, which were stimulated and led not least by writers and artists who fought courageously against tyranny, the portrait of Eliade that we now possess is especially regrettable. For, as we know, the number of intellectuals who were on "the wrong side" in the last half-century is not negligible. Even now, during the chaotic transition to a civil society, there are intellectuals in those newly liberated societies who speak about the necessity of "good doctrine" and "iron discipline," about the need for a powerful state, a sacred authority, and so on. The fight against the canonization of Power is as difficult as ever. Had Eliade testified truthfully to his involvement with totalitarian ideas and actions, his testimony would have had a great impact, especially at this moment.

II

The fourth volume of Eliade's journals, a book of modest length, ends shortly before his death in 1986. It fits smoothly into the series, and has the same structure: the most important events of the day are laconically noted and linked to his teaching, to his scholarly and literary work, to his travels, to conferences, and to the people he meets. As Larry McMurtry noted about an earlier volume, "This is not a journal of personality, much less of gossip. Eliade doesn't give the impression that he is too good, either for personality or for gossip, but merely that he is too busy, too absorbed by the work at hand."

Though Eliade's journal summarizes his every activity (it even includes a datebook, which it sometimes resembles), it does reveal moments of melancholy, even of suffering. With advancing age, discretion, impersonality, and other strategies of evasion are some-times abandoned. In the entry for November 19, 1983, for example, we find the following admission: "I can't lift heavy books from the shelves, I can't rummage the file folders. . . . Why have I been punished for—and through—those things I have loved all my life: books and writing?" Melancholy is usually associated with a lack of energy: "I suffer from melancholy provoked, as usual, by . . . what I *must* do now immediately."

The reader of *Journal IV* is often aware of the burdens of age and illness, the diminution of the extraordinary capacity for work that Eliade had maintained throughout his long life. The presentiment of the end is stoically treated with daily intellectual activity, and an often Olympian effort at retrospection. "I'm afraid my exaggerated [candor] and [modesty] minimize a certain conduct (from earliest youth) which was not lacking in *grandeur* and nobility," Eliade wrote in June 1980.

If there are underlying themes running through the feverish daily activity described in the *Journal*, they are the two subjects that obsessed him, in this last period as in his whole life: books and Romania. As Wendy Doniger correctly emphasizes in her affectionate epilogue to *Journal IV*, "The primary focus is books; people come second." The drama of the approaching end focuses more on the books that Eliade will not be able to write than on the people from whom he must part. Here he speaks of the inevitability of the end, there he divides up his library with supreme calm and meticulous care; and together such passages create a moving portrait of the essential scholar. The people close to him must have found it difficult to accept his devotion to the books he lived with so closely, but books were the ruling passion of his life, from an adolescence of insatiable reading (he developed a system of gradually cutting back to a minimum of sleep in order to make more time for reading and writing) through his insomniac old age, when the magic in books still had the power to invigorate him.

For a student of magic like Eliade, there was an odd premonitory relationship, an interdependence, between the destruction of books and the coming of death. A dream that he recorded on July 21, 1979 included typically surrealistic scenes: an elegant gentleman in a coffee shop surrounded by a multitude of bizarre little animals, a manuscript reduced to a sandwich for mice that cannot be stopped from eating it, his own futile panic, and so on. This nightmare came true, in a way, in the strange fire that destroyed his office library at Chicago's Meadville/Lombard Theological School in December 1985, four months before his death. Dream and reality seemed to join in a somber warning that time was running out.

It seems probable, as Doniger suggests, that Eliade considered his work more important than his life, and that he saw the destruction of his books as a warning that "it is not long now." Still, he did not conclude that his life had lost its meaning, and he published his many memoirs and journals. This perdurability can also be seen in the relationship that Eliade maintained with Romania, and with what might be called Romanianism. To the end of his life, he wrote his literary works and his memoirs in Romanian. His relationship with the Romanian language and culture (as well as with Romanians living at home and abroad—it is notable how many he met with, or kept in touch with, from like-minded thinkers to communist officials or former Legionaries, from admirers and students of his work, friends and relations, to all kinds of strangers) reflects a lively and lasting interest, and more, a deep sense of affiliation.

In a meticulous monograph on Eliade, *Mircea Eliade: The Romanian Roots*, which appeared in 1988, Mac Linscott Ricketts, who is also the translator of some of these volumes, made a useful observation about Romanianism:

> Romanianism . . . was a term that in the mind of the [Romanian] public was associated with the ultra-right-wing political philosophies and programs. All the parties of the extreme right . . . invoked it in their propaganda. Ordinarily it signified chauvinism, anti-Semitism, policies for restraint of minorities, anti-

communism, and enthusiasm for Italian fascism and German National Socialism. Eliade believed the word, which he found in the writings of nineteenth-century nationalists he admired.
. . . had signified originally something "above" politics, and that it had been debased by political parties in the twentieth century.

The fact of Eliade's nationalist affiliation, its magnitude and its durability, should be stressed not only because he spent more than half of his life outside Romania, writing in other languages and living as an émigré of international renown, but also because he represents a case of broad significance for Romanian intellectual life, even for the fate of Romania as a whole today, yesterday, and perhaps tomorrow. Eliade was not a scholar who built an impenetrable wall of books between himself and the real world. He was always concerned with the fate of his native land, and he possessed a clear vision of the social and political ideal that he wished for Romania.

It is understandable that Eliade often thought, toward the end of his life, about his relationship with the country that he left but could never abandon. "I kept thinking of what I would have suffered had I remained in the homeland as professor and writer," he noted on October 10, 1984. "If it hadn't been for that *felix culpa*: my adoration for Nae Ionescu and all the baleful consequences (in 1935–40) of that relationship," he continued with odd candor. The thought was repeated (and the formulation about his "happy guilt," too) in the last pages of his *Journal*, on August 29, 1985: "I think of myself: without that *felix culpa* I'd have remained in the homeland. At the best, I'd have died of tuberculosis in a prison."

Now, Nae Ionescu was, in the words of Professor Virgil Nemoianu of Catholic University of America, "a minor but lively Socratic thinker [who] advocated a kind of vitalistic existentialism (an irrationalism that was not foreign to concepts borrowed from Orthodox

Christianity) . . . and ended up as a supporter of the Iron Guard. . . ."
It would be naïve to imagine that Eliade's adoration of this mentor
of the fascists in Romania was the only reason he could have been
arrested and convicted in the postwar period (although it would
have been sufficient cause). If an excuse for his arrest and conviction by the communists was needed—thousands were arrested without ever knowing what their crimes were supposed to have been—it
could easily have been found in his journalistic activity during the
time that the Legion of the Archangel Michael, and after it the Iron
Guard, was active in Romanian political life.

The Legion of the Archangel Michael was the original name of
the Romanian fascist movement that later became famous as the Iron
Guard. Among the many crimes it committed was the often mentioned barbarous "ritual murder," on January 22, 1941, of 200 Jews at
the Bucharest slaughterhouse, as the "mystical" murderers sang
hymns. (Marshal Ion Antonescu, once the fascists' ally, eventually
dissolved the Iron Guard in 1941, though anti-Semitic murders did
not cease under his military dictatorship.) At that time the left-wing
press called Eliade a "fascist" and a "Legionnaire." Indeed, a number
of serious charges could have been brought against him after the war
by the communist authorities. There were his attacks on communism and on the Soviet Union, his disputes with the left-wing press,
and his scandalous sanctification of the "martyrs" of the Spanish
Civil War (those who fought for Franco, naturally).

Just as serious was Eliade's eulogy of Antonio de Oliveira Salazar,
the dictator of Portugal, whom he apparently wanted to propose as a
"model" for Antonescu. His book on Salazar was written and published in 1942, when he worked at the Romanian embassy in Lisbon.
In other words Eliade's file would have been filled to bursting if the
communist authorities had wanted to justify severe punishment. Of
the accusations of "fascism" continually brought against Eliade by
the left-wing press, Ricketts writes shrewdly that "in a sense, Eliade's

critics—unjust though they were—saw more clearly than he himself the direction in which his thinking was taking him."

If his health had withstood the hard years of imprisonment, Eliade would have been freed in the 1960s, like others who shared his way of thinking, and like them he would have been the "beneficiary" of the far more malignant policy of "retrieved" values that formed the basis of the new cultural policy of Romanian communism. He would have been allowed to publish at least some portions of his old or his new books. He would have been favored with respect and with the "tolerance" reserved for "useful" Romanian intellectuals. He might even have received the calculated "encouragement" of communist officials, who found the old ideas of their former right-wing nationalist opponents useful sources of justification for their own new ideological orientation.

For the ideological apparatus of Ceauşescu's Party initiated, in the mid-1960s, a systematic study of the Iron Guard experiment. The communists envied the Guard's former popularity, and they adopted its slogans as their own: "the national revolution" in place of the "international" one; the totalitarian state centered around a *Conducător*, or Leader; the discrediting of democracy; anti-intellectualism; the repression of liberalism; and so on. The enemy of Ceauşescu's nationalist-Communist Party was not right-wing extremism, it was democracy. The democratic and rationalist directions in Romanian thought (that is, the principles of the democratic-bourgeois revolution of 1848, the sarcastic humor of the great Romanian writer Ion Luca Caragiale, the legacy of the important literary critic and social thinker Eugen Lovinescu, and so on) came to be a favorite target of the "witch-hunters" in Bucharest, along with the "decadent influences" of the West, around which the omnipresent Securitate tried to throw a cordon sanitaire.

But Eliade never returned to Romania. In the West, his status as an anti-communist probably protected him for a while from unpleasant questions about his relationship to fascism. In the end, however, the questions came. They were raised not by the communist enemy, but by the democratic society that Eliade had always regarded with deep skepticism. And they required a reply, not least because public opinion is stimulated by unsatisfactory answers to probe further. Eliade's confrontation with his past was not pleasant, even if it was not as dramatic as it might have been under a totalitarian system.

III

Echoes of these confrontations appear in the last volume of the *Journals*. On June 6, 1979, Eliade writes:

> I learnt that Furio Jesi has devoted a chapter of calumnies and insults to me in his book that has come out recently, *Cultura di destra* [Culture of the Right]. I learned long ago that Jesi considers me an anti-Semite, fascist, Iron Guardist, etc. Probably he accuses me also of Buchenwald. . . . It makes no difference to me if he abuses me in his book (I shan't read it, and therefore I won't respond to it).

His annoyance is so great that he drops his cool scholarly attitude and denounces as libelous a book that he has not even read, that he does not intend to read, so as not to be obliged to reply to it; and he invokes Buchenwald in a wry tone that is, to put it mildly, inappropriate.

A few weeks later, on July 4, 1979, he has resumed his blasé mask, and we find an evasive reply in his *Journal*. "Barbăneagră relates to me that Jean Servier said to him recently: that from Israel they have received precise instructions that I am to be criticized and attacked as a fascist, etc. Jean Servier, says "Barbăneagră, was indignant. . . . I believe it, but there's nothing to be done." Is this annoyance—passed off as irony, transmuted into tired self-pity—a sign of vulnerability, or guilt, or some higher detachment from the claims of ordinary life? To those who knew Eliade as an affable émigré of delicate sensibilities and stylized civility, always sociable and receptive ("the last man in the world to have a totalitarian thought," said one of his friends), such accusations were inconceivable. But it is not easy to triumph over such an accusation, if you cannot prove it false.

The infamous human experiment known as Nazism—with its hysterical propaganda, its arrogant brutality, its devastating warfare, its extermination camps—cannot be removed from the context in which it arose. In a period of economic, political, moral, and intellectual crisis, it offered a simplistic, violent, "radical" solution. Nazism did not at first mean the crematorium; it developed slowly, slyly, cruelly, to its sinister culmination. (At the opposite pole, or so it seemed, was communism, which derived its totalitarianism from the humanism of an egalitarian and rationalist utopia.) Still, there *were* those who saw from the start the horror of the totalitarian project, and they must not be forgotten as we strive to comprehend the collective or individual guilt, happy or otherwise, of all those who were "fellow travelers" with the missionaries of horror. There were some men and women who had real clarity of vision. We might cite, for example, one pre-Holocaust opinion, not a philosopher's or a writer's, but a journalist's: the American journalist Dorothy Thompson, who was expelled from Germany by Hitler for her anti-Nazi writing, considered Nazism

> a repudiation of the whole past of Western man. It is . . . a complete break with Reason, with Humanism, and with the Christian ethics that are at the basis of liberalism and democracy.
> . . . In its joyful destruction of all previous standards: in its wild affirmation of the "Drive of the Will": in its Oriental acceptance of death as the fecundator of life and of the will to death as the true heroism, it is darkly nihilistic. Placing will above reason; the idea over reality; appealing, unremittingly, to totem and taboo: elevating tribal fetishes, subjugating and

destroying the common sense that grows out of human experience: of an oceanic boundlessness. Nazism—that has my consistent conviction—is the enemy of whatever is sunny, reasonable, pragmatic, common-sense, freedom-loving, life-affirming, form-seeking, and conscious of tradition.

If we knew how Eliade would have responded to such a view during the years of his connections with the Romanian fascist movement—with its specific references to the Christian ethic, to the oriental vision of a heroic death, to the "Drive of the Will," and to the tribal rituals of blind subjection to the Leader, all of which were so important to the Legionary movement—it would help to explain why so many of the eminent Romanian intellectuals of his generation chose this sinister affiliation. It would also help to explain how a stubborn conservative intellectual is transformed into a right-wing fanatic, in the way that a humanistic, "progressive" intellectual is transformed into a simplistic and militant communist. Does the fault lie simply with the confusion of a society in crisis, a society that could not consolidate its democracy or offer a coherent "faith" to those who were exposed to the temptation of these radicalisms?

Eliade always avoided a clear analysis of his militancy. About these potentially unpleasant matters, he preferred ambiguity and evasion. Even about less controversial matters, about scholarly questions on his view of the history of religions, he sidestepped direct confrontation or open, concrete debate. "From the articles which Ioan Culianu has dedicated to me, I understand, that in recent years the 'methodological' criticism brought against my conceptions of the history of religions have increased" (September 15, 1985). Eliade gives the impression that it was only by this indirect means that he learned of the objections to his method. "I've never replied to such criticism," he says, "although I ought to have done so." He promises himself that he will do so to explain "the confusions and errors," but he knows that he will not, for "I'm afraid I'll never have time."

When he is called a Nazi or an anti-Semite, when he meets the stony weight of accusations that simplify the story of his life, Eliade's tendency to withdraw is even more marked. To be sure, there is dignity in silence, and there is delicacy, not just cunning, in evasion: but in silence and in evasion there is also much that is reprehensible. To retract one's former beliefs, to denounce the horrors, to disclose the mechanisms of mystification, to assume the burden of guilt—probably few are sufficiently clear-eyed and courageous for this. But it is precisely those few who do have the courage for such a confrontation with the past who justify the stature of the intellectual.

In order to be truly separated from the errors of the past, one must acknowledge them. Is not honesty, in the end, the mortal enemy of totalitarianism? And is not conscience the proof of one's distance from the forces of corruption, from totalitarian ideology? In his *Memoirs*, Andrei Sakharov confessed without embarrassment his youthful admiration for Stalin. The honesty of that admission was precisely the honesty that enabled that great scientist and humanist to achieve a profound understanding of the nature of the communist system, and to become its unyielding critic.

When questions do not come from within, they come from without; but in the end they come. It is a matter of constant surprise, perhaps, that Eliade's "enemies," and not his admirers, posed the questions. Would it not have been more natural that his admirers should have been his most exacting judges? (On July 23, 1979: "C. Poghirc comes to see me. . . . He talks also about the campaign against me in Italy, provoked by F. Jesi. The aim: to eliminate me from among the favorites for the Nobel Prize.") And why is it, we must also ask, that those who have borne honest witness to the totalitarian tragedy have emerged largely from the victims, and only rarely from the victimizers? After all, the latter are the ones who could definitively establish the essentials of the evil.

The recent collapse of the totalitarian communist system probably will not bring about a fundamental change in this sad pattern.

People would always prefer to discuss innocent suffering rather than their own responsibility for it.

IV

"Between a tradition of thought and the ideology that inscribes itself, always abusively, within it, there is an abyss," write Philippe Lacoue-Labarthe and Jean-Luc Nancy in their interesting book *The Nazi Myth*. Even if we may question such a categorical claim, their argument should be heeded:

> Nazism is no more in Kant, in Fichte, in Hölderlin, or in Nietsche (all of whom were thinkers solicited by Nazism)—it is, at the extreme, no more even in the musician Wagner— than the Gulag is in Hegel or in Marx. Or the Terror, with all simplicity, in Rousseau. In the same way, and whatever its mediocrity (by whose measure its ignominy must however be weighed), Pétainism is not a sufficient reason to invalidate, for example, Maurice Barrés and Paul Claudel. Only to be condemned is the thought that puts itself deliberately (or confusedly, emotionally) at the service of an ideology behind which it hides, or from whose strength it profits: Heidegger during the first ten months of Nazism, Céline under the Occupation, and a good many others, at that time or since (and elsewhere).

"A good many others . . . and elsewhere" indeed. Romanian fascism may have been different from Hitler's or Mussolini's, but it retained the same principal characteristic: "an amalgam between rebellious emotions and reactionary social ideas," as Wilhelm Reich said.

The extremes of nationalism and religious militancy that gave rise to the Iron Guard (and to its earlier and later variations) could already be observed in the confusion following the Treaty of Versailles after World War I, when Greater Romania was created. The inclusion of the new provinces (Transylvania, Bucovina, Bessarabia) suddenly added to the country not only Romanians who formed the majority in those provinces, but also significant minority populations (Hungarians, Jews, Germans, and others). Thus it was not frustration over defeat, as for the Germans, or discouraged inertia, as for the Italians, that turned an old Romanian nationalism into a violent and fanatical extremism. Romanian extremism was the result of territorial success.

Violently anti-Semitic Romanian fascism, calling itself "Christian" and "moral," took advantage of a fragile parliamentary democracy and sought its electoral base among the peasants, who were neglected and frustrated at a time when Romania was embarking on industrialization and modernization. The movement was responding to the same appeals that Hitler's National Socialism made: to find an identity and to construct a mythology. Today we would call the fascism that developed in Romania—which ritualized a death cult and Christian sacrifice, violently excluded all "foreigners," idealized the rural life, rejected democracy, individuality, and modern Western civilization—a Christian Orthodox fundamentalism with a terrorist structure.

Many of these ideas could be found in the traditions of conservative Romanian thought. And important Romanian writers of the nineteenth and twentieth centuries had expressed a similar vision in journalism and philosophy. From the national poet Mihai Eminescu through B. P. Hasdeu, Nicolae Iorga and Octavian Goga, Eliade and his friend, the thinker and writer Constantin Noica, the fact that leading names in Romanian culture could be claimed as standard bearers for right-wing extremist movements is a deep and unfortunate measure of Romanian public opinion and Romanian political choices. The political writings of these figures did not directly incite their readers to murder (though their intolerant and hate-filled language reaches unbearable levels of violence in some of their nationalistic texts), but they certainly pushed in the darkest directions.

"Mac Ricketts has come for three days . . . Two evenings we dined together. He keeps asking me questions. There are periods still only partially understood: for example, the accusation and allusions to my 'Nazism' (anti-Semitism) in the years 1938 and 1939. I try to explain for him certain articles, conversations, and events of those years." This is an entry for March 1984. Ricketts, a former student of Eliade's at the University of Chicago, has devoted to his mentor two massive volumes of thorough documentation. He does not always grasp the implications of the byzantine political atmosphere of the time and the place, or all the historical ramifications of nationalism in its Eastern Orthodox variant, but he has provided a large quantity of carefully researched material, and has tried to draw fair and balanced conclusions.

Ricketts is careful to list precisely the occasions on which Eliade dissociated himself from certain violent actions based on narrow concepts or fanatical strategies, but in the end he accepts the truth of the documents he has so passionately studied. "Many of the ideals for the Legion were identical to those Eliade had long been advocating." "Returning to one of his favorite themes, the mission of Romania, he finds it embodied in the Legion's Program." "In his new found enthusiasm for the Legion, which for years he had classed as just another right-wing political extremist group, Eliade lost his sense of perspective and overlooked the flaws in its doctrines and practices." "Eliade wrote about the 'new aristocracy' being constituted by the Legion." "The longest pro-Legionary article bearing Eliade's name is one that he has denied writing . . . Actually the pseudonymous piece probably contains nothing Eliade would not have agreed to at that time; it appears, in fact, to have been based very closely on articles he had written in recent years . . There can be no doubt that, at this time, he did hope and believe in the triumph of the Legionary Movement." Finally, Ricketts summarizes Eliade's view this way:

> Democracy has been unable to inspire in the people a spirit of fervent nationalism—to make of them a strong, virile, optimistic nation, imbued with a sense of mission and destiny. Being a foreign import, democracy is concerned with matters that are not specifically Romanian concerns: with "abstractions" such as individual rights, rights of minorities, and freedom of political consciousness—and these, Eliade says, do not strike at the heart of "Romania's problem."

Ricketts also provides the English reader with significant quotations from Eliade's journalism. Some examples:

> To me, then, it is entirely immaterial what will happen to Romania after the liquidation of democracy. If, by leaving democracy behind, Romania becomes a strong State, armed, conscious of its power and destiny—history will take account of this deed.

> The Legion member is a new man, who has discovered his own will, his own destiny. Discipline and obedience have given him a new dignity, and unlimited confidence in himself, the Chief, and the greater destiny of the nation.

> There are a great many revolutionary impulses that have been waiting for thousands of years to be put into practice. That is why the Son of Man descended: to teach us permanent revolution.

There are still other pieces, not included by Ricketts, that Eliade published in the Romanian press of the time that could have been cited, such as this comment, which appeared in the newspaper *Vremea* on December 18, 1936, in an article called "Democracy and the Romanian Problem":

> In the name of this Romania that began many thousands of years ago and will not end until the apocalypse, social reforms will be enacted with considerable brutality, every corner of the provinces now overrun with foreigners will be recolonized, all traitors will be punished, the myth of our State will extend all across the country, and the news of our strength will stretch beyond its borders.

Or this one, from an article called "Eulogy for Transilvania," which appeared in *Vremea* on November 29, 1936:

> From those who have suffered so much and been humbled for centuries by the Hungarians—after the Bulgarians the most imbecilic people ever to have existed—from these political leaders of heroic martyred Transylvania, we have expected a nationalist Romania, frenzied and chauvinistic, armed and vigorous, ruthless and vengeful.

Even more citations from Eliade's writings of the 1930s can be adduced, about the "terrifying murders" of which the weak, corrupt, powerless, and still youthful Romanian democracy was guilty; about "the advance of the Slavic element from the Danubian and Bessarabian regions," or the fact that "Jews have overrun the villages of Maramures and Bucovina, and have achieved an absolute majority in all the cities of Bessarabia."

In sum, there are countless such pronouncements, some even more ridiculous and even more disgusting. Today these phrases sound absurd, infantile and aggressive, but we must not forget that such "irrationality" was made legitimate in its time by a summary and deviant "logic" that furnished instant "solutions" to long-unresolved social conflicts. It is no coincidence that, in the confused and oppressive period before the war in Europe, when even long-established democracies were tottering, this kind of extremist impulse turned up in one form or another even among many intellectuals. Rebellious spirits, and those with a reactionary social vision, were especially vulnerable to this kind of messianic and simplistic solution. The unhappy spectacle of the fragile democracy in Romania, paralyzed by internal contradiction and by the complicated situation abroad, added to the dilemmas of a long and troubled national history, in which identity crises and easy identifications with a utopian and totalitarian ideal have together worked much harm.

Mircea Eliade was a writer and a scholar. That is why his "case" deserves our special attention. It is certainly true that the work of the writer and scholar exists in a separate domain from that of the militant reactionary journalist of the interwar period. Again, "Nazism is no more in Kant, in Fichte, in Hölderlin, or in Nietzsche (all of whom were thinkers solicited by Nazism)—it is, at the extreme, no more even in the musician Wagner—than the Gulag is in Hegel or in Marx. Or the Terror, with all simplicity, in Rousseau." Eliade's literary work is extensive and uneven. His scholarly work is written for specialists. To draw a connection between his scholarship and his "fascist" period, to cast an inquisitorial eye on "suspect" details in his many learned studies, would be to provide a perfect example of totalitarian methodology.

Indeed, during the period between the wars, the leftist Romanian press labeled some of Eliade's novels "fascistic," an example of just such abusive and fanatical simplification. (In his monograph, Ricketts ably rejects distortions of this kind.) Writing about the case of Paul de Man, Denis Donoghue recently observed that "it would answer injustice with injustice if one were to assert that Deconstruction is compromised by de Man's wartime journalism. The current attempt to smear Deconstruction by denouncing de Man is sordid."

The same may be said of any attempt to smear Eliade's scholarship with his politics.

Many literary critics in Romania and elsewhere have stressed, moreover, the humanist value of his literary work: the stimulating and mysterious ambiguity of his prose, his magical fantasy and enigmatically coded reality, the free play and the dreamy compassion of his writing. But this does not diminish the questions that must be raised. Quite the contrary, it aggravates them. Literature must meet primarily aesthetic criteria, not moral ones, just as scholarly work must meet scholarly standards. But journals, memoirs, autobiography: such strictly personal reckonings cannot avoid the ethical test.

The contrast between Eliade's fiction and his fascist journalism is as pronounced as the contrast between Eliade the supporter of the fascist Iron Guard and Eliade the respected intellectual of later years, remembered by his friends in the cordial and cosmopolitan atmosphere of his American home, always hospitable and affable with colleagues and acquaintances of all races and faiths. No one could see (and perhaps Eliade himself managed to forget) the hovering ghost of another time, another personality.

And so the issue that the *Journals* avoid returns persistently to haunt them. Eliade's "happy guilt" does not refer only to his remembered adoration for Nae Ionescu; in old age, after all, the nostalgia for youthful joys and passions often goes beyond acceptable limits. (Eliade's friend, the Jewish writer Mihail Sebastian, was also in his youth an admirer of Ionescu, but he would probably have recalled his admiration differently in 1985.) It is harder, however, to excuse a passage like this one from the *Autobiography*:

> I don't know how Corneliu Codreanu will be judged by history. The fact is that four months after the phenomenal electoral success of the Legionary movement, its head found himself sentenced to ten years at hard labor, and five months after that he was executed—events that reconfirmed my belief that our generation did not have a political destiny.

Corneliu Zelea Codreanu was violently anti-Semitic and anti-democratic, and he committed odious murders. Yet Eliade appears to be uncertain, four decades after the war, in Chicago, how history will judge him. He is still fascinated by Codreanu's electoral "success," he fails to mention the murders committed by this "martyr," and he does not hesitate to identify himself with that "generation" and even its political destiny. And the same treatment is accorded the Leader's "lieutenants" the martyrs Ion Moța and Vasile Marin, slain in January 1937 as volunteers for Franco in the Spanish Civil War (dramatically evoked by Eliade at the time and later recalled as "models" of sacrifice in the Legion's view). It was really a case of retaining an outlook. Eliade's conception of the best social and political solution for Romania seems to have remained constant. It was a traditional and conservative vision, "fundamentalist" in its orthodoxy ("I don't believe in God, I believe in Jesus"), skeptical about democracy and modernity, tied to ethnicity and to the cultural values of the place.

V

Alexander Solzhenitsyn's recent call for a Slavophile Russian state comes at a time when the old conflict has reawakened in Eastern Europe between the "separatists" and the "integrationists," between the supporters of independent states and the "Europeanists." In Romania this dispute was tragically manipulated during the years between the wars. Now it is reappearing in a changed historical situation, pitting those who want integration into Europe against those who want to strengthen the national state and the national character.

The right is still no smarter, though, than the left; it learns neither from its own disasters nor from those of the other side. Nor are the intellectuals always capable of protecting their illusions, ideas, and aspirations from evil associations, notwithstanding their own grievous experience. In the 1970s, according to his friend Noica (as reported by Katherine Verdery of Johns Hopkins University), Eliade encouraged Professor Edgar Papu, from his distant American home, to launch a debate in Romania about "protochronism." This debate was launched initially to emphasize the Romanian contribution to world culture, and more generally the role of small isolated cultures in stimulating important intellectual achievements. It gradually degenerated, however, into odious, ideological, "patriotic" pressure, similar to the pressure of Stalin's requirement that the Soviet press discover new aspects of the "supremacy" of Soviet culture over Western culture. This debate occupied the Romanian cultural scene for some fifteen years, and led to one of the most sinister campaigns against the intelligentsia by the Ceauşescu regime.

The political schemers, of course, soon bridged the abyss between Eliade's thinking and their own immediate interests. Which does not make his unhappy guilt (involuntary, this time) any less. Eliade was, after all, an intellectual with much experience in such matters. In contrast to his great predecessors in Romanian culture (such writers and thinkers with a similar right-wing vision as Eminescu, Hasdeu, Vasile Pârvan, and Iorga), Eliade had the "advantage" of witnessing the Holocaust, the unfolding of Stalinist genocide, the horrors of right-wing and left-wing dictators. Eliade lived the longest part of his life in a democratic society, in which he could see that, besides its economic and intellectual achievements, and despite its many shortcomings, democracy is the only system in which there can be a dialogue between the right and the left, even in their extremist forms.

In its everyday, domestic aspects, the reality of "totalitarian" systems such as Nazism and communism has been far more complicated than is suggested by the classifications and the denunciations. Honesty requires those who have lived with "true socialism" to reject simplistic recrimination, which is more likely to cut off than to help an understanding of the truth. The current spectacle of millions of former Party members in Romania now madly reciting anti-communist slogans is moving, because it forces us to think twice before returning to our comfortable categories. How quickly these people forget not only their own guilt, not only the unhappiness of those who were truly oppressed or marginalized by the totalitarian powers, but also the many "happy" moments enjoyed during their somnolent complicity. Guilty pleasures? Happy guilt? It would be hard for these opportunists, past and present, to admit to this kind of ambiguous happiness, just as hard as it probably was for many Nazis —genuine and "convinced" Nazis who only in retrospect were forced to acknowledge the horror, and to speak of their happy Nazi youth, of the demonstrations, the balls, the lectures, and the other ecstasies of their own *felix culpa*.

An honest and critical analysis of the significance of Eliade's life would have been important to the whole of Romanian culture. Banned in Romania for the first decades after the war, Eliade began to be "retrieved" in the 1970s. This was not without complications: though Ceauşescu's "National Stalinist" regime sought the kind of nationalist legitimacy that the Legion had enjoyed, the last leaders of the communist "old guard" could not forget the political orienta-tion of their old enemy. It is now known, for instance, that in 1937, on learning that the student Gogu Rădulescu, a communist who later rose to become vice-president of the Council of State and a member of the executive of the Romanian Communist Party under Ceauşescu, had been detained at Legion headquarters and beaten with wet ropes. Eliade not only expressed satisfaction with this barbarous "punishment," but said that he would have put out Rădulescu's eyes.

Yet Eliade's literary works began to be reprinted in Bucharest, and gradually some of his scholarly works appeared as well. Despite its author's political past, and despite its title, *The History of Religious*

Ideas was distributed in "atheistic" Communist Romania "through institutions" to a list of the "privileged" selected by Party officials. Eliade began to meet not only with Romanian writers, but also with Romanian "officials," even with representatives of the Romanian government. Though Eliade's political past was not to be discussed in Romania, his work was so respected and his personality so fascinating that his name gradually made its way into many publications and into the work of many intellectuals. It was taken up, too, by the noisy nationalism that had for some years appeared in several journals (*Săptămîna, Luceafărul, Flacăra*), which, protected and even encouraged by repressive officialdom, practiced a genuine cultural and "patriotic" terrorism.

In 1982, a black year for Romanians under Ceauşescu's leftist-rightist dictatorship, I saw Eliade's play *Iphigenia* performed at the National Theater in Bucharest. The play had first been performed in 1941, another black year, and was published again in Romanian in 1951 by an expatriate right-wing press in Argentina. As in 1941, no doubt, the tension outside the theater, and the mood of the audience, its fear, disgust, exhaustion, and despair, combined with the play in a most unfortunate way, so that it seemed a kind of dark exaltation of "sublime" death for a glorious "cause."

"There is a real campaign beginning in the West to unmask Mircea Eliade's ties to the extreme right during the period between the Wars," wrote the Romanian dissident Dan Petrescu in the final years before Ceauşescu's fall, in an essay smuggled to the West. "This may at least lead, as it did for Heidegger, to increased popularity for his work." Petrescu went on to exclaim, "If only the collaboration of Romanian intellectuals with the present regime—which is anything but leftist—can be discussed one day. Then we'll see a show!" Indeed, Ceauşescu's regime was anything but leftist, and the same was true of the members (about four million of them!) of the Communist Party, which had no decisive tradition in Romania. But that show is now running, and it has become grotesque. Everyone proclaims his own innocence, his own suffering. And some of the loudest of those are the former "intellectual" servants of the dictatorship.

Romania's current problems with democratization must bring to mind the country's complicated history: the old identity crises and the addiction to extreme solutions are working together again to prolong the post-totalitarian impasse. Still, some encouraging effects of the transition to democracy can be seen. The free press isn't entirely nationalistic and provincial. It contains many voices that warn against the new dangers of political manipulation and against the old dangers of narrow-minded nostalgia and isolationism of the extreme right-wing ideology. Some esteemed intellectuals have created the Group for Social Dialogue, a critical forum that scrutinizes and debates the dismantling of the social-political institutions of the totalitarian state, and which follows and encourages the still timid phases of structuring a civil society. Although the old Nomenclature and the old-new secret police are smartly and efficiently using their network for enriching their comrades and building a shady alternative to democracy, the future cannot be, is not, the past.

Like other countries in the region, Romania will soon look to NATO and the European Community for help with her evolution, and the public discourse will certainly be influenced by this. Yet the way will be neither short nor easy. The country has to examine its history before starting a new future. There have been too many unhappy choices in the past and their consequences for the last half of a century, if not longer, cannot be ignored. The transition toward an open society will probably be marked by corruption and opportunism, greed, demagogy and manipulation, traditions that it will be difficult to override in this new, unstable and weak phase of democracy. But the darkness of dictatorship will surely still be vividly remembered, at least for a while, and that will help to energize hope. As Havel said: "Hope is not the conviction that something will turn out well, but the certainty that something makes sense, regardless of how it turns out." The potential for Romania's renewal is there, it has to be stimulated and guided to its fulfillment.

The time may be coming when the fascist period, as well as the communist period, can be analyzed clearly. If today there can be open and lengthy discussion of great writers such as Mihail Sadoveanu, George Călinescu, Tudor Arghezi, and Camil Petrescu, and of their compromises with the communist regime, would it not also be appropriate to analyze the voluntary involvement in the fascist movement, the "happy guilt" with all its consequences, of writers and intellectuals like Mircea Eliade? Instead, during the past year, the sacralization of the thinking of Nae Ionescu and Mircea Eliade, with their lasting guilt, has proceeded apace in Romania's large-circulation right-wing press (though a critical approach to that generation may be found in the new democratic press, as in the recent and important essays by Alexandru George, especially one called "White Bolshevism").

All this is more important now that communism is no longer a real danger in Romania. In a sense, indeed, it never was: Ceauşescu's Stalinism gradually became a camouflaged nationalist dictatorship. But the forces of totalitarianism in Romania still appear strong. The bankrupt collapse of the totalitarian "left" has much to teach the "right," even if the nationalistic right seems not yet ready to learn the lesson. The Romanian Parliament's recent rehabilitation of Ion Antonescu, Romania's wartime dictator and ally of Hitler, is a scandalous and unprecedented event in postwar Europe and a dark warning about the political future of the country.

And yet Romania means more than just Ceauşescu or Codreanu or Antonescu, more than the green-shirted terrorists of the Legion or the miners of the Securitate.* There still lives in Romania, or so we must hope, a legacy of democratic thought. It was stifled for

---

*In 1990 some ten thousand miners, manipulated by the old apparatchiks as political provocation, invaded Bucharest and terrorized the inhabitants.

many decades by right-wing and left-wing dictators, but it retains a deep relationship with European culture. The new generation thirsts for freedom and prosperity. There is hope for Romania, but it can be nourished only by a clear commitment to democracy and an unambiguous transition to a civil society.

Translated by Alexandra Bley-Vroman, 1991

Note

1. Mircea Eliade, *Journal I, 1945–1955* trans. Mac Linscott Ricketts (University of Chicago Press). *Journal II, 1957–1969* trans. Fred H. Johnson Jr. (University of Chicago Press). *Journal III, 1970–1978* trans. Teresa Lavender Fagan (University of Chicago Press). *Journal IV, 1979–1985* trans. Mac Linscott Ricketts (University of Chicago Press). *Autobiography Vol. 1, 1907–1937: Journey East, Journey West* trans. Mac Linscott Ricketts (University of Chicago Press). *Autobiography Vol. 2, 1937–1960: Exile's Odyssey* trans. Mac Linscott Ricketts (University of Chicago Press).

BLASPHEMY AND CARNIVAL

In 1970, Emil Cioran, the iconoclastic philosopher who had left Romania three decades before and won postwar fame in Paris, wrote in a letter to a friend from his youth about his nostalgia for the illusions of those who stayed behind. "I never cease to wonder that after so many trials you have managed to keep such evident composure. Nor is yours a unique case. I can guess the secret of so much vitality. Without hell, no illusions."

After so many years in the West, and despite the glory he achieved, Cioran felt old and worn out. "We pay dearly for not having suffered. We believe in nothing," confessed the nihilist in his Parisian refuge, where he had fled in the wake of the great European and world upheaval. Before, in Bucharest, he had contemptuously savaged the corrupt Romanian interwar democracy and—like his friends, the philosopher Constantin Noica and the writer Mircea Eliade—had ardently supported right-wing extremism.

Writing to his former friend in Romania, Cioran also referred to the sacrilege he had once committed against the French poet Paul Valéry, an unjust text in bitter opposition to his early admiration for Valéry, who had dominated the spiritual aspirations of his youth. Curiously, however, his blasphemy, he says, "was quite well received in Paris, where people like to demolish all reputations, even legitimate, even justified. Especially those."

He seemed unhappy at the lack of scandal, at the lack of people taking offense. No one had called him a vampire from Dracula's land, an alien, unworthy Wallachian who had tarnished the splendors of French culture with his barbarous, parvenu frustrations. On the contrary, Parisians adopted his paradoxes with delight and considered him a great stylist of the French language. Had he written an irreverent article in Romania, about, say, the national poet Mihai Eminescu, the outrage would have been instantly felt; he would have been treated as a rootless cosmopolite, an immoral, atheistic renegade. And the scandal would very soon have focused not only on the abject person of the blasphemer but also on the conspiracy of which he was a part, the classic, timeless, pagan, Masonic, foreign conspiracy aimed at undermining the values of a universally misunderstood and abused nation. The fact that he came from a family of Romanian Orthodox priests, or that he had once written that he would commit suicide if he were a Jew, would naturally have been cited as the usual cover for betrayal.

There is, we have to admit, something touching about the canonization of representative cultural figures. And in a world that is constantly losing its ideals, this may even pass for a sign of spirituality. But piety and taboos are structurally alien to culture, which, as we know, is essentially creative and questioning; on the other hand, even from a theological perspective, the quasi-religious canonization of certain nonreligious figures is an act of impiety, a vulgar substitution, itself almost a blasphemy, which expresses people's need for myth, illusion, and subterfuge.

Without hell, no illusions indeed; all the more so if society is passing through a severe crisis of identity and structure. This is what is happening in countries that belatedly face modernity, with all its tensions, promises, and failures. The Islamic world, large parts of the ex-communist world, but also many other tumultuous regions of our unbalanced planet are in this unenviable position.

The Viruses of Critical Thinking

Amid the explosive uproar of frustrations, even literary debates may become the pretext for violent appeals for a common unity and, of course, for excluding those carrying the viruses of critical thinking and individualism.

Take, for example, the reactions produced by the Russian writer Andrei Sinyavsky's attempt to clean Pushkin's hallowed literary monument of the disfiguring dross that had accrued to it from Slavophile orthodoxy and Soviet propaganda.

The mythologizing of Pushkin seems to have begun immediately after his fatal duel with D'Anthès in 1837. At the poet's funeral, admirers fought to carry off sacred strands of hair from his whiskers and head. But the official canonization took place at the unveiling of the great Pushkin's statue in Moscow in 1880, and half a century later, in 1937, it was ratified at the Soviet festivities marking the centenary of the poet's death. In 1880, Dostoyevsky, gratified by an impressive grouping of 100 women surrounding the huge wreath that he had to hang around the statue's neck, had proclaimed Pushkin a prophetic emblem of Russia, to the accompaniment of the shouts and tears of the crowd. Pushkin, Dostoyevsky said, would show "the way out of European ennui." He represented "the universally human and unifying Russian soul." He "uttered the ultimate word of great, universal harmony, of ultimate brotherly accord between all tribes according to the laws of Christ's gospel!"[1]

In 1937, an editorial in *Pravda* announced that "Pushkin is completely ours, Soviet, for the Soviet power inherited everything that is best in our people. . . . In the final analysis, Pushkin's creation merged with the October socialist Revolution as a river flows into the ocean."[2]

Compared with this ideological-political appropriation of the national poet, the spectacle of admirers overcome with grief at his funeral, or the marketing of numerous products with the name Pushkin (cigarettes, shoes, chocolate, vases) on the centenary of his birth in 1899, appears as no more than a naïve, homely carnival.

For a genuine dissident like Sinyavsky, courageous exposure of Soviet hypocrisy and terror (for which he suffered years of prison and then exile) needed to be supplemented with a critical examination of the "national emblems" that still provided the iconography for the idealization of Russian identity. The "Pushkin myth" has proved over more than 150 years to have had an enormous potential for mystification and manipulation, and to nullify this is the ultimate aim of Sinyavsky's *Strolls with Pushkin*.

A huge hagiographic literature had depicted the national poet of Russia, and then of the Soviet Union, as a martyr, a man of the people, and a social model, ignoring his distinctive and truly great characteristics as an artist and human being. In the introduction to Sinyavsky's book, the Russian scholar and translator Catherine T. Nepomnyashchy writes,

> Pushkin had been sacralized, forged into the center of a secular cult which none the less drew its emotional force from the wellsprings of religious zeal. Around the figure of Pushkin an entire cosmology was cultivated, a black and white universe divided clearly between heroes and villains who were defined ethically by their relations with Pushkin and served to validate him politically through their own allegiances.[3]

It is easy to understand why not only a dissident, but also a great admirer of Pushkin such as Andrei Sinyavsky, could not accept the canonical legend of the poet's life, or the metamorphosis of his work into a national ode. "What we might term 'Pushkin for the mass reader,'" Nepomnyashchy writes,

> was the most widely propagated version—the one most clearly implicated in the official mythology. This was the Pushkin whose verse every Soviet child began to memorize as soon as he or she began school, if not before, and whose biography, reduced to something of a simplistic catechism, was a standard part of the school curriculum. The emphasis here, as in virtually all Soviet humanities schooling, was on rote learning of canonical texts—favoring those of Pushkins works that could

easily be made to support the official image—and canonical interpretations of those texts.[4]

To recover Pushkin as a great artist required restoration work to remove the numerous layers of cosmetics.

Sinyavsky is not shy about the truth, and it is this that lights up the exceptional personality of the great poet.

> Pushkin gradually renounced, without exception, all the conceivable purposes that are generally imposed on art and opened up the way to an understanding of poetry—negative to its very core—according to which poetry, "by its very nature lofty and free, must have no other aim but poetry itself." Precisely because this art is free and obeys only "the movement of momentary, free feeling" (as Pushkin called inspiration), it has a habit of slipping through the fingers that embrace it too tenaciously, even if they are fingers of those who worship the beautiful, and it does not fit into its own pure definition.[5]

Not by chance did Sinyavsky begin the iconoclastic "strolls" with his beloved Pushkin when he was serving seven years of hard labor for "anti-Soviet agitation." He would transcribe fragments of his study in letters to his wife, and thus to the world outside his prison cell—real "anti-Soviet agitation," and much more besides, as its impact in the post-Soviet period demonstrates.

In the West where, as Emil Cioran believed, people like to demolish all reputations, legitimate or not, Sinyavsky's book was considered an original and scrupulous restoration of Pushkin's true reputation as an artist. "Brilliant, stimulating, intriguing," wrote Laurence Binyon in the *London Review of Books*. "An ardent and fastidious attack on philistinism in all its forms," Susan Sontag declared on the dust jacket. "By our standards, there is nothing scandalous about Sinyavsky. His every sentence is full of discernment and common sense," explained John Bayley in the *Times Literary Supplement*.

On the other hand, Russian standards, probably linked to the suffering and illusions that still make the writer both prophet and educator, have given rise to a different type of reaction. Take, for example, Igor Shafarevich, author of the scandalous volume *Russophobia* (1989)—a kind of anti-Western, anti-liberal, anti-Semitic manifesto, in which the great Russian people are seen as besieged by an alien minority that, in alliance with the demonic West, is bent on subverting the people's religious traditions and destroying the Russian nation. In an article entitled "A Phenomenon of the Emigration," Shafarevich urged Russian readers to demand the outlawing of Sinyavsky, much as the Islamic fundamentalists outlawed Salman Rushdie.[6] It was not quite a death sentence, as in Rushdie's case, but Sinyavsky was compared to him and placed in the same category.

By taking the pen name of Abram Tertz, a once-famous Jewish pickpocket from Odessa, Sinyavsky had already issued a dual challenge: a Jewish name and the Pushkin critique. The name reminded people that the writer had been considered a criminal by the Soviet authorities, sentenced for reading and writing forbidden books. But it also recalled the age-old fate of the Jew in Russia, as alien, renegade, and apostate, so similar in many ways to that of the artist. (The Russian poet Marina Tsvetaeva once said, "In this most Christian of worlds, poets are kikes.") Referring to Mikhail Bakhtin's vision of the art of the carnival—which Sinyavsky considers applicable in a broader sense to art in general—Sinyavsky maintains that the provocative name Abram Tertz was also in fact "an example of carnivalization," of a clownish metamorphosis.[7]

Alexander Solzhenitsyn saw in the "childish playfulness" of Sinyavsky's book a sacrilege specific to an émigré and "aesthetic nihilist" who, through Pushkin, was attacking authority itself, the foundation of society.[8] Other writers, too, from Russia and the Russian emigration, thought it inadmissible that Sinyavsky should have challenged a literary icon on a par with the icons of the Orthodox Church.

Many of Sinyavsky's violent critics have stressed the difficult circumstances of the moral crisis through which Russia and Eastern Europe have been passing since the end of communism. That he brought out his iconoclastic text in such ill-fated times seemed to many to add to his guilt. Thus, in January 1990, speaking on Soviet television, the conservative critic Vladimir Gusev argued that the scandal was not so much due to the text itself; "it was the context of the publication that was strange."[9] And what was the context? "Pushkin is one of the last saints left to our people in this spiritually tragic time."

This was similar to the point of view expressed by Ernst Safonov, editor of *Literaturnaya Rossiya*, in a debate at Columbia University in May 1990: "When all of these holy things are trampled, when there are no more icons or very few, Pushkin is one of those icons. He is an icon equal to the icons of the Church."[10] For his part, the rural fiction writer Viktor Likhonosov said, "an attempt was once again made on Russia," and he thought it perfectly natural and understandable that the publication of Sinyavsky's study "was like a bomb exploding."[11]

A preoccupation with social and moral problems has always been part of the Russian intellectual tradition. This served in the Russian press as an excuse for the uproar that Sinyavsky caused when his attempted restoration of the real Pushkin seemed to remove the great poet from that tradition.

In Romania, by contrast, the image of the writer as a "pure artist," belonging to the elite and far from the madding crowd, is accepted and even admired. Social-political commitment, like the whole sphere of moral problems, seems rather tedious, if not suspect—and is not necessarily tied to—is sometimes even harmful to—creativity. Creativity usually focuses on aesthetic achievement, spiritual heights, and a kind of condescending aloofness from immediate reality. Many Romanian intellectuals appear more proud than upset to see themselves propelled into a lofty sphere of unshakable composure.

Irritation occurs, rather, when the troubled life of one of their more esteemed representatives reveals that, instead of shutting himself up in the ivory tower of his own books and projects, he has taken a passionate interest in his nation's destiny, ready to be politically active on the terrain of his age, not uncommonly in far from honorable company. Even if the debate starts from a premise contrary to the one in the Sinyavsky case, it may trigger an equally violent reaction—as did the previous essay on Mircea Eliade.[12]

Although my essay deals with the former and current implications of the intellectual's involvement with totalitarian ideology, and so is strikingly different from Sinyavsky's study of Pushkin, its public impact inside the country was no less shocking—and an almost burlesque relationship, at once unintentional, spicy, and eloquent, subsequently developed between the two.

I wrote and published the article after the collapse of communism in Eastern Europe, when it had become evident that nationalism, which was being utilized as a major weapon in the winning of electoral support, was staging a powerful political comeback in that part of the world. Legitimacy was being sought in the writings of some illustrious cultural precursors, to be presented as new propaganda for public worship. It is no accident, for example, that since the overthrow of Nicolae Ceauşescu a party such as the "Movement for Romania"—which proclaims its continuity with the fascist Iron Guard—has required applicants for membership to take an examination on the work of Eliade and other scholars with similar political views.

I thought it necessary to remind those who did not know, or who wanted to forget, about the tragedy to which the nationalist option once led. The differences, as well as the similarities, needed to be brought out between nationalism and the more recent communist catastrophe, which, not surprisingly, was uppermost in everyone's mind.

Arousing Passions

The essay, "Happy Guilt," discusses Eliade's persistent "amnesia" about his political commitment in the interwar years, and the strange, vaguely nostalgic way in which his last writings before his death evoked the "happy guilt" of his youth. The text, as I have said before, deals only with the autobiographical writings. But these are far from insignificant, given that Eliade himself considered not only his work but also his life to be important, devoting to it successive volumes of memoirs and journals. My own memories of the time in "socialist" Romania when everything was "politicized" probably explain, at least in part, why I limited myself in this way and avoided analysis of Eliade's scientific or literary work.

The arguments of those who appreciated my essay were not very different in the East and the West. It was the arguments of those who objected to it that differed so much, and it may be of interest to compare them. In America, many readers considered the text too restrained, too subtle, too qualified. Such comments, however, remain a long way from the stupefying interpretation of the *Los Angeles Times:* "In an ambivalence that reveals Manea's determination not to overlook political complexities, he is hesitant to embrace popular democracy as the clear alternative to totalitarianism . . . and even sympathetically presents the philosophy of Romanian writer Mircea Eliade that democracy has been unable to inspire in the people a spirit of fervent nationalism."[13]

Publication of "Happy Guilt" in Romania, in 1992, however, aroused militant passions. Although the essay is focused on established facts and testimony, it met an audience that seemed quite unwilling to accept this. The legacy of the nationalist tradition had been obscured and manipulated by the communists for more than forty years, and today nationalism presents itself with an aura of legitimacy, mystery and martyrdom to a public in the throes of an identity crisis and thirsting for a new communitarian mythology.

Some felt it was a "luxury of remembrance" to call into question the values and excesses of nationalism. It seemed to them preferable to idolize great thinkers who had at some time been affiliated with the extreme right, but who could become spotless new parents for the masses orphaned by the collapse of a paternalistically socialist society. To express doubts about their immaculate spiritual biography became a kind of outrage, a hostile and offensive provocation.

Exposure of the horrors of communism was, to be sure, an urgent task but it also evidently fulfilled a complex role of exorcism. In 1945, the Romanian Communist Party had only a thousand or so members. By 1989, it was, in percentage terms, the largest in the entire Eastern bloc, with a membership close to four million, among whom it would have been difficult to find a thousand true believers. A broad, comprehensive debate about left and right totalitarianism—that is, a simultaneous exposure of the horrors of nationalism and native communism—seemed too much for people recently freed from oppression and yet so eager for new protective illusions. (*Without hell, no illusions.*)

"Blaspheming" the Idols

"Happy Guilt" was immediately seen in 1992 as a blasphemy directed against the great national values. In a chain reaction of indignation, with predictable anti-Semitic spurts, the few voices that dared challenge the general hysteria found themselves overwhelmed. And today, more than three years later, the uproar is revived from time to time by fresh distortions, in an inventive and inexhaustible carnivalizing of blasphemy.

In the ranks of the nationalist-communist press, where the author has been variously described as a "traitor," "the dwarf from Jerusalem," or "common trash," a paper such as *România Mare* owned by the nationalist parliamentary star C. V. Tudor, ex-bard of the Ceaușescu couple, has published an explicit declaration of faith:

"Yes, indeed, we are fighting to make Mircea Eliade sacred . . We are fighting to rehabilitate Marshal Antonescu, President Ceauşescu."[14]

It would be wrong to think, however, that cheap nationalist-communist speechifiers were the only ones to take offense. Judging by reactions in the press, "Happy Guilt" also incensed quite a few intellectuals, even those professionally trained in critical reading and interpretation. Nor was there any lack of invective in papers of a more "democratic" character. Certainly more elaborate, perhaps even more subtle, they depicted the author of the scandalous essay now as a "detractor," now as an "American propping himself up against the White House wall," now as a "follower of Ceauşescu," and now quite simply as a "policeman of the mind."

The Group for Social Dialogue, an intellectual nucleus of the opposition, prefaced its three-part publication of "Happy Guilt" in spring 1992 in its journal, 22, with a foreword by the deputy editor. Just back from the United States, he described the text as "tolerant and full of nuances and subtleties."

But once the last part had appeared, just three weeks later, he found himself compelled to explain that the Eliade essay had mostly aroused "reactions of disapproval and indignation." There had been hysterical anonymous phone calls, in which patriotic voices warned that those guilty of publishing such blasphemy would account for it "when the time came for judgment."

But 22 also made it clear that there had been a reaction from well-known cultural dignitaries, "people with some weight in our public life" who, without being named, were identified as "Romanian intellectuals who think in terms of a Judeao-Masonic world conspiracy." They did not merely express indignation or disapproval, but, according to 22, claimed that the publication of the essay on Eliade actually "served the dark purpose of demonstrating to certain circles abroad that Romanians are racist, anti-Semitic, and chauvinist."

It is hardly cause for astonishment that the extremist publications saw in "Happy Guilt" a confirmation of what they expected from international circles hostile to Romania. The true surprise was the general reaction of the Romanian press, including opposition magazines, strictly cultural publications, and so on. "Extremist" echoes in the left/right press (it is hard to distinguish between the two in the current political landscape in Romania) differed only in tone and style from the reaction of supposedly democratic individuals and publications "with some weight in public life." Those "circles abroad" that are said to decide Romania's unjust fate would, I believe, have been able to make equally good use of many of the reactions in the country's "democratic" press in their sinister attempts to promote an unfavorable image of Romanians as intolerant.

Faced with public indignation and assorted threats, the editor of 22 now hastened to explain that the text praised to the skies three weeks earlier "does not *by a long shot* represent the point of view of the magazine 22" or of its staff. Barely two weeks later, this revelation was followed by a fresh piece in 22 under the same signature, "Mircea Eliade—A Hero of Our Time," which clarified a few more things. The new article adopted Eliade's view that the rightist Iron Guard movement had been "essentially ethical and religious," preoccupied with services, requiems, mourning fasts, and prayers, guided by "blind faith in God's omnipotence," and obsessed "only with love." In this context, of course, it was not surprising that for the Bucharest journalist, the essay he had so recently considered "tolerant and full of nuances and subtleties" now "tended to drive Mircea Eliade away from sympathetic understanding in Romania, instead of bringing him closer to it."

As we can see, unlike the Russian reaction to Sinyavsky's book on Pushkin, the Romanian response to my essay on Eliade is better exemplified by the democratic and cultural press than by the much too crude and foul-mouthed nationalist press. The reason for the different reactions may be that Russian culture is traditionally obsessed with ethical and social questions, whereas Romanian culture often seems to be seduced by the delights of ambiguity, of a subtle and coded aesthetic game.

In this connection it is (probably) worth mentioning an original last-minute intervention in the debate, serialized in 1994 under the title "Mircea Eliade and his Detractors," in the Bucharest cultural review *Luceafărul.* The Romanian literary critic who wrote this piece located Eliade's "detractors" among leftists of every stripe, homosexuals, Jews, and exiles. He believed that "Happy Guilt" was part of a huge American conspiracy to obscure the guilt of the United States for its treatment of Native Americans, blacks, and the Vietnamese by focusing attention on Europe and its great cause for guilt, the Holocaust.

This broad and ever-shifting diversion required the constant discovery or invention of celebrated anti-Semites for the new Holocaust archives and museums springing up all over America. "Happy Guilt" was thus seen as part of an active worldwide plot, and the exile, N. M., had simply proved his loyalty to his adopted country.

The name Salman Rushdie was mentioned but once in the long press campaign in Romania against the essay on Eliade. Again, there was a striking difference from the aggressively moral and Slavophile slogans in Russia equating Rushdie's novel with Sinyavsky's literary study of Pushkin. The "essentially moralistic themes" in my article were said to have been stimulated by censorship and "fundamentalism, which corrodes the foundation of culture."[15] So, it is not Mircea Eliade's tiresome pro-fascist propaganda of the 1930s that is inquisitorial, but rather attempts to discuss his case against the background of nationalist revival in the Eastern Europe of the 1990s.

This carnivalization reached its peak in an absolutely original idea: the twinning of Rushdie and Eliade, in a staggering operation of twofold distortion, as jointly sacred. Salman Rushdie, who aroused the dogmatic fury of Islamic fundamentalists against the blasphemy of his anticanonical *The Satanic Verses,* and Mircea Eliade, whose dogmatic political texts fit perfectly into the fundamentalist canon of an extremist, totalitarian movement claiming to be essentially Orthodox Christian!

For all the wild manipulation, however, the invocation of Rushdie's name was not altogether inappropriate: neither in the case of the outrage at Sinyavsky's study of Pushkin, nor in the reaction to my essay on Eliade's political and autobiographical writings. For in the end, the great Rushdie scandal also began as a "literary affair" associated with an émigré—as did the incomparably smaller and more "local" scandals discussed here. And like these, it facilitated a significant comparison between how "blasphemy" is defined and perceived in societies that have been closed and in those that have long been open.

On its first publication, the novel *The Satanic Verses* did not shock the West. When its author was sentenced to death by the Iranian dictator Khomeini, he was, of course, fervently defended in the West, in the name of basic human rights and democratic principles. Sinyavsky's study of Pushkin was appreciated in the Western press as a solid and interesting piece of research, perfectly legitimate and of real use. My essay on Eliade's political commitment in the 1930s and his ambiguous memoirs about that period was regarded by Western readers, amid the present political confusion in the world, as a revealing critical reflection on the guilt of an intellectual led astray by suspect extremist affiliations.

The authors of these texts—writers exiled in the West, and thus hybrids of belonging and estrangement—had the poignant opportunity to feel in their own skin the moral, historical, psychological, cultural, and religious conflicts that their homelands were experiencing.

"Happy Guilt," instead of stimulating analysis of the responsibility of intellectuals who aid and abet political extremism, was rejected as an insult to the Romanian nation. Sinyavsky's book on Pushkin was received as an act of spiritual vandalism designed to separate the masses from their sacred national poet, an outrage to the messianic mission of Russia's great literature, its very pride and soul. Rushdie's novel, though a work of fiction, was not accepted as such even by Western clerics, and became the pretext for a fanatical instigation to crime on the part of the fundamentalist militants of Islam. The demonic "disorder" of democracy, the freedom to doubt and debate, pragmatism and diversity, appear to the theocrats as mortal dangers to Islam and the Koran—just as provocations to undermine ethnic cohesion appear intolerable to those who believe in the paternalistic authority of the Nation.

Demonizing Difference

In all these cases, the natural exercise of the intellect—whether focusing on moral interrogation, aesthetic research, or epic creation —was elevated to the rank of blasphemy simply because it challenged the comforts of spiritual routine and convention. In the end, as the Australian scholar David Lawton points out, "blasphemy is an orthodox way of demonizing difference, in order to perpetuate violence against it." If blasphemy can be seen as "a discourse that includes those who purport to be offended by it," then it is no wonder that "literature, representation and reading is [sic] potentially blasphemous."[16]

The demonization of difference is actually quite common. Its dark, blind, fanatical carnivalization may even reach the point of crime (as in the Rushdie case). PEN figures show that in 1993, 89 writers were murdered around the world, 150 were in prison, and 216 were under investigation.

Where there is no possibility of dialogue, blasphemy is simplification. The impact of blasphemy is all the greater, of course, in closed, authoritarian societies. In the silence of submission and the cold of dogma, the void is suddenly filled with panicky alarm. Anything that conflicts with the communitarian canon becomes blasphemy. Through careful manipulation and surveillance, the authorities maintain at any cost the narcissistic illusion of homogeneity and cohesiveness. Everything foreign or unusual becomes a source of danger to be negated and shut away—in the name of the ideal of perfect cohesion.

One might repeat Cioran's "without hell, no illusions" for too many of the characteristically closed, authoritarian social-political systems—even for countries suffering the painful transition from a closed to an open society. It may be that suffering strengthens belief but, at the same time, lends power to illusions. As has often been pointed out, however, the effect of illusions is so painful that it seems an involuntary homage to skepticism.

In closed, authoritarian societies, there is an obsession with blasphemy which assists the artificial cohesion imposed by the system, while carnivalization is the acting out of its dark, oppressive, fanatical consequences. In pluralistic democracies, on the other hand, blasphemy is rapidly diluted, whereas carnivalization becomes more widespread in the frivolous forms of entertainment imposed by mass consumption.

The existence of ever broader individual liberties, combined with an acceptance of diversity, effectively cancels out the risks of blasphemy in the society as a whole ("people like to demolish all reputations, even legitimate, even justified"). It is hard to imagine, in the varied cultural market of the West, that something like the Rushdie affair could be triggered by even the most unconventional, iconoclastic, heretical, indecent, or provocative book—or painting, sculpture, music, ballet, photography, or film. The emancipation of thought and taste goes together with increased tolerance, but also with ever more widespread indifference.

Nevertheless, the longing for an idealized community remains active in modern democracies; perhaps not in society as a whole but certainly in numerous closed groups. Communitarian narcissism generates suspicion and cult worship; sectarian formations sometimes present staggering similarities to the totalitarian model. The technique of mind control, the absolutism of power, the doomsday scenarios, the mystical exaltation going as far as ritual crime: these are the truly baneful characteristics of many closed groups in the open society.

The 900 suicides in Guyana in 1978, the 80 who died as a result of the authorities' brutal and stupid attack on the Davidian sect in Waco, Texas, in 1993, and the 48 who perished in 1994 in the Swiss castles of the Order of the Solar Temple are just the tip of an iceberg of social pathology. The growing number of local militias and religious and communal tribunals in the United States is also a part of this phenomenon.

Illusions and delusions can themselves create hell. Quite a few people wonder, for example, whether the disturbing rise in cases of "repressed memory," cited in the numerous reports of child abuse, does not resemble the witch hunts of several centuries ago. In volatile and suggestible persons, the psychosis triggered by "child abuse" films can become an obsession with satanism, a twisted form of regaining cohesion and protective authority through belief. "A religion is a sect that has succeeded," said the French historian Ernest Renan. And in their closeness and isolation, sects do have militant global visions.

Bad Taste and Cultural Innocence

In the open society, the public expression of frustration and illusion takes on carnivalesque aspects in the simplistic political debate. You do not know what to think more strange or ridiculous when, in response to the serious educational problems of young people under attack from violence, drugs, and precocious sexual initiation, the Christian right argues that the reintroduction of school prayer will make things better, while the liberal left seems to accept the idea of giving teenagers classroom lessons in masturbation. The cacophony of bad taste and cultural innocence is often overwhelming, obliterating any chance for a substantive exchange of opinions.

Yet the advantages of an open society can also be experienced in crises. In a democracy, the authorities would never aim to intimidate every voice into silence; here, the abolition of dialogue seems to be less of a real danger than the loss of meaning. The dominant tendency is for values to proliferate and rapidly perish, and it is no wonder that the end result is insignificance. But individualism, competition, and unhindered confrontation sustain an energy of self-affirmation that undermines centralism and absolutism, the essential premises of closed societies and their dark disorders.

Gradually, by opening itself to ever more finely shaded demands of the individual that may border on eccentricity, the democracy of late capitalism accepts outrage and thereby limits its effects. Blasphemy can operate only in restricted areas and sectarian groups. At the macro level of an open and heterogeneous society, blasphemy cannot resonate except in the form of scandal—scandal that is instantly carnivalized through commercial promotion, channeled to a broad public, and reduced to a routine product.

As the power of blasphemy has become more negligible, the field of the carnival has become larger. Freed from the pressure of blasphemy, society has opened itself to the prolific forms of carnival: the dozens of television channels on which ordinary people "confess" to millions of viewers; the nonstop "talk shows" about everything under the sun, complete with tears, laughter, and applause, where the scandalous becomes mere planetary gossip that grotesquely fuses together the unusual with the farcical, all too common vulgarity with suffering, intimacy with stupidity, authenticity with parody, exhibitionism with frustration. The television audience's Pantagruelian consumption—the omnipresent and omnipotent monster of trivialization—compresses the earthly Babel into a huge village fair.

"Televised" reality becomes a self-devouring "proto-reality" without which the real world is not confirmed and therefore does not exist. The selection process is harsh, the cacophony deafening, the images volatile; the ephemeral remains sovereign. The fierce competition to break through the sound barrier of attention seems all the more futile, the wilder it becomes. The trial of the sports star O. J. Simpson, accused of an atrocious crime, attracts more attention than the American president's speech about the barely flourishing State of the Union. The frontier between good and evil is ever harder to glimpse.

Every day, the thousands of new items about people agitating for rights, recognition, revenge, and fame demonstrate an ever more cynical renunciation of dialogue. Chosen at random, any such piece of news comes to illustrate the carnivalesque hysteria of today's world, in which fanaticism is not necessarily religious, or necessarily antireligious, because it does not necessarily have any meaning other than the release of a huge frustration.

Cohabiting with the Outrageous

Unfortunately, one can see an increasingly pronounced blurring of the meaning of opposites. The reverse of closed-mindedness sometimes appears to be merely its complement. And culture seems to be ever more visibly losing "the insistence of the ideal" (what the English critic George Steiner once called "the blackmail of perfection")—that is, the nonmystical relationship, not infrequently adversarial and always contradictory, but in any case profound, between religious spirituality and the spirituality of culture.

The perception of outrageousness is being lost; we are now reaching a routine cohabitation with the outrageous. Always permissible, made banal, it is even becoming in a way indispensable. The elimination of all criteria, hence of all limitation, has destructive effects that are incalculable and, above all, seem hard, if not impossible, to stop.

The horrors of this century do not seem to have marked only "the death of God." As George Steiner rightly observes,

> Much has been said of man's bewilderment and solitude after the disappearance of Heaven from active belief. We know of neutral emptiness of the skies and of the terrors it has brought. But it may be that the loss of Hell is the more severe dislocation. . . . To have neither Heaven nor Hell is to be intolerably deprived and alone in a world gone flat. Of the two, Hell proved the easier to re-create. . . . Needing Hell, we have learned how to build and run it on earth.

A world that has more in common with a carnival, however, than with an over-perfect hell. Carnival aspiring, without success, to blasphemy.

In the great free-market carnival of the modern world, nothing appears audible unless it is scandalous, but nothing is scandalous enough to become memorable. An imperfect world, to be sure. Its citizens undoubtedly have enough grounds for dissatisfaction and concern. Sometimes they receive strange confirmation of the privileges they enjoy when they look at the ever more numerous exiles coming to live among them. The majority of these exiles have known captive man in the dark carnival of tyranny, before being able to contemplate free man and the not always happy carnival of liberty.

Without hell, no illusions. The memory of their life stories is the memory of a perverse and closed utopia, in which individuality as such was blasphemy.

What Exiles Remember

Exiles living in the West know the alternative to the often stupefying spectacle of man in freedom. They recognize, of course, the huge differences between a closed society, distorted by terror and misery, and an open society, distorted by selfish competition and trivial publicity; between a manipulated collectivism and a well-trained individualism. They will never forget that totalitarianism, not democracy, provoked the Holocaust and the Gulag, and the Cambodian and Chinese genocides, and that ethnic and religious fanaticism provoked the Bosnian tragedy.

But after the defeat of fascism and the collapse of communism, the open society itself is in a deep crisis, it seems, with the loss of decency, of humanitarian and fair principles, of generosity and grandeur. The need for an enemy (ethnic enemy, ideological enemy, gender enemy, religious enemy) both drives and confuses people, whether they are in a society obsessed with lies or in a society obsessed with money. Demagogy, censorship, bigotry, and cynicism survive, under different labels, even in the market of the free world.

The exiles are not the only ones to recognize the dangerous hidden similarities between closed and open societies. The Western man is now their fellow man, as they are his. And all of us know that playing with hell and illusions is not the best way to avoid hell or to overcome costly illusions.

Translated by Patrick Camiller, spring 1996

Notes

1. As quoted in the "Introduction" by Catherine Theimer Nepomnyashchy to Sinyavsky's *Strolls with Pushkin* (New Haven and London: Yale University Press, 1993), p. 32, which appeared after its partial publication as "Progulki's Pushkinom," in the Russian journal *Oktyabr* (April 1989).

2. Ibid., p. 37.

3. Ibid., p. 38.

4. Ibid.

5. Sinyavsky, *Strolls with Pushkin*, p. 145.

6. Igor Shafarevich, "A Phenomenon of the Emigration," *Literaturnaya Rossiya*, September 8, 1989.

7. As quoted in Catherine Theimer Nepomnyashchy, "Andrei Sinyavsky's 'Return' to the Soviet Union," *Formations*, 6 (spring 1991), p. 13.

8. See his comment on *Strolls with Pushkin* that appeared in *Vestnik Russkogo Khristyanskogo Dvizheniia*, 142 (1984), p. 152.

9. As quoted in Nepomnyashchy, "Andrei Sinyavsky's 'Return,'" p. 13.

10. Ibid., p. 35.

11. Ibid., p. 36.

12. My Eliade piece appears here on pp. 92–118 above.

13. *Los Angeles Times*, May 24, 1992.

14. *România Mare*, March 20, 1992.

15. "Mircea Eliade, Culture and the Inquisitions," 22, no. 12 (1992).

16. David Lawton, *Blasphemy* (Philadelphia: University of Pennsylvania Press, 1993), p. 202.

17. "Some Notes Toward the Redefinition of Culture" in *Bluebeard's Castle* (New Haven and London: Yale University Press, 1971).

CIORAN

In the spring of 1990, I was invited to attend the Salon du Livre in Paris, on the occasion of Albin Michel's publication of my first volume in French, *Le thé de Proust.*

The year before my trip there, I had got to know a friend of Cioran's, Edouard Roditi, a fabled pilgrim of letters. It seems he had written to Cioran about me. One day he showed me a surprising message that had come from Cioran, in French, dated September 25, 1989.

> Mon cher ami,
>
> Thank you for your letter, which has come at just the right moment. Just a few days ago I was struck, or rather deeply shaken, by Norman Manea's piece. It is the best thing I have read on the Romanian nightmare. . . I left Romania fifty years ago, and it is mainly out of masochism that I take an interest in my origins. How can one explain that the shallowest of all nations should have such a destiny?

Cioran was referring to my essay "Rumänien in 3 (kommentierten) Sätze" ("Romania—Three Lines with Commentary"), which had just appeared in the German magazine *Akzente.* The same issue had also carried a piece by Cioran entitled *"Begegnungen mit Paul Celan"* ("Encounters with Paul Celan"), a coincidence which probably prompted what he wrote to Roditi regarding "the right moment."

Naturally, I wrote Cioran. I have always considered him a great writer, even if I have had some doubts about his philosophy. He answered with an extremely cordial letter in which he did not forget to stress that his leaving Romania had been the most intelligent act of his life. ("C'est de loin l'acte le plus intelligent que j'aie jamais commis.") And, of course, he advised me to come to live in Paris, too ("l'endroit idéal pour rater sa vie").

When I telephoned him upon arriving in Paris, he invited me and my wife over to 21 rue l'Odeon, for dinner.

This fierce cynic, who delighted in overturning axioms and canons, values and virtues, was a short, thin, frail man, both amiable and courteous. He, who had written that he would have killed himself had he been a Jew and who rejected God while admiring the Führer and the Romanian fascist Zelea Codreanu, the "Captain" of the Iron Guard, came across as modest, gentle, polite. The sharpshooter so adulated by French literati lived in a student garret. He told us that until a lift was installed a few years earlier he had heroically scrambled up the stairs several times a day—even after midnight when he returned from his long solitary walks that were well known to the district policeman.

My intention was not to ask him anything but to leave him at the mercy of his own nature and words. Still, if the opportunity had arisen, I should have been happy for us to discuss, for instance, the "barbarity of enthusiasm," one of his many striking phrases in *Le Mauvais Demiurge*. I thought that, even for a nihilistic prophet of the apocalypse, it might have been interesting to consider the relationship between his youthful enthusiasm for barbarism and his later determined skepticism of civilization, progress, and democracy. But we did not get on to such complicated and important matters. He seemed to have prepared himself for a relaxed Mozartian evening, drugged with beauty like the Parisian spring. His gaze and gestures, seeking and bestowing admiration, were directed with a delicate touch of gallantry towards my wife, Cella. . . .

Yet, his conversation was not lacking in sarcasm. Although he was briefly exhilarated by the anti-Ceaușescu "revolution" of 1989,

Romania still remained to Cioran "the space of failure, where things were ruined for good"—comments he repeated with visible pleasure. Less expected, given that this was our first meeting, were his caustic remarks about old friends—especially the Romanian philosopher Noica. With excitement in his voice, he enjoyed describing the servility and grotesque flattery in the Maestro's dealings with fellow professors, students, and friends; nor did he hold back from telling us, virtual strangers, about some embarrassing visits that the author of *The Romanian Sense of Being* used to make in his way around Paris. According to Cioran, who seemed more condescending than disgusted, the "transcendental" thinker Noica played the role of a loyal defender of the "Greatest Son" of Communist Romania. "What is this you've got against Ceauşescu, eh?" Noica (in fact, Cioran's old comrade) is supposed to have asked with almost pious astonishment. Apparently, Noica also kept a little notebook in which he jotted down the names of everyone he met and talked to in Paris, so that later, returning to Romania, he was able to show these notes, as a sign of gratitude, to his connections in the secret police who had given him a passport to travel abroad.

The evening continued after midnight, amid anecdotes and paradoxes, under the spell of a host unstinting in verve. "What you need now are some literary prizes. Awards! In Paris you arrange literary glory over dinners. At restaurants, the best restaurants." He could not possibly accept, as he saw it, the scandalous slipshod behavior of my publisher who had failed to arrange fancy promotional lunch and dinner parties for an author who had come all the way across the ocean. His physical frailty seemed offset by a robust high-born suppleness. He had an open, welcoming air and was enamored of Paris and his local *quartier*, happy to enjoy the benefit of a civilization that he never ceased to mock.

Nevertheless, the French publishing house did something for its guest. The next day, Albin Michel had arranged a photo session with Mme. Giles Rolle, a well-known professional. "I know your fellow countryman, Emil Cioran. I have photographed him, too," she told me cheerfully. "Some of the pictures came out really well— disastrously well." Cioran had looked at them with delight in his eyes, continued Mme. Rolle, and had then torn them all up. "For- bidden! Prohibited! Me, Cioran, smiling? No one should ever see Cioran smiling."

Unfortunately, I wasn't in touch with Cioran after that trip to Paris. Some years later I heard of his long, slow agony, the senility in which the former iconoclast and cynic was peacefully slumbering. The exile who had learned perfect French, becoming one of France's most brilliant contemporary stylists, had suddenly lost his linguistic refuge and had started to speak in Romanian again, the language he had been so happy to abandon half a century ago. Was it a new form of Alzheimer's disease? It certainly was, as the Romanian writer Ion Vartic remarked acutely, a "successful regression," about which Cioran had always dreamed. A way of regressing to the state of the unborn and, at the same time, a way of unknowingly returning from exile, coming home to his pre-birth homeland. "Unconscious- ness is a homeland," Cioran himself had written.

Then, in an irony of fate, the world's major newspapers announced the death of this skeptic who had always stressed his indifference to glory and his boredom with the paradoxes of posterity.

In a *New York Times* obituary, Susan Sontag—one of the first in America to write about Cioran—observed that he had practiced "a new kind of philosophizing: personal, aphoristic, lyrical, antisys- tematic." She illustrated this with a characteristic Cioran quote: "However much I have frequented the mystic, deep down I have always sided with the Devil, unable to equal him in power, I have tried to be worthy of him, at least, in insolence, acrimony, arbitrari- ness and caprice." It was a quotation that combined his rebellious vitality with the provocative seduction of his phrases, their twisted glowing spikes, the nervous shudder, the icy irradiation of his ever- youthful prose, his gnomic solitary thought.

I, too, was asked to characterize Cioran. I recalled that one evening we spent together, and the question I did not manage to ask him. In a few sentences, I tried to relate Cioran's evolution to the evolution of our contemporary world, to the watershed represented by World War II. In the issue of the *New York Times* dated June 22, 1993, my comment appeared as a laconic statement: "He was a brilliant rebel and a challenging misanthrope who tried again and again to awaken us to the nothingness of human existence."

Soon after his death, a stormy controversy (called by some participants "Cioran's second death," although it might have been seen rather as a rebirth) arose in the French and Romanian press. It focused on the political extremism of his youthful misanthropy and rebellion, his involvement with Romanian fascism, his outrageous statements about Hitler and Zelea Codreanu.

Readers were reminded that he wrote in 1937, "No other politician of today inspires a greater sympathy than Hitler . . . Hitler's merit consists in depriving his nation of its critical spirit," or what he said, in 1940, at the commemoration of his beloved "Captain," whom he saw as a kind of new Messiah: "With the exception of Jesus, no other dead figure was more present among the living."

In 1995, Gallimard published *Cioran, l'herétique*, Patrice Bollon's balanced critical analysis of Cioran's life and work. The book provoked a violent debate in the French newspapers. Jean-Paul Enthoven wrote that "the second death of Cioran promises his orphans a vast loneliness"; Bernard-Henry Levy described a meeting, in 1989, at which Cioran seemed very cautious in talking about his past and quite uncomfortable when asked about his extreme right-wing militantism of the 1930s and 1940s. Cioran was passionately defended by Edgar Morin, André Comte-Sponville, and François Furet. The latter wrote: "Cioran is a great writer and a great moralist, whatever his ephemeral commitment to the Iron Guard was." Finally, Alain Etchegoyen explained, on a French television program, without any trace of irony, that "Cioran's main regret was well and nicely expressed through his silence and his pessimism. Opposite to the penitent Stalinists, he had the merit of discretion. The Stalinists maintained their arrogance, which isn't necessarily a philosophical habit."

In Romania the debate was enhanced by the publication, after the collapse of communism, of Cioran's entire work, including part of his hitherto unknown correspondence. And the appearance, after his death, in France, of two posthumous books, *Mon Pays* (Gallimard, 1996), and *Cahiers, 1957–1972* (Gallimard, 1997) was, of course, extensively commented on in both countries. These books show that, unlike his fellow Romanian intellectuals with whom he was associated in the right-wing political movement (Eliade, Noica), Cioran was, after the war, continuously obsessed with his "guilty" youth. He viewed his political commitment to the extreme right-wing "Revolution" as a mixture of craziness and stupidity, due to the suffocating environment of his mediocre and apathetic homeland, an oppressive dead end, without past or future. "My Country! I wanted, by hook or by crook, to cavil at her but she wasn't even there for me to cavil to," he wrote in the early 1950s. Thinking again and again about his country, his countrymen and himself, Cioran concludes, in obvious disgust: "I hated my country, I hated everybody and the entire universe: so that, in the end, nothing was left to hate but myself: which I did, in the devious way of desperation." And he adds: "When I look back . . . it is another man whom I abjure now, everything that means 'Me' is now elsewhere, two thousand leagues away from what I was."

As ambiguous or superficial as his statements may still sometimes be (he thought, for instance, that the "error" of the Iron Guard was "to conceive a future for a place without one," transferring their guilt onto the country and its people, even while he still believed the Iron Guard's martyrs "achieved for themselves a destiny which exempted their country from having one"), it's obvious that, after the war, Cioran was ashamed and burdened by his past political commitment, and that he kept his distance, in fact, from any political connections.

Yet, what still proved to be an impossible, never-ending, complicated, and troubled process was the taming of his genuine, innate nihilism. For better or worse, his nihilism remained the energetic spiritual force behind his creative writing, behind its originality and style. He kept his lonely struggle alive, as a writer, as a performer, a clownish philosopher mocking philosophy, I would say, a solitary *apatride* with a Buster Keaton mask, and as a seducer, of course, even if the seduction was rarely obtained through virtuous means. He was ever the Devil's advocate.

The Romanian writer Marta Petreu remarked recently, in a rigorous essay, "*Doctrina legionara si intelighentia interbelica*" (Apostrof, 1998), that Cioran was a heretic even as he was a supporter of the Iron Guard. Knowing too well that the political project of the Iron Guard meant, in the end, a total suppression of freedom, he still wanted to be a "free man": claiming for *himself* the right to rebel, to be different, unique, above the mob. His "elitism" seemed to be, as Marta Petreu emphasizes, the essential reason for his ultra-reactionary political views of the 1930s and 1940s. "An epoch of boundless liberties, of 'sincere' and extreme democracy, lingering indefinitely, would mean an inevitable collapse of humankind. The mob wants to be ordered about," Cioran wrote in 1937.

Readers will recognize the obvious separation and also the lasting connection between the young and the old Cioran. Already aging, he seems, at the time of writing these "notes," more sensitive to human suffering, more vulnerable and even more tolerant. His loneliness and lucidity still play with negation, even in some frivolous form, but his melancholy runs deeper as the consequence of a painful knowledge that the end of his earthly, pagan adventure is near. He seems, indeed, "more inclined to accept even the liberal democratic Western world with its quintessential injustice, with its vermin of businessmen and shopkeepers, with its freedoms," as Matei Calinescu wrote in an excellent study, "Reading Cioran" (*Salmagundi*). And yet, Cioran still thought, in 1960, in *History of*

Utopia that: "'Freedoms' prosper only in a sick body politic: toler-ance and impotence are synonymous."

As a master of paradox and, therefore, an "anti" type of thinker, a fighter of banality, canons, and standards, common sense and com-mon taste, Cioran always followed his stubborn "anti"-ness, even when the result was not necessarily of real spiritual relevance. "Being paradoxical—embracing ideas and opinions that go against the grain, that are shocking to the common sense or to what is more or less gen-erally accepted—becomes an imperative, a categorical aesthetic (and implicitly amoral) imperative, as it were. A certain kind of (theo-retical) extremism is always involved," proposed Matei Calinescu.

This may also be a key for reading some of the fragments from *Cahiers*. It may contribute, in a way, even to the understanding of the most scandalous statement, such as "There is something worse than anti-Semitism: it is anti-anti Semitism." What exactly does Cioran mean by this? Does he equate anti-Semitism with the gas chambers? Does he see anti-anti-Semitism as a profitable "show," a false rhetoric and demagogical militancy? And can these two be compared? He doesn't qualify the terms: neither dark or frivolous or boring anti-Semitism, nor cheap or vigorous or inflated or boring anti-anti-Semitism. The reader should be reminded, at this point, that Cioran's relationship with Jews and their fate was never simple. He never wrote about the Jews in the consistently harsh way he wrote about his fellow Romanians, and we, probably, cannot ask for more from a zealous nihilist and a heretic. Yet, his statements about Jews were always ambiguous and often held double meanings.

In 1937, when Romanian anti-Semitism was booming and the generic iconoclastic Rebel-Cioran was already a supporter of the extreme right-wing political movement, he proved ready to adopt the "banal" view that the Jewish "antinational spirit" was, of course, a threat to the country. He added, however, that another threat was Jewish "superiority." This was a quite daring "paradoxical" state-ment, at a time when anti-Semitic laws were based on the assumption of the *inferiority* of the "Jewish race," but it was not necessarily a statement of sympathy or solidarity with the "enemies" of his country. Similarly, he wrote, then, that anti-Semitism was "the greatest tribute paid to the Jews."

During and after the war, Cioran was, it seems, shocked by the Jewish tragedy, by what happened to his Jewish friends (the novelist Mihail Sebastian, who remained in Bucharest; the Romanian-French poet Benjamin Fondane, killed at Auschwitz; the Romanian-German poet Paul Celan, who committed suicide in Paris). In his postwar essay dedicated to the Jews ("A People of Solitaries"), which Susan Sontag considered "surprisingly cursory and high-handed," Cioran attempted a kind of codified dialogue with his prewar texts on the same topic. "I found myself loathing them with the fury of a love turned to hate . . . I had only a bookish commiseration for their suffering, and could not divine what was in store for them."

We may assume, perhaps, that after stating in *Cahiers* "I am metaphysically Jewish," he had forgotten, however, that he had also introduced himself, in the same notes, as a Mongol, a Hungarian, a Slav, a Central-European, people not known as great friends of the Jews or of "anti-anti-Semites . . ." He thought he might allow himself the kind of statement with which some real Jews, well known for their bittersweet humor and sarcastic self-criticism, would have agreed. So, gambling with negativity, playing tricks on himself and on the entire world . . . equating anti-Semitism with anti-anti-Semitism (and, hard to believe, *even less* than equating) seemed, probably, simply too easy for that promoter of any and all "anti" impulses.

Translated by Patrick Camiller, 1998

THROUGH ROMANIAN EYES: A HALF CENTURY
OF THE *NRF* IN BUCHAREST

When the Romanian poet Benjamin Fondane left Romania for
France in 1929 he did so, as he himself declared, because "he
couldn't bear living in a backwater French cultural colony any
longer"; he wanted the Center.

The witticism gives a sense of the prestige that the *Nouvelle
Revue Française* (NRF) held in Romanian cultural circles at the
time, a prestige that remained intact even after the imposition of a
communist dictatorship in Romania by its victorious neighbor to the
east. By then, however, the prestige was measured in absence. The
famous journal was no longer available outside of a few libraries
here and there; even then it was held under lock and key, and
available for consultation only by special authorization.

A grotesque and tragic episode with profound implications for
today's *NRF* anniversary celebrations* would take place in 1957
when the magazine published Emile Cioran's "Letter to a Faraway
Friend," a text that reflected the *NRF*'s commitment to encompass
the widest possible range of cultural issues. Not for nothing had
François Mauriac referred to the role of the journal as a "rose des
vents," or Compass Rose.

The addressee of Cioran's letter was unnamed but the text followed upon a series of recent epistolary debates between Cioran
and his friend and fellow thinker Constantin Noica. Before the war

*This text was written for these celebrations.

both of them had been sympathizers of the Iron Guard. Against the advice of his friends, Constantin Noica unwisely posted a reply to the message from Paris in December of 1957. Aware (but belatedly, I would say) of the risk to which he had exposed Noica, Cioran blocked publication of the response; the text circulated only among the circle of Romanian exiles in France.

Cioran lived in the city he adored, but indulged in a melancholy shaded with sarcasm when it came to the "domestication" of his old rebellious and nihilist tendencies; condescending about the free world, he didn't deny himself its pleasures. As for Noica, he survived in a communist totalitarian regime that, while opposed to the one he had earlier supported, often resembled it in numerous, terrifying ways. As a flash of wit that made the rounds of Bucharest in those years had it:

> Captain!
> Don't take it so hard.
> In the Communist Party
> You'll still find the Guard!

Its author would soon be charged in the Noica treason trials convened by the Military Tribunal.

If the same skepticism regarding democracy and its moral and spiritual vacuum can be discerned in both correspondents, Cioran is obviously "resigned" to living in a free, prosperous society, whereas Noica denounces the decadence and betrayals of the West and asks to what extent the "necessity" of a totalitarian regime should not be accepted, even if the cost is the renunciation of freedom. Both of them, of course, rue the absence of utopian idealism or ambition in the day-to-day Western postwar world.

"We find ourselves faced with two types of intolerable societies," writes Cioran in "Letter to a Faraway Friend":

... the abuses of yours permit mine to persevere in its own abuses, to set its own horrors quite effectively against those your society practices. The central criticism that can be addressed to your regime is that it has ruined utopia, that principle of the renewal of institutions and of peoples. ... In the end, a life without Utopia becomes unbreathable, at least for the masses. Without some new delirium in the world, the danger is that we turn to stone. ... The difference between regimes is less important than it may seem: you are alone by force, we are alone if uncoerced. Is the gap that great between hell and a deplorable paradise?

The essential theme of freedom is treated with jaded wariness: "For those of us who possess it, it is just an illusion, because we know we're going to lose it and because it is, in any case, meant to be lost." Cioran even believes that rather than let the East have "the privilege of realizing the unrealizable," the West should humanize and liberalize communism "and gain the power and prestige of the most beautiful modern illusion."

Noica sees in communism the "message of Europe itself," and in a sense the pain-racked transformation of the Russian soul into a Faustian soul. In the decline of the West, the philosopher perceives the death of the "esprit de finesse"; the triumph of communism appears to him to be the victory of the "esprit de géométrie." And so he says in this warning to his former comrade: "You would prefer to sink in the 'esprit de finesse' rather than consent to logical barbarity." Although the Pascalian shorthand does not do full justice to the issues involved, it does at least point to a conceptual opposition that had become familiar in debates between proponents of "Eastern" and "Western" political ideology. For the captive in the East, the problem of European man seems to be the reconciliation of Pascal with Aristotle, of freedom with necessity. The socialist utopia "would quite precisely give necessity back to man . . . along with the risk . . . that a number of freedoms might be taken away from him." The choice of the socialist "utopia" would entail "an attempt to remove man from the 'alienation' caused by wealth," or comfort. Noica is not unaware of the sickness of a society that "even as it constantly evokes Hegel and contradiction as the principle of life, is not only unable to bear the contradictor from outside and fears him, but would actually go to any lengths to stifle the contradictor who naturally arises from within." He pleads for "collaboration," in the conviction that the friend on the other side will acknowledge the vapidity of the standard Western values and the "banality" of an "exile which risks making you nostalgic, patriotic and sentimental," whereas his own brand of exile, "in his own world, but a world emptied of itself," is preferable, because more "subtle." Noica's conclusion is clear: "All things considered, exile [in Noica's own world] is better here."

The so-called "better" aspect of internal exile under a dictatorship was something Noica would unfortunately soon experience; and the skeptical Cioran would over the coming months discover just how different "hell and a deplorable paradise" could be.

As was their custom, the commissars and technocrats of the Party could easily have found in the letters of Cioran and Noica, in their critiques of the bourgeoisie, of the institutions of democracy and its vacuity, quite enough material to manipulate in the service of their own propaganda. But the official reaction was quick and harsh. After the publication of a few inflammatory pamphlets in the official press, Noica and a group of twenty-two others, most of them his friends, were arrested and charged. Among them were notable personalities in Romanian intellectual circles.

The order referring Noica's case to the courts was issued on December 1, 1958 and mentions that the detainee "kept up relationships with the legionnaires Cioran Emile and Eliade Mircea among others." It was claimed that he received from them "documents hostile to the popular democratic regime of the People's Republic of Romania, documents he then reportedly spread widely among his circle of friends and acquaintances during secretly organized meetings in his home." The philosopher was accused of "writings whose content is hostile to the government," of transmitting them to his friends and associates in his country and "by illegal means" to "legionnaires that fled to France for the purpose of publishing them." He was said to have set the tone for hostile conversations "in the pursuit of the violent overthrow of the popular democratic regime of the People's Republic of Romania." The hostile documents referred to by the penal investigator of the Securitate who drew up the charges were books published in France by Cioran and Eliade; a manuscript of Noica's entitled *Povestiri din Hegel* (Tales from Hegel), another manuscript on Goethe; and, of course, Cioran's *NRF* "Letter to a Faraway Friend" and Noica's unpublished response.

Then followed the interrogations, the torture, the forced confessions, the manipulations: a sinister system of incarceration for the prisoners and terror for their families.

After Stalin's death and the famous Khrushchev report, the Soviet bloc seemed to enter a period of relative détente. In his novella of the same name, Ilya Ehrenburg called this period "the Thaw." Still, the Communist Party lived by its own meteorology: spring in Moscow, Prague, or Bucharest remained an iffy proposition, and cataclysms took no account of the seasons—we need only recall the autumn of the Hungarian Revolution in 1956.

Not for the first time, Romania found itself in 1958 in a byzantine situation. Having succeeded in convincing Khrushchev to withdraw from Romania the troops stationed there through the Warsaw Military Pact, the country's leaders needed to prove that they were in complete control of the country. In 1954, Molotov told Gheorghiu Dej, General Secretary of the Romanian Communist Party: "You won't last three days without the presence of the Soviet army in Romania." The Romanian Communist Party needed to show itself master of the situation, so as to avoid internal rebellion and any attempt to depose the Stalinist group in power, as had already occurred in neighboring countries. Internal terror was about to stiffen.

This was the atmosphere on February 15, 1960 when testimony at the Military Tribunal began in the sinister Noica trial. Referring to the accusations and to Noica's *Povestiri din Hegel* manuscript, the military prosecutor emphasized its "fascist content" and the "attempt to rehabilitate ideology with the practice of fascism." Noica's manuscript about Goethe supposedly "rid [Goethe's] works of everything useful to the people, larding them instead with foreign [that is, legionary] theses." The "Letter to a Faraway Friend," received by the accused in an "illegal" manner from abroad, was said to have a "subversive content, full of irony." As for Noica's reply, it would be shown to be "far more hostile than the article by Cioran Emile."

The prosecutor added for the edification of the audience that "Cioran Emile is an old man with dull teeth, whereas Noica is the spitting image of a hungry wolf with razor sharp fangs."

Noica was condemned to twenty-five years' hard labor while others also received stiff sentences. They would be paroled after four years, during yet another period of "liberalization," but many would then be forced to become informers for the Securitate. Noica published three conversion texts and undertook "the collaboration" he had earlier asked for in his letter to Cioran. He would go on to publish the rest of his writings under Ceaușescu's regime, becoming a sort of guru to young intellectuals hungry for culture. Today he is considered Romania's most important postwar philosopher.

On his first visit to Paris in 1972, the philosopher surprised his friends and admirers in the Romanian exile community when he asked them to take him off the pedestal where they had placed him, saying, "I have eliminated the ethical from my universe." After their reunion, Cioran would say of his old friend: "He has the soul of a disciple, a perfidious disciple. How could he ever understand that I have abandoned everything he defends? I can't discuss anything with someone who teaches illusion, who does not suffer with and from the passage of time, and learns from it nothing at all. I ask of my friends that they do me the favor of growing old." The reference to the political illusions of youth and the status of the disciple are reminders of the old nationalist ideological obsessions of writers who were supporters of the extreme nationalist, pro-Nazi Iron Guard.

Mircea Eliade was comparably severe with a Noica entrenched in his roles as hermit and mentor and indifferent to the always more terrible reality around him, convinced as he was that Ceauşescu represented the "national way." Eliade also alluded to Noica's bitterness at his and Cioran's guilty silence during the heinous trial in Bucharest that, without intending to, Noica's old comrades had provoked. Eliade's justification—that had they said anything publicly they could have been accused by the communists of being "legionnaires"—seems willfully naïve, since despite such pathetic prudence the communists unmasked their past as right-wing legionnaires anyway. The simplest solution would have been to acknowledge publicly their former erring ways and disavow them, thus freeing themselves to attack totalitarianism of every stripe, including the communist dictatorship.

When, in later years, he came upon the draft of his 1957 reply to Cioran, Noica exclaimed: "How savage life is, how savagely beautiful." It is not incongruous, perhaps, to take up his exclamation ourselves in paying deserved homage to an eternally young Lady *NRF*, on the celebration of her glorious anniversary.

Translated by John Anzalone, October 2008

BERENGER AT BARD

In the fall of 1989, at Bard College, New York State, I started a course entitled "Eastern European Writers." I had selected mostly authors who, like me, were exiles: Milosz, Koestler, Kundera, Danilo Kiš, Ionescu. I was thus trying to liberate myself from the confusion of the oriental-communist degeneracy (whose imminent implosion I, in fact, did not foresee) and still remain connected to my distant homeland.

The besieged man had finally escaped from the Colony of Rhino. He had got tired of shouting by himself, crouched in the cell of his room and deafened by the trampling of the street guards: "I will resist, I will not surrender! It's my duty! I will stay that way to the end, no matter what, to the very end!"

He had finally run from the black wind of disaster; he had not resisted. The big words had fled too, as guilty as he. The prisoner did not prove to be a "superior" man, as he had dreamed of being. He was just a poor lost man, too attached to petty survival.

The passage from the state of contraction in Rhinoromania of the ninth decade to the state of expansion on the great stage of the free Carnival had not been easy. The liberating shipwreck had also been a siege fraught with doubts and anguish.

In 1989, the transitional passage suddenly unfolded into bracing sunshine, under a clear and fresh sky.

July 9, 1989 was a glorious day in the wanderer's calendar. The small brown Honda, battered and tenacious, drove heroically through the gates of the American college—a paradisal enclave of trees and flowers and small houses in which teachers and students were practicing the traditional didactic Glass Bead game.

I was given the gold key to my lodging that very same day. As in a fairy tale where the wizardly benefactor imposes a deadline, I was offered refuge for an entire year. Everything seemed to have come together under a lucky star. Time was eminently hospitable, as in my distant or more recent youth. That spectacular summer, with its sun that had turned solemn and imperial, heralded the beginning of a new era.

Exile is also an initiation into simulacrum, an exercise in inventive theatricality. This is what interior exile is about, the solitary man's alienation within the ubiquitous totalitarian masquerade. But what of exile proper? On the new stage, the newcomer had been cast in a role he had never played before. Professor! . . . In a foreign world and a foreign language, in front of a foreign audience.

The idyllic academic enclave could not dispel the exile's doubts; it only rebuked them, every day, through the majestic peaceful woods and the perfect sky. With every dusk, the hospitable summer months were bringing the debut closer, the meeting with the public, scheduled for that fall.

He had many doubts. He wondered how he could avoid the old role that had made him famous. "The Lost One" . . . Not yet at home with life? With its confused forces? Lost, any way, anywhere, any time?

When I opened the door to the classroom, I was amazed by the casual, typically American look of my young audience. Quite a few of them were barefoot. . . . The relaxing effect of the superb September afternoon or the pleasure of annoying the Martian who had been trained on his bizarre native planet according to strict rules.

The dialogue with the students became natural quite soon. Despite a certain cultural deficit, most of them were bright and open to anything new. They had been educated in and for freedom;

they were accustomed to the critical spirit and defied preconceived ideas, even the most honored. Gradually, my new position was moderating into its own routine.

Toward the end of the semester, around November, when in Eastern Europe the Berlin Wall and the walls within ourselves were being broken to pieces from one day to another, something out of the ordinary happened in my class.

Among the midterm papers, I had received one on Eugen Ionescu's *Rhinoceros.* Hesitating to evaluate it, I decided to read it to the class, without disclosing the author's name, then to ask them to comment on it and suggest a grade.

There was nothing spectacular in the beginning:

> Berenger cannot believe his eyes when his close friend, Jean, joins the epidemic sweeping their village and transforms himself into a rhinoceros. As the horn swells on his forehead and guttural moaning bulges from his thickening throat, the frantic Jean sings the blessing of freedom to a bewildered Berenger. "Morals! I'm sick of morals! We must go beyond moral standards. Nature has its own laws. Morals is [*sic*] against nature!" From a responsible obedient citizen who ostracized Berenger for his senseless rebellion, Jean has become a raving reactionary. He gradually turns green as he denounces the societal structure he so vehemently protected as a human. Along with the release of his human form, Jean is released from the laws and the rules he had been conditioned (forced) to uphold. Berenger is terrorized. Before him stands the man who had always symbolized order—a man he had felt too weak to imitate. Berenger cannot get beyond the absurdity of this revolution against the human condition. He is terrified to admit that the RHINOCEROS could be making a valid, self-satisfying decision of rejection."

However natural and acceptable it seemed, the last sentence was somehow already announcing the novelty.

The class sensed the potential turn; the silence was complete. I read the last sentences again, before going on. "Berenger cannot get beyond the absurdity of this revolution against the human condition. He is terrified to admit that the RHINOCEROS could be making a valid, self-satisfying decision of rejection."

Attention grew keener, I felt that.

> He is terrified to admit that the RHINOCEROS could be making a valid, self-satisfying decision of rejection . . . Could Jean, a model citizen—a pillar of social strength for Berenger himself—be choosing to betray the established code he so religiously upheld? To Berenger's horror, the choice is imminent. He grasps at analytical solutions to a social crisis. He is responsible for making up his own mind, he will procure his destiny and suffer the repercussions: to become a Rhinoceros or to remain a human being. Suddenly, life before the commotion seems safe and logical to Berenger, as he watches Jean go stampeding through a brick wall. The fact that he had, for all intents and purposes, rejected society through his alcoholism is buried under the weight of his fear. He clings dearly to that same societal structure, as if to a rope over an abyss. Though he openly admits condemnation of his social stratosphere, Berenger isn't strong enough to allow his own release. He holds on to the life he hated to avoid the wave that would wash him into the life he does not understand.

Curiosity and tension were rising in the class. The true surprise was not so much the reversal of an accepted interpretation as the rigor, the paradoxically reversed common sense and the logic of the demonstration.

> Berenger maintains that his friend Jean "must have made a mistake" because he (Berenger) is unable to find a more valid

reason to choose, and because he cannot comprehend his old friend's desire for a "new life." Whether or not the "mindless" life of the Rhinoceros is a more satisfying one or a (better) more stimulating one is irrelevant. Berenger choosing not to sacrifice his identity is unfounded because he makes it on the basis of fear. As he finds himself the last remaining human being, he retains his obstinate skepticism. "I'm the last man left, I'm staying that way to the end. I'm not capitulating." Berenger's refusal to "capitulate" is hardly an honorary one. Fear of change constrains our progression. To choose a life of bondage to certain misery—a life of constriction (as Berenger's was): "I just can't get used to life," is a coward's choice. Berenger cannot be credited with "maintaining his integrity or identity." He maintains nothing but the pathetic life he so detests that for him is safe, and turns his back on an opportunity for revival.

The professor had hurried over the last few sentences in embarrassment. He already knew the text and was terrified that he would sink into his thoughts again, as when he first read it. *"I can't get used to life."* All too often he had himself whimpered such words back home as well as here, in the new World, and in the new life which he did not feel prepared for.

Preserving his identity? Out of fear? Really?

Yes, he hurried over the last sentences as if he hoped to shut out the dilemma, the thought that had been left behind, in the words that he had dragged after him from the other end of the world and that continued to crawl after him, with him, in him, endlessly.

How "European" the traditional interpretation of the play seemed all at once!

The reader had admitted his duplicity, his proposed aspirations, gradually perverted by the sinuous twists of prudence, but he knew how much the American sentences expressed the American mythol-

ogy of renewal. The natural and the sudden surprises, the regeneration of the daily travesty, the complete changing of one's appearance, personality, preferences, the need to "get ahead," at any cost.
Avoiding lament, accepting challenges, no matter how unfavorable,
but not defeat. Assuming destiny individually, yes, one could say so,
as his new fellow American countrymen were saying.

> Throughout this crisis Berenger is concerned, not with the
> human condition, but with his own. The people of his village
> transforming into Rhinoceroses affect Berenger's own life.

Yes, it was true, I knew how it was when Rhinoceroses multiply
around the solitary man.

> He maintains that, had it happened elsewhere ("if only it had
> happened somewhere else"), it could have been discussed log-
> ically and rationally. There was even the potential for it to
> become instructive and educational in its sensibilities.

Indeed, had it happened elsewhere . . it would have been a logical,
instructive discussion, but encircled, under siege, one barely has the
strength to breathe.

> However, because it involves Berenger on such an immediate
> level, he is unable to deal with the situation on any basis of
> integrity. His fear of the disruption of his own existence blocks
> out his ability to be rational.

Yes, it blocks it, perhaps. It would have been reasonable to give
up everything, to run finally, to free himself from everything and
from himself, to start all over again in a new world and in a new life.
Integrity . . integrity had existed, though! The isolation, the contraction in the narrow cell of the room preserved integrity—at least
partly. One must not forget that! No, one cannot forget the sacrifices
and risks of solitude, that's what the professor was thinking.

His fear of the disruption of his own existence blocks out his ability to be rational . . . the concept of structural unity and of independent responsibility for choice, that lays the foundation for democracy, would be obsolete . . . again we are shown Berenger's character to be one lacking the strength to sustain his own moral freedom. He is certainly no advocate who would sustain the freedom of society.

But he is, poor thing! He is, he certainly was, and he has remained a dreamer, a champion of freedom. That's what he is, that poor bastard.

A eulogy for "the revolutionary" symbol, embodied by the cruel "renewing" disease of rhinoceritis? An indictment of the anti-hero Berenger? My student was overturning the premise that was so dear to the author, his admirers, and the reader, lost in that tumble and that American lecture room.

Although with difficulty, the professor was giving up—he had to admit it—this hero of non-abdication, non-giving-up, to the humanity of his ambiguities; he had discovered the vulnerability of the lost ones long ago and far away, not only in Ionescu's tragicomedy but also in the comedy—not lacking in tragic aspects—of everyday life in socialist Rhinoromania.

Do ambiguities and vulnerability hinder us and put an end to our "progress?"

No, the professor did not voice his doubts. He continued to listen to the alien sentences that emerged from the clear handwriting, the black ink, the lined notebook, and evasively phrased in the adventurous phonetics of his new role.

Berenger shouts for his neighbors-turned-rhinoceros to maintain the laws established by humans. ("Stop it! . . . Noise is forbidden in these flats! Noise is forbidden!") Berenger did not maintain these laws himself; he drank consistently, missed work, appeared socially delinquent, and yet, in this time of upheaval, Berenger grasps on to the "social code" for dear life. Lacking the ability to live up to the original social status, he is certainly not ready to adopt a new set of standards however revolutionary or progressive it may be. These weaker members (such as Berenger) will hold a society back in a time of revolutionary change.

"New set of standards," "revolutionary change" "progressive" . . the terms certainly had a different meaning for the young audience than the one perverted for so long in the Colony of Rhino that the improvised Eastern European professor kept thinking of.

He was smiling questioningly and aloofly and confusedly, looking down at the lined sheet of paper, preparing himself to pronounce the new-old words: "radicals," "conservatives," "conventionalism," "duty"—barbarisms twisted and turned in the Dada confinement, with hammer and sickle, until they could no longer be pronounced, except in the Rhinoceros Circus.

After being an outcast himself from a society with strict standards, those same conservatives take Berenger's place as radicals and he, in turn, clings to their conventionalism. With the breakdown of society, Berenger's former social stance is disqualified. Berenger seems to have adopted the ultraconservative views expressed earlier by Jean. ("A superior man is the one who does his duty.") Suddenly, he is obsessed with man's obligation to society—a notion he previously acted against.

The iconoclastic commentary on the iconoclastic literary work ended with a verdict to match:

The utter absurdity of Ionescu's plot that a town full of respectable citizens turns, one by one, into a herd of stampeding Rhinoceroses, lends itself well to the simplicity of its message. Ionescu uses the character of Berenger to illustrate man's tragic incapacity to accept change and the growth and improvement that inevitably accompany it.

The professor stopped. He seemed amazed by the words "growth and improvement," as if he had heard them for the first time. In fact, he heard a series of muted words in another language. Berenger was then called Eugen Ionescu, a terrified witness of the rhinocerization of too many of his friends. To him, the fascist legionaries in their rhino-green shirts were "enchained beasts," embodying "the bestiality and endless stupidity of mankind and cosmos," while their songs were "an iron roar, with iron and gall, spitting gall and iron."

He nevertheless regained the blank tone that the text preserved for the conclusion:

> Berenger, seemingly the most dissatisfied, is the first (and the last) to refute the new ideology. By fear, human beings are held back from progression.

Fear? Yes, certainly there had been fear too. But not only that. Not just fear, he could swear, swear—not just fear!

He was ready to swear in front of the youthful audience in the New World that disgust and lucidity and integrity too, yes, yes, integrity too, yes, yes, ambiguities and vulnerability too had kept the poor outlaw far from the "progress" of the New Man, the New Life, and the New Ideology.

The reading had stopped. The political actualization of the famous play had been realized in the very last sentences of the text:

> For twenty years a wall stood blocking change in East Germany. Not until this year was the last "Berenger" overrun by the Rhinoceroses, and the wall removed, opening up space for growth.

Perplexity should finally have burst out. Did the Rhinos remove the wall? Didn't they actually build it? . . . What kind of "growth" did they want? asked the cricket buzzing imperceptibly in the East European's thoughts and in the American sentences read to the American youngsters.

No one seemed in a hurry to comment. I remembered the school of long ago, in the homeland of long ago and far away. "Get back to your seat, moron," the Teacher Rhino would roar at the silent class. The iron roar and the iron words of gall had made me shrink in my desk, ashamed at the shame of the classmate standing at the blackboard, and terrified that the same thing would somehow happen to me all too soon.

One of the rights the exiled had discovered in America was exactly this: the right to . . . "stupidity." Stupidity, ignorance, candor, and innocence—cultural, political, social, and other. The nerve with which aberrant beliefs, feelings, and experiences are being proclaimed! And the sacrosanct justification: "This is my opinion!" The void full of "self-esteem," in which landmarks, comparisons, and inhibitions are annulled; any admonition becomes "paternalistic," and therefore unacceptable. Certainly the show is not necessarily funny. And yet, the uninhibited display of qualities and defects is quite rich in revelations (even that "stupidity" is not always as foolish as it seems).

The inexhaustible energy of self-achievement is the hallmark of American democracy. A people's democracy (how could it be otherwise?), therefore also "vulgar" and "stupid," but impetuous in its renewing vitality.

The exile had not forgotten the words of a poet who returned to socialist Romania after spending a year in America and who, when asked what seemed to him unique, unrivaled, one single thing, just one, finally answered, overwhelmed: "The status of the ugly woman. It is the only place in the world where this does not seem to be a handicap, where it does not become a reason for being excluded or frustrated or made fun of. . . ."

Such digressions went through the exile's mind as he waited for a student to comment on the paper he had just read to the class.

They were so quiet, the vast silence was difficult to break. I insisted, however, that I wanted to hear their opinions. I finally received several brief and cutting criticisms of the troublesome thesis.

I then passed out small slips of paper, asking the students to give the paper a grade and explain their reasoning. They did not have to sign the slips, their opinions would remain anonymous.

At the end of class, as the students were heading out the door, the author approached me with a pale face. I had guiltily watched how she stood the trial, stoic but also hurt. I apologized for not having asked her permission to read her paper in public and not warning her of the referendum.

She did not seem bothered about such formalities. Her discontent was about something else. "How can they say I'm a fascist? You may not know, but I'm Jewish!"

No, I did not know and it did not seem very important to me. This is not what it is all about, I said, this is not about ethnicity or even about "fascism."

She had indeed ignored the antifascist or anti-communist meaning of the play, as well as the numerous historical, not just ideological, connotations. The real question remained, however, whether the reasoning was sound. That is what I tried to explain to the slight and silent young woman in front of me. I was hesitant to tell her that in fascist legionary Rhinoromania, as well as in the socialist one, her point of view had been validated not only by the party propaganda but also by certain famous thinkers and artists.

Back home, I started looking at the students' slips of paper. Despite the harsh criticism expressed in class, the grades given to the paper were good, even very good: B+, A, A−, B.

The comments were also worth paying attention to:

Well-written, provocative, well-defended, and plausible—if it weren't for the mindless uniformity of the Rhinoceroses. This poses the problem of "good" totalitarianism. I can't present a contradiction to the views here, even though I can't agree with them, and in total I give an A for entertaining and disturbing provocativeness.

Well written, but sounds like it was written by a Rhinoceros. A convincing argument but something tells me she missed the point.

This slip of paper indicated that the author of the paper had been identified ("she") and added a hesitant B/B−.

A/B+ was not accompanied by a commentary. One slip of paper did not have a grade but, in beautiful handwriting, asked:

Transgression or transcendence? The student could either be a Stalinist or a fascist, but not a revolutionary. Yes, there are reasons to make noise in a stifling society, but the "transgressions" are neither progressions, or revolutions. Fascist character is partly rebellious, of course; the question is that the (justified, I suppose) rebellious impulses are manipulated by reactionary social groups. Change for the sake of change is not praiseworthy.

Another A/B+ was justified as follows:

Fear is not the only reason for which he doesn't become a Rhino. But a good point.

Finally, an A included a brief note that seemed addressed to the East European professor:

Although I had a different interpretation I find this one to be very interesting, subversive, and not unfounded.

Obviously, the class had not been apathetic at all. Nor was it lacking in suppleness of perception.

The East European also had something to learn, as it were, from his students' spirit of fair play.

I kept in touch with Nancy after she was no longer my student and even later when, having received a master's degree in fine arts from Bard, she went to Japan, where she taught English for a while.

I also kept in touch with her paper. In 1996, I had the opportunity to subject her thesis to a re-evaluation.

Many things have changed with regard to Ionescu over the years. An open adversary of Romanian nationalism, he was condemned immediately after the war, before communists took complete power, for "insults" against the state and the nation. He had indeed expressed his disgust for the Army, the Church, the Law, demagogy, immorality, the tyranny of the parvenu, and yet again, the "angel-like figures of Romanian nationalism." But also for the "refined" intellectuals, fascinated with the base nature of the Beast.

He did everything to escape his rhinocerized homeland:

> Anything could have happened. I could have died; I could have been convicted; I could have become a dog too; I could have been possessed by the Legionaries' devil. When I left the country, I had the feeling I had saved myself from fire, earthquake, ocean waves, whirlpools. . . . It seems to me I had not seen people for a long time. I was awakening from a nightmare; I was escaping from hell. . . . Everything is fine when the nationalistic homeland is far away.

His work, which was banned under Stalinism, was briefly recovered during the interval of "liberalization" in the mid-1960s, due to his "humanism" and "antifascism." Later on, it was exiled again because of its antitotalitarian subversiveness and the author's intransigence toward the Carpathian Clown's dictatorship. Published again in their entirety after 1989, his writings have remained a source of perplexity and suspicion for any "national" institution and also for some consumers of pop-cultural products.

Ionescu's death, in 1994, sanctioned not his return to his native country, but his separation from a whole world that was no longer his.

To the very end he had been a fierce enemy of death in all its forms. He kept dreaming of avoiding the unavoidable. "The truth is to be found in the imaginary," he repeated. While constantly reasserting his Christian faith, he never failed to add that "I could never believe enough. . . . I am like the one who prays daily: Lord, make me believe. . . . The truth is in the imaginary." In the end, he resigned himself, as revealed by his will, which *Le Figaro* published the very day he died: "Perhaps there will be joy afterwards. . . ."

In the years following the collapse of the Wall between the two Europes and the two worlds, *Rhinoceros* had garnered not only the well-known antitotalitarian meaning but also a "democratic" and "American" connotation—in the light of the new wars between sexes and minorities of all kinds, each group fighting for a distinguished and privileged identity.

Class and race struggles had been replaced by other conflicts and slogans. . . . This was no longer about absolute, totalitarian oppression, it was about militant simplifications, not reflecting greater tolerance of insecurity, vulnerability, imprecision, ambiguity, and skepticism. The horn of rhinoceritis can be recognized today in the party membership card or badge, in the fundamentalists' cross, star or crescent, but also in the extreme ideologization of difference.

Seven years had passed, as in the stories of prophecy. The lost one, the wanderer, was still at Bard. The green and the red Rhinos had gradually moved on, and his homeland, still not immune to old and new types of rhinoceritis, had receded farther and farther into the distance. Yes, the exile was in the same place, but less exiled than before. Moving away from his former biography proved beneficial more than once; the exile Eugen Ionescu had been right.

In 1996, the class at Bard no longer resembled that of seven years earlier. Soon after the fall of communism in Eastern Europe, the college had initiated a program of academic exchanges, and every year a number of East European students had come to Bard to study for two semesters.

During the 1996–97 academic year, I was teaching a course entitled "Danube—A Literary Journey." This time Ionescu was accompanying his fellow writers Musil and Kafka, Koestler and Krleza, Kiŝ and Canetti. The literary journey along the Danube dealt with "Central European" authors; in their books, we were trying to discover the spirit of "Mitteleuropa" in relation to the ever-changing reality of here and there.

The class was almost equally divided between American and East European students. From the very beginning, the seminar discussions benefited from the stimulating tension between the "subtlety" characteristic of the Old World and the open, realistic, efficient "practicality" of America.

Ionescu's metaphor seemed shocking to the Americans and already partly "outdated" to the Europeans. The voluble student from Tbilisi argued that Beckett's plays seem more radical to him than Ionescu's because the Irish author accepted no compromise with the so-called humanism of hope, while the female Czech student saw in the Logician's rhinocerization a necessary "liberation" from the monomaniacal idiocy of ignoring reality.

I promptly recalled the image of Ionescu as he appeared in 1979, when I first met him. It was the same image evoked more than half a century before by Mihail Sebastian, his friend and a friend of his friends, whose rhinocerizing delirium these two contemplated together in Bucharest in the 1930s and 1940s. "I can't get used to life . . ." the playwright who found it even harder to get used to death seemed to say in 1979, just as in 1941. Then, listening in Cismigiu Park in Bucharest to a broadcast of a speech by the Great mustarchioed Rhinoceros from Berlin, Berenger had turned pale, then white, and fled in terror. "I can't! I can't," he was whispering, terrified by the besieging barbarism around him.

I gave up my initial idea of discussing the significance of the rhinoceros in the imagery of antiquity with my class. I had been going to talk about Alexander's apocryphal letter to Aristotle (quoted in Flusser's memorable book *Judaism and the Origins of Christianity*, 1988), in which the unusual animal, larger than an elephant and with three horns, is evoked by the name the Indians gave it: "odontotyrannos." The fabulous apparition is also mentioned in the writings of the neo-Pythagorean Philostratus and, even before him, in the Jewish apocalyptic literature and in the Book of Daniel 7:7 where the monstrous "odontotyrannos," seen with the same eschatological horror and fear, embodies—in its "steel teeth and bronze claws"—the all-destructive force the modern tyrants would regenerate with renewed vitality. I was not at all sure that such pedantic clarifications would not bore my audience.

But the provocative, unconventional pages of the student of seven years earlier could be useful again, I believed. I therefore tried the "Nancy test" on the new class too. The grades she had received in 1989 from her fellow students were not very different from those given by their successors in 1996. Nor were the commentaries too different either:

> Her arguments seem to be well-supported, her indulgence can be justified. The paradox she depicts coming from the hero's fear of change which then also necessarily means a reabandonment from the society the same way as in the non-rhinoceros one, is very well posited.

> Is the disregard for its historical context a conscious decision? The analysis of the main character (his inconsequence, therefore, weakness) seems even more satisfying than the traditional "humanistic" approach (what saves him is "humanity" i.e., weak-

ness, thoughtlessness?) Surely this interpretation is far more optimistic, however, leaving out the bitterness and tragedy (for, after all, there is no victor). A brave, provoking attempt.

The paper is one-sided. In fact, becoming rhinoceros is not, according to the internal logic of the text, an improvement. But the originality and brilliancy of the paper is beyond any question.

Some valid points on the subject of Berenger's about-face and his hypocrisy in defending the "civilization" he cannot believe in, but she gravely misreads "rhinoceritis" by interpreting it as "progress" of a liberating nature; also, she ignores the way language in the play functions as a rationalizing suprastructure, and accepts the characters' statements at face value.

Awful. However, her assertion that the actions of a society rely completely upon the balance Rhinoceroses/Berengers at any given time for any given cause/extreme was clear.

This paper is a somewhat irresponsible piece of proto-fascist propaganda. It fails to provide a means of entering the text by neglecting: 1. the distinction between collective (in a non-coercive way) political/historical change and violent conformist suppressions of otherness, and 2. the actual psychological impact of the concrete historical situation that Ionesco is allegorizing.

We could even have discussed some of the theses of the students of 1996. A Polish female student focused on "the rhinocerization of language" in Ionescu's play ("The Intransparency of Language in Rhinoceros"), analyzing language as a "dramatic object," revealing its own absurdity and gradual loss of meaning, its capacity to convey ideas and sentiments, in the absence of an appropriate idiom. A crisis of human relationships, which are finally automated by clichés and redundancy.

What the thesis of seven years earlier brought, however, was the shock of turning the interpretation "inside out." Was this turn in Ionescu's spirit? "The right to stupidity?" How "stupid" was yesterday's stupidity? And today's? I would have liked to have taken up the question with the father of the absurd drama. The fundamental right to candor, doubt, challenge, failure? Forms of freedom, that is, of individuality? I suppose Ionescu would have had a lot to say.

I had seen him in passing during a visit to Paris at the beginning of the 1980s, on an evening that I would spend with Marie-France, his graceful and devoted daughter. He came into the hall for a few moments, lonely and vulnerable, just to meet me. We only exchanged a few unimportant words. There was an affectionate absence on the sad Charlot's face, a sort of not necessarily alcoholic dizziness.

"Already drunk, after several cocktails (on a Saturday morning), he starts talking to me about his mother," Sebastian wrote in 1941. Over forty years had passed, it was a Saturday evening, not morning, but the tormented inner self seemed to ask for relief this time too, "as if a burden would lie heavy on him, as if he would smother." The burden, perhaps a secret rusted by time but still bleeding, was that "precious leper" who was born of a Jewish mother.

His face seemed to bear the trace of that absolute grief of understanding human reality. His "confidence" in man's ability to save himself, despite the horrors he himself produces, clearly had been the result, not of naïvety or optimism, as the student from Tbilisi believed, but of the ultimate need to "force" the gods' grace.

When we went into the street, Marie-France told me about Ionescu's meeting with an important Romanian fiction writer. After skeptically inspecting the roomy apartment, located in the heart of

Paris, at Boulevard Montparnasse 96A, the visitor from Bucharest expressed his disappointment that a writer of such standing and a member of the French Academy had not been given a villa with a garden and adequate atmosphere, as socialist Rhinoromania's "classics" were. The member of the French Academy did not seem offended. He called Marie-France and asked her to show the guest her small room too, so that he could see that the apartment had one more room. . . .

I was only half listening to this meaningful anecdote. The noble sadness of his face, which I had seen in one of destiny's moments, was haunting me. *I can't get used to life.* Inside myself and from all around I could hear Berenger's voice reading the author's unforgettable face.

Translated by Liviu Bleoca, 2000

MADE IN ROMANIA

The last time I saw Saul Steinberg was a year ago, in February. I had invited him and his friend Prudence to dinner, along with two women friends of mine from Milan, a city to which he felt close. A few days later, to thank us, he sent my wife, Cella, and me a copy of a map of interwar Bucharest that Prudence had found in the New York Public Library.

The communication, as so often before, bore his unmistakable mark: the large white rectangular envelope had been folded in half, into a square; at the top left, the sender's name, street, city, state, and zip code had been stamped in blue ink; at the top right, beneath a row of six 32-cent stamps showing the American flag, a label had been improvised out of what looked like sand-colored wrapping paper. On it the artist had drawn a box and written FIRST CLASS. In fact, the label had come from a roll of masking tape and matched two similar scraps at the bottom and the right of the square. The bottom half of the envelope was covered with six black lines of calligraphic handwriting, indicating the person and the address to which it was to be sent. It seemed a typical Steinberg collage.

The large-scale map folded inside the envelope was a black-and-white photocopy. The gift was accompanied by a note: "*Dragii mei,* A map of Bucureşti (NY Public Library) the center—enlarged. The map has no date, but from some signs, I can guess, it is 1924 ca. I've marked my Strada Palas, Liceul Matei Basarab, Circul Sidoli, etc. We both enjoyed the evening. *Cu drag,* Saul." As usual, the body of the text was in English, but the salutation ("*Dragii mei*"—"My dear friends") and the sign-off ("*Cu drag*"—"Affectionately") were in

Romanian. With a red pencil, he had drawn an arrow from his Strada Palas to Strada Rinocerului (Rhinoceros Street).

He also spoke to me on the phone about that map, in which he had located the magical Palas district of his childhood. He seemed deeply affected by the past—by the sonority of the old street names, to which his rumbling voice and wonder-filled annotations indeed restored a degree of exoticism and fascination. His voice took on musical inflections as he kept repeating the name *Gentilă, Gentilă,* a street close to the market that we both remembered well. Then more street names: *Fetiţelor* (Young Girls), *Gîndului* (Thought), *Graţioasa* (Gracious), *Zefirului* (Zephyr), *Vişinelor* (Sour Cherries), *Parfumului* (Perfume), *Trifoiului* (Clover). He said *Graţioasa* several times and continued with *Dimineţii* (Morning), *Stupinei* (Apiary), *Turturelelor* (Turtle Doves).

He kept returning to the Palas district and wandering off to names he discovered with delight to be still in his memory or that he saw hypnotically for the first time. "*Concordiei* and right next to it, look, *Discordiei.* So . . . Concord and Discord! And here we have *Trofeelor* [Trophies], *Oiţelor* [Little Sheep], *Olimpului* [Olympus], *Emancipata* [Emancipated]. Listen, *Emancipata!* Isn't it wonderful?" *Emancipata.* We were speaking English: he did not seem comfortable conversing in Romanian, but he liked to throw in a Romanian word here and there and savor it. Our discussions about Romania always confirmed an affectionate complicity of minds, but for me they were also a constant challenge to rethink the past with the fierceness and seriousness of despair that the past deserves.

Saul had wanted to accompany me on my 1997 trip to Romania. He thought himself too frail to undertake his long-postponed journey into the past alone and wanted the companionship of a much more recent émigré. Before I set off, he had sent me a copy of a map of Bucharest on which he had drawn a circle around the Antim-Justiţiei neighborhood. There were a few lines of explanation: "Apr 12, 97. Dear Norman, Here is my magic circle: Strada Palas off

Antim—Strada Justiţei crossing Calea Rahovei (now George Geor-
gescu!). Cella had told me that nothing remains—but have a look if
you have the time. Bon voyage. *Cu drag*, Saul."

Saul told me that he went instead to Milan, the city of his youth,
which he thought would serve as a "safer" and less overwhelming
substitute for present-day Romania. He did not return, it seemed,
any happier than I did from Bucharest. He had found not the city of
his youth but a vulgar and noisy place that not even his small,
expensive, and well-situated hotel could render more appealing.

In the spring of 1999, weighed down by the difficulties of writing
A Hooligan's Return, about my trip to Romania, I thought that Saul's
memories, with their inimitable blend of the sardonic and the emotional, might help me find the right tone for an over-complicated
subject. Even at the time of my trip I sometimes saw him as an
essential figure in the exile's dilemma, helped in his difficult adaptation to new places and codes by the resentments that his native land
had bred in him, yet constantly troubled by the memory of his
magical initiation into existence in the old place, in childhood.

Our first real conversation had taken place some seven years previously. It was more of a conflict, in fact. New to America at the time,
I was invited—and even went—to a number of parties in luxurious
houses where the artistic elite of the city of my shipwreck gathered.
We had already been introduced to each other a few times on such
occasions, but we had never done more than exchange a conventional word or two. The short gentleman with a bald patch, glasses,
and a mustache was simply dressed yet with a touch of eccentricity,
whether in the color of his muffler or the shape of his hat. My hosts
presented me to him as a "Romanian," thinking that this would make
me more to his liking, but not surprisingly it appeared to have the
opposite effect. He reminded me of Tudor Arghezi, a prominent
Romanian poet of the interwar period, who had had an enviably long
creative life. It was not just Steinberg's morose air, chary of words, but

the boredom he displayed so readily at the approach of strangers—
and, more than once, in the face of people familiar to him.

The sardonic Arghezi would probably have liked Saul's drawings
of crocodiles: not only the type that stays alive by feeding on itself and
digesting its own tail, but also another type—or the same—placed in
the service of the symbolic as well. That crocodile bites with sawteeth
into the cry "HELP," inscribed on an abstract baguette loaf. The
despairing man's cry is the link with the assailant who has seized him
as prey. "The vulnerable part of the man in danger," Saul writes, "is
the cry for help, which is the part by which the crocodile holds him
and which has the function of an appetizer. What do I want to say?
That he who cries his terror becomes the victim of his statement."
Skeptical and sometimes cynical to an extent that intrigued conversational partners, Saul guarded his vulnerability, avoiding confession
and complaint alike.

Our quarrel took place at dinner. Someone asked me to describe
the situation of writers in Romania during Ceaușescu's last decade,
and as I began to speak I heard, across the table, a voice interrupting
me: "But how can anyone be a Romanian writer? Is there such a
thing as Romanian literature?"

Two quotations immediately came to my mind: Montesquieu's
famous question of the eighteenth century—"How can anyone be
Persian?"—and the words of Camil Petrescu, a Romanian writer of
the 1930s—"With heroes who eat five olives in three weeks and
smoke one cigarette in two years, with a little market tavern in the
mountains and a farm with three pigsties belonging to a teacher in
Moldova, no novel or even literature can be made."

"When did you leave Romania?" I heard myself heatedly ask.

"In the thirties," the Romanian replied.

"In those days there was already a generation of distinguished
modern writers," I said, and I went on to name a number of important Romanians, among them Rebreanu, Blecher, Urmuz, and, of
course, Ionescu.

"Maybe, maybe," he replied. "It's been many years since then. I'm not up to date on Romania."

That was probably the beginning of our friendship. It would seem that Saul regretted his rudeness that evening. Several times he gave me to understand that his affront had been one of those stupid social games he usually despised, although he sometimes fell back on them at parties because they had won him pleasant, if temporary, female company.

He grew lonelier with age, as the number of people with whom he kept in touch continued to diminish. He went through periods of depression. I really drew closer to Saul Steinberg, I suppose, on the morning when he called me and, having asked how I was, commented on my conventional reply in a way that cast a different light on the evening of our argument. "You can't be well. I know you can't. We carry a curse—the place we come from—we carry it inside us. It doesn't heal easily. Maybe never."

I was surprised to hear this near-confession on his part. He had been in America for more than half a century, happy to have come and to have found here purpose and fame. Yet the Romanian wound did not seem to have healed, although, as I later discovered, there was more to it than merely the horror, scorn, and resentment evident in his crude opinions the evening of our confrontation.

Anti-Semitism was one theme he did not fail to mention, as if it were an inseparable part of his native geography. He treated it with disgust, as a hideous and incurable disease or an emanation from natural waste seeping into every pore of social life; it poisoned its victims, too, inuring them to the surrounding hatred, training them in a constant bargaining that deformed their characters forever. He spoke with acrimony of both the primitive aggression of the persecutors and the humbleness of the persecuted, with their grotesque accommodation that combined pitiful little domestic pleasures and oozing hypocrisy.

As we became friends, he also began to tell me about his family, his school, and his schoolmates. Neither his relatives nor his friends were safe from his irony, and this irony also seemed to contain self-pity for the misfortune of his ridiculous place of origin; an attachment that passed insidiously, one might say, into a view of the world in general, including even the America he so much admired. One name alone enjoyed the perfect intangibility of love: that of his adored sister, Lica. He did everything he could to get her out of the communist hell of 1950s Romania and, subsequently, to make her life easier in France.

"The Land of Dada," as he called Romania, reappeared more and more often in recent years, not only as "the dark land" or "the land of exile" (as he wrote in a letter to his old school friend Eugen Campus) but also as the land of his childhood, that "miraculous time" beyond recall even for a childlike artist fascinated by the magic of its set pieces and clowning.

The street of Calea Griviței, where an uncle of his apparently had a watchmaker's shop, came back to life as a bewildering initiatory realm. Even eighty years later, he remembered vividly the smells of cobblers' workshops and shoeshine booths, spice stores, dust and perspiration and a nearby railway station, pickles and pies and Romanian-style kebabs and the hairdresser's shop.

He frequently woke me with a 'phone call, presumably holding a Romanian dictionary on his knees. "*Cacialma.* What would you think?" he would ask about the word for "bluff." "Obviously a Turkish word, no? Like *mahala* [slum district], like *sarma* [stuffed cabbage], *narghilea* [hookah], or *ciulama* [chicken in white sauce]. But what about *cică* [a contracted form of 'it is said that']? And then there's *cicăleală* [teasing]. Or *cișmea* [fountain]. Turkish, both of them, right? *Colibă* [hut] is Slavic. And the linguistic influences of these words: professions are German, flowers French, but *rastel* [gun rack] comes from the Italian *rastello* [rake], or *rastellum* in

Latin. And *seară* [evening] and *searbăd* [tasteless] and *zi* [day] and *ziar* [newspaper] and *zînă* [fairy]. But *zid* [wall] is Slavic, and so is *zîmbet* [smile]. . . ."

He discovered strange words whose exotic sound seemed suddenly to bring back the time and place that had formed and deformed us. "I can't manage to make my peace with the language," he wrote in 1988 to Eugen Campus, who was living in Israel. And in another letter that same year, referring to his relations with his native country, he recognized "a complexity that caused me confusion in my childhood—I should have liked to be normal, that is, primitive."

In his last years, more and more frequent incursions into Romanian confirmed his fascination with the language and the aura of his early life. To me, too, he said that in his youth he had wanted to become a writer but that lacking a language even later on, he had turned to writing through images. We were joined in our plight, he was saying, but the suggestion of kinship did not stop there. "We can't be Americans," I was told more than once.

The Romanian archives that Saul kept in his apartment and that I consulted after his death show a far from dimmed memory of the inaugural place and time.

The genealogical tree sketched in his hand on large drawing boards maps a large Jewish-Romanian family. His paternal grandfather, Nathan, who had children from both of his two marriages, was born in Russia and lived in Buzău, Romania, where he worked as an army tailor, and where Saul himself spent his early childhood. His only son from the first marriage emigrated to America and founded a new family there, while the children from his second marriage, two sons—Martin and Harry—took the same course and went off, respectively, to New York (as a printer) and Denver, each eventually producing a sizable family of his own.

Most of Nathan's offspring, however, stayed in Romania. Saul's maternal grandfather, Iancu Itic Jacobson, lived all his life in Buzău as a wine merchant; some of his sixteen children died young, but the others spread to France, America, Israel, and, above all, to different parts of Romania, as typographers, watchmakers, engineers, binders or sellers of books, one even as a croupier. In the graphics of this meticulously documented genealogy, Saul appears with his arms outstretched toward Hedda Sterne (the wife from whom he was separated but not divorced) and Sigrid, his companion of many decades.

The Romanian postcards that he collected (first through an agent in Queens, New York, then through an art dealer in Amsterdam) display the same obsession with his native country: picturesque views from the interwar years of Romanian towns and villages and spas. As I looked with amusement at a market sequence with halva sellers ("Alvițari. Marchands d'alvita, Editura Mag. M. Rosenbaum, București"), I was inevitably reminded that when Saul first came to our house, he arrived not with the usual bottle of wine, or the even more usual box of bottles, as he would later, but with an old colored postcard of interwar Buzău.

Both before and after the war, Saul's letters from his parents, still in Romania, are full of a great affection and concern, especially after he was forced by new anti-Jewish laws to leave his beloved Italy and go to America. They confirm the same painful connection to that common Romanian past from which he and eventually they were severed and liberated.

One can see why a winter journey to the Soviet Union in 1956 had a powerful meaning for the tourist Saul Steinberg. "That winter in Russia was a trip for my nose," Saul confessed, "a voyage to the odors of Eastern Europe and my childhood—beautiful ones of winter and also of elementary school, police station, disinfectant, the terrible odor of fear which at that time, with Stalin only recently gone, permeated Moscow and Leningrad and even the countryside.

Those ancient smells and emotions were like a visit to my past, a travel in time."

The adult's journey was also the child's journey. Among Saul's envelopes, letters, Romanian identity papers, documents, and other relics, I found a recent photograph that looked as if it had been extracted from a Bergman film: the elderly Saul Steinberg holding the hand of a child, himself as a boy. A collage, then, a bewildering sequence from the lost and yet never lost Proustian time of childhood.

"By putting oneself in the uncomfortable position of the immigrant, one is again like a child," explained the New World immigrant. "I am among the few who continue to draw after childhood is ended, continuing and perfecting childhood drawing." The place of exile was childhood itself, but a miraculous one full of visions and magical effects. Saul Steinberg discovered his homeland ("patria," as he used to say) in America precisely in this sense of liberty and play and substitution, openness and creativity—and also farce. Stunning mutations, dreams and versatility and spectacle, energy and illusions, oceanic solitude, ingenuity, devastating despair.

The basic infantile mythology of this modern Land of Promise offers us, in his cartoons, an Uncle Sam in the posture of the Sphinx and a Statue of Liberty in a nightgown, but it also offers us the consumerist extravaganza of toy objects in the man-made landscapes, the man-made birds and crocodiles and cats and pencils and movie stars, and finally that inexhaustible "self-made man" himself, master of the great universal trick: METAMORPHOSIS.

To the artist—forever a child, as Brancusi put it—America is offered not just as the fable of inexhaustible contemporary reality but also as a cognitive adventure in which the newly shipwrecked Crusoe, a stranger and an adult infantilized by the shock of dislocation and dispossession, learns what it is to be an American. In this sense, both Harold Rosenberg ("The United States was made to order for Saul Steinberg") and Arthur Danto ("The travels were undertaken in the spirit of learning how to be an American") are right.

It is not by chance that the immigrant arrived on this side of the Atlantic with a passport he had faked, nor is it by chance that many images in the artist's repertoire are of wandering. Saul Steinberg admits: "What I draw is drawing, [and] drawing derives from drawing. My line wants to remind constantly that it's made of ink." His work is the coded autobiography of an estranged foreigner, a child now "cosmopolitan" and "cosmic," hidden in anonymity as in celebrity, who plays with a series of different identities for himself, a parodic combination of masks, surrogates, and othernesses.

We may find significant the frequent appearance in the artist's work of fingerprints and images made from fingerprints, as well as of identity papers, rubber stamps, diplomas, signatures, pictures of post offices (in Charlotte, North Carolina; Nashville, Tennessee; Kansas City, Missouri; Lynchburg, Virginia; and Canal Street). In *The Passport* (1953), the oval-shaped fingerprint that stands in for the human face is completed with a collar and tie, the exile's emblematic image.

Nothing "natural" seems to attract his attention, unless it is part of "artificial" nature, man-made in the same sense that the artist-demiurge creates objects by situating them in parodic relation to their model (when there is one), in a nonstop juggling routine. Saul is a juggler with reality who, through art, makes his public aware of ordinary things.

Among the many captivating "trifles" scattered in Saul's files, I found a dollar bill with which he had once tested the efficiency of the US mail. He had put a strip of paper with his address and a stamp directly onto the banknote, tossed it in a mailbox, and then probably waited with an adventurer's impatience to see the result. The postal workers put it in an official envelope and sent it on.

Saul Steinberg remembered Romania as a place of peasants in folk-loric dress, mustachioed cavalry officers in parade outfits, children in school uniforms with their official numbers on their sleeves, for ease of identification and denunciation, a place where a Dadaist alloy was created out of frustration, hedonism, and grief.

"Land of masquerade," "land of operetta," "land of exile" . . . even perhaps the Dark Land? In a drawing from 1975 that he gave to Eugen Campus, the schoolboy appears in quasi-military cap, collar, and boots, with his registration number LMB (Liceul Matei Basarab) 586 on his arm. He is making his way down Strada Palas to the solemn Institute of Instruction. A rural landscape, with drainpipes, stovepipes, and barrels. The street fauna are humbly domestic: dogs, cats, chickens, "real" geese (not the man-made geese later created across the ocean). People peer awkwardly and suspiciously through windows. The props are meticulous: a briefcase in the boy's right hand, inkwell and pen holder in his left hand, satchel on his back with a ruler sticking out like a gun.

The clue here may lie in the satchel. According to another schoolmate, the recruit's first appearance in the schoolyard was not as ordinary as the simple provincial scenery would suggest. In reality, it was a stunning debut. The satchel with which he came armed at the beginning of that school year was also an identity card (of a sort never seen before). On the flap the schoolboy's exotic name was printed in large black letter: STEINBERG. Of course, it drew dizzily admiring looks from his new schoolmates. But the precocious public assertion of identity was actually an innocent premonitory farce. The mark had been imprinted on the satchel by the workshop that produced it, STEINBERG Bookbinders, which belonged to his father, Maurice Steinberg, in anticipation of the name that would be printed in the memory of his contemporaries and in that of vastly more admirers in the future.

Translated by Patrick Camiller, February 2000

AN EXILE ON SEPTEMBER 11 AND AFTER

That morning I was at Bard College, about one and a half hours from New York City. I was preparing my afternoon seminar, "Exile and Estrangement in Modern Fiction." I only heard about the brutal attack on America towards noon. Most professors canceled their classes. I asked my students whether we should go ahead as planned with Nabokov's novel *Pnin*, call off the class, or discuss the event rather than the book. Their presence showed that they didn't want to be alone, and I assumed that the theme of exile would allow for a wide-ranging discussion of today's world—a world in which estranged people, and not only they, are obsessively looking for a lost center, even reacting hysterically to their own tensions, trauma, and mystifications.

"You are sixteen students, an even number," I said. "If half of you decide one way and the other the opposite, you may also need my vote. However I vote, some of you would not be happy. Those who are not happy can still join the discussion, accepting the dialogue as a compromise. Or they can leave the room and even blow up the building." A prolonged, tense silence followed. The majority of the students were still in shock. Finally, they chose dialogue. For some of them, it was indeed a compromise. This seemingly trivial situation mirrored the global alternative, the essential choice: democracy or war against it.

Democracy is, in fact, an often tedious search for compromise, a complicated enterprise in domesticating aggressiveness. Compromise is not acceptable to everyone, as the nihilistic "messengers" had proved that morning. Their answer had been crime, the urge to blast the world apart.

Democracy is not a utopian project and is not Paradise; even religious fanatics locate Paradise in heaven, not on earth. It's not at all surprising that one of the obvious results of democracy is incoherence—a form of freedom, probably. The unavoidable contradictions and conflicts, the inequalities and frustrations of democracy—of freedom—as well as the widespread resentment of the "demonic" and much-envied America may explain, at least partially, that terrible September 11 event.

Religious, as well as many non-religious, militants keep reciting America's shortcomings and the disaster of future "globalization." For better or for worse, globalization is already part of our everyday life, through television, computers, antibiotics, exotic travel. In many underdeveloped and poor countries, or in countries with authoritarian, oppressive rule, quite often the resentment seems not against globalization, but against the lack of it. Globalization doesn't mean ethnic, ideological, or political unification, but a metageographical network with all its promises and risks. It would be useful and important to debate such issues, not blindly to reject the concept itself with simple-minded militancy.

In their own way, the fundamentalists are also suggesting a kind of globalization. Not a democratic one, of course, but a totalitarian one. The real question remains as to what kind of "globalization" might be offered as an alternative. Surely not the mystical, totalitarian patriarchy of the Middle Ages that negates dialogue, difference, dissidence. The "holy" war for the restoration of obsolete, collectivist traditions is part of Islam, but also part of Christianity and Judaism and the fundamentalism of other religions. It is only due to the large number of Muslims and the role of the Mosque as a guide for many illiterate believers that the danger in the Muslim world seems greater.

Yet, I think we should avoid the idea of an irreconcilable battle between the Christian-Jewish tradition that celebrates human life, with all its ideals and warts, and the Muslim fanatics, to whom death appears the holiest fulfillment. We should hope, rather, for a structural change in the Muslim world, for a gradual and essential modernization of its social landscape, and do our best to accelerate such a change.

The cult of death is not strictly a Muslim phenomenon. Extremists of the European right celebrated it before 1945. We are now as familiar with the reactionary nationalistic revolution of fascism and Nazism as with the communist one, known as "progressive" and internationalist. It isn't difficult to imagine where the return to such projects may lead. The question about Islam is still more puzzling: do we really know Islam?

I suggested to my students that they start a dialogue with their Muslim colleagues. It is important that Muslims themselves, not followers of other faiths or atheists, explain whether the belief in Allah implies an apocalyptic war against all "infidels"; or was the terrorists' clever use of religious slogans an excuse for their criminal undertaking?

In these horrible times, New York was damaged, shocked, traumatized. They were days of siege and emergency. But the citizens and institutions of this great city remained courageous, and the incomparable metropolis gradually began to pulsate, to return to its old rhythm. I truly felt American, even more so than when I was granted citizenship, and I truly felt a New Yorker, deeply connected to the daily life and the symbols of my new domicile. This modern Babylon—with a large Chinatown, with large Russian, Jewish, Italian, and Indian enclaves—symbolizes not only America and its ideals, but the entire modern world. It is not accidental that people from eighty countries died in the Trade Center.

More than a few, in America and elsewhere, are demanding that America submit itself to the strongest criticism for its sins and disasters, its arrogance and superficiality, its materialism, vulgarity and wealth. Self-scrutiny and self-criticism should be undergone as a matter of course for every sound nation. But whoever believes that "America" consists of a horde of arrogant and domineering "patriots" does not understand that at every level it is made up of countless Americas. Its unyielding diversity often confuses strangers, and even Americans, forcing them to adopt a childish reductionism. To use simplistic "emblems" of anti-Americanism means to ignore the great American scientific, cultural, economic, and social achievements and its past and present indispensable contribution to world democracy. Would our planet be better without America? I doubt it. I rather hope that in the near future the American Muslim population will become the point of reference for the Muslim world, as has happened with Jews, Latin Americans, Koreans, and many others in this country.

I recall a writers' conference in Amsterdam, at the beginning of the 1990s. Since I was the only participant from the United States, I was taken for a "Yankee," although then I did not even have American residency. After my speech, a renowned Arab author from Israel mentioned a few incidents of discrimination against his fellows in America, then turned to me and asked in front of the audience: "Is that a democracy, sir?" I was tempted to ask him, in turn, what he was comparing America with. With Arab states, for instance, corrupt monarchies and brutal dictatorships? But I only told him that I was speaking for myself, as always, not for any group or country. "Yes, I think America is a real, often trivial, essential democracy," I said. "A popular, dynamic democracy that forever reinvents itself. But it is not a perfect country." And I added, "I spent most of my life in a faraway country in a society that claimed to be perfect. I would prefer never again to share such a privilege. I am glad to live in a country that is as imperfect as its citizens are." When I finished, I suddenly remembered that the one American novelty I really was enthusiastic about from the start was the absence of identity cards.

America has, of course, not a few disturbing sides, but in the history of world powers it doesn't find itself in too bad a place. A comparison with the Ottoman Empire, the Tsarist Empire, or the Soviet Union and the Third Reich suffices. Certainly, America provokes frustration, envy, injustice, and even hatred. But its principles are deeply humanistic, supported by a sort of religion of dialogue and pragmatic compromise. The American spirit furthers competition, often tough competition—but it asks of the victor not to allow the loser to sink too low. America has helped many peoples and countries, even former enemies. It is hoped that this will happen in Afghanistan, as well, to speed up a drastic social and political change.

So many people who try to understand and accept the terrible habits and deeds of closed societies in faraway countries and civilizations should also try to understand the contradictions and conflicts, the errors and disasters of a free society. This would also mean, in the end, understanding the unsettling potential of human beings—not only elsewhere, but here, in our proximity, at the core of modernity.

Political errors and new options should be discussed more and more in the near future in relation to the premise, cause, and consequences of the September 11 terrorist attack. This must be an open and also a self-critical discourse of a sort that is unthinkable in the terrorists' countries of origin.

An American military victory alone would mean another huge diversion. The major event of September 11 should force us all to rethink major questions about ourselves, and the national and international social-political environment.

As much as I hope for a serious debate on this matter, I must confess that I sometimes find myself stupefied by the scandalously frivolous old/new anti-capitalist and anti-American slogans. They seem to say: "The attacker is always perfect." The victim, in this case America, has taken the guilt upon itself, has done regrettably bad things, so we should blame it for its imperfection.

We should not forget that we are under attack by the brutality and barbarism of a deluded enemy, for whom human life does not count and who can rely on fellow believers and other extremist ideologies. The threats from the centers of the fanatical movement are a serious danger to the entire free world. This is a fact we should no longer allow ourselves to ignore.

I would hope, as I have already said, for much more than an American military victory. What we all expect is a more secure and open world, a change for the better—which means a lawful and fair society—in some of the Islamic and underdeveloped countries, and an enhanced democracy in many other places as well as here at home. America needs to do its best in this direction. Otherwise this unusual battle may result, in the end, in another trivialization of tragedy.

Translated from the German by Eric Grunwald and
Edward Kanterian, February 2002

THE WALSER DEBATE*

Of course, the Holocaust is not exclusively a German problem. While it was a crime perpetuated by the National Socialists, it has a significance that goes beyond geographical boundaries and historical fact. The question of German guilt, especially now, after unification, remains a moral obligation for this country, whose current and future generations have a right to learn about what happened in the past, but also to be assured that they themselves bear no direct responsibility for it.

Every four or five years, I offer a seminar at Bard College entitled "Literature and the Holocaust." I don't teach the course more frequently because I wish to avoid developing rhetorical routines I could fall back on in discussing this difficult topic. The first thing I tell my students is that the Holocaust is not only a Jewish tragedy, though it was above all a tragedy for the Jews. The Holocaust was a tragedy for the Germans as well, and, indeed, for all mankind.

*The German writer Martin Walser, in his acceptance speech on receiving the Peace Prize of the German Booksellers' Association at the Book Fair in 1998, warned against the "permanent representation" of the Holocaust in the mass media as an enduring argument against Germany and the Germans. He also spoke of the media's use of the Holocaust as a "moral cudgel." Walser's speech has provoked a broad controversy in the German press and a high rate of popular approval. However, some intellectuals and Jewish representatives have criticized his way of mentioning only German "shame" (never "guilt"), of suggesting that foreign pressure, not Germany's inner postwar evolution, has imposed the Holocaust Memory, and of using the term *Errinerungsdienst* (memory service) that echoes the Nazi term *Arbeitsdienst* (labor service) or *Wehrdienst* (military service).

I can understand Martin Walser's irritation. No doubt it was provoked above all by the way in which the memory of this tragedy has repeatedly been commercialized, trivialized, and even instrumentalized to various ends (including political ones). I have to say that for a Jew—above all for one who has his own memories of that horror—it is not easy to come to terms with the sensationalist notoriety that surrounds this terrible wound and shame. I see this matter rather differently than do the activists of many Jewish and non-Jewish organizations who, with the melodramatic pathos of the "good cause," invoke the catastrophe again and again, to the point of exhaustion, until all that remains is tedium.

When I arrived in the United States, I was surprised to see what a huge quantity of literature had been written about the Holocaust. Bit by bit, a fully-fledged industry had come into being to keep the memory alive. Enough survivors were ready to participate in bizarre, theatrically earnest exorcisms which took the form of ostensibly spontaneous discussion sessions before all sorts of audiences. But I also found people who took a critical, even sarcastic, approach to this mechanism of supply and demand.

On my own, I came to combine tolerance and skepticism in my attitude toward the freedom of expression enjoyed by the masses in this consumer democracy. That I (like Walser, presumably) would have preferred to keep alive the memory of this tragedy in a different way doesn't much change matters. After all, what would the alternative have been? If poetry did not cease to exist after Auschwitz, why should other expressions of life in its various manifestations cease, whether they belong to the "higher spheres" or are of more banal, "humble" origin? Without this "lower sphere," life could not go on. The Holocaust, after all, did not become well known primarily through sophisticated forms of representation.

As overwhelming as it was, the Holocaust did not put an end to the course of human existence. Life went on, outside the sphere of memory, but also within and in relation to it.

Reactions to the Holocaust are no less various and contradictory than other human responses, for even this barbarism was the work of humans, not demons: it came neither from hell nor out of nothing. Some sacralized the tragedy, others denied its existence; some suffered silently from the wounds they bore, still others took it as a basis for investigation, pity, hate, revelation, revenge, despair. Unfortunately I am not religious, but I must confess that the Jewish prohibition on pronouncing the name of God or making images of him has always struck me as somehow more appropriate than the naïve fairy tale iconography of other religions. Perhaps I'd have been satisfied to have the catastrophe known as "the Holocaust" similarly enshrouded in a solemn, dignified silence. But I am not sure if there can be any solution to this dilemma.

Perhaps Samuel Beckett described the problem best. Not long after the war, in 1949, he wrote "There is nothing to express, nothing with which to express, nothing from which to express, no power to express . . . together with the obligation to express." In the more than fifty years that have passed since it took place, the general public response to the Holocaust has changed from silence to a more and more open and insistent reappraisal, to the current state of saturation. Expression has taken a variety of forms: documents, memoirs, reminiscences, diaries, debates, novels, poems, films, plays, works of art. Many of these works are minor, but many are original, authentic, and striking. The substantial repercussions in the mass media, sparked less by the most significant works than by the products appealing to the general public, have kept the memory of these events alive in the public imagination.

This dilemma was brought home to me in particular by the success of *Schindler's List*. I entered the movie theater curious and apprehensive. The audience, primed by the full-blown advertising campaign, awaited the film in reverent silence. When it was over, the optimistic finale received tumultuous applause as the dead and the living came together to sing about a dream come true: the thousand-year-old hope which had become Israel, a home to yesterday's refugees. Surely only a very few members of the audience recognized in this didactic Hollywood cliché the very same solution that social realism had once offered for all artistic, and not only artistic, dilemmas in the communist world. And just as few, apparently, were those who were taken aback by the simple "functionality" of the picturesque characters, the spectacular improbability of their relations to one another, and the film's whole ineffably kitschy aura. (Seen from such a perspective, the hero's long melodramatic final speech to those he's saved reaches far from enviable heights.) Even fewer of the satisfied consumers who had partaken of this cheap trick were able to offer resistance to the trite, moralistic message of this commercial masterpiece by invoking their own experiences in the concentration camps.

That so few were able to resist guaranteed the film's success: a success, one could perhaps say (and this would not be the only paradox of the reality we live in), that will ensure the memory of the Holocaust for coming generations, who will have neither their own memories of this tragedy nor any reason to occupy themselves with it.

The applause in the movie theater, which gave the film's consumers the agreeable sensation of participating briefly in a victory, continued afterwards at the live ceremony in which the director, smiling among the spotlights, received his Oscar—a scene that would have deserved to be spliced into the film. In his acceptance speech, the recipient of the award reminded the audience that there were still a good 300,000 surviving "Holocaust experts," and encouraged schools, nursing homes, and cultural institutions to use them and popularize their sufferings. Needless to say, I was more horrified than flattered by my sudden promotion to the "endangered experts" category.

Subsequently, the award-winning director initiated the project of a vast Holocaust Archive, a laudable endeavor that well befits our time. The film's therapeutic and profitable happy ending made possible a new, philanthropic phase in our day-to-day lives, a charitable result that will, of course, in turn receive deserved applause—even in Germany. The Spielberg Archive, we are told, might even serve as a welcome substitute for the controversial Holocaust Memorial in Berlin. A good solution, many say.

Is this a good way of diverting the "moral cudgel" that has been repeatedly raised against Germany and the Germans in the trivial mass media of which Martin Walser spoke? Is this an alternative to the "monumentalizing of German shame" which Walser, perhaps rightly, so fears?

Although I understand why Walser is fed up with the media's primitive representations of the Holocaust and German guilt, it would be difficult for me not to distance myself from his position on several counts.

If it had been a German politician giving expression to these patriotic concerns, I'd likely have been more understanding. In the case of a writer—above all one of Walser's standing—whose calling it is to scrutinize the ambiguities, the dark side of human nature, such a view of the historical "German shame" (and guilt) seems strange to me. It would have been inconceivable for a politician to write a text like "Brother Hitler," in which the great author and great German Thomas Mann displayed, as in *Doktor Faustus* or in the "Novel of a Novel," not only the good side of Germany and the Germans, of which he was so glowing an example, but also its bad side, which he debated with exemplary lucidity during the last decades of his life. I have difficulties believing that Martin Walser reads this text any differently than I do.

Assigning an individual to the permanent role of victim or perpetrator certainly entails alienation. As we know from the case of the Jews, who have always been the world's scapegoats, the assignment of such a role is unbearable. Even more grotesque is the situation in other countries. Unlike Germany, Japan has never engaged in a critical reassessment of its past, but has continued to hold up the terrible symbol of Hiroshima, with no mention whatever of the barbaric massacre of Chinese citizens in Nanking, where the Japanese Army engaged in horrifying acts of bestiality.

But don't we *still* have to ask ourselves whether the Holocaust has rightly come to serve as a moral cudgel, regardless of what Miss Media, this frivolous, cynical, omnipresent concubine of modernity, has to say about it? And do we not have to ask ourselves where exactly the danger of "monumentalizing the shame" would lie, whether or not the guilt in question is German?

Baudelaire says that the Devil's most clever trick is to convince man that he, the Devil, does not exist. In our case, one might say that memory may constitute a trap if the evil in man is forgotten, the "shame" (and guilt) that ought to accompany mankind's many demonic acts. Should we just go on filling the world with monuments to "heroism," that is, with glorifying commemorations of deeds which, seen from the "other side," from the point of view of other nations (or even one's own), meant defeat, death, loss of honor and home. What does a monument in honor of a German victory over France mean to a Frenchman, and vice versa? And what is the meaning, for a German, of a monument to a peasant revolution in which thousands of German lives were lost at German hands? Would not this, too, be a "monumentalizing of German shame" (and guilt)? Not to mention the countless massacres that have been carried out between and within various peoples in the name of brotherly or neighborly love.

Would not, then, these "Monuments of Shame" be at least as instructive, if not even more so? Ought not the people of all nations be reminded again and again what man is capable of doing to man? "Ignominy," not only "Heroism." Complementary aspects of historical fate—a complementariness that ought to be unsettling, even now. Would it mean an end to the "glorious" unity of the state, or would this state finally be compelled to reconsider its role and aspire to the highest good, namely the unconditional respect of the rights of the individual, regardless of whether or not this individual lives in one's own or in some other society?

Young people in Germany should not have to bear the burden of a guilt for which they were not responsible. Yet why should they surround themselves with the aura of a heroism which they have equally little to do with? How does a monument to an ignominious event (i.e., the Holocaust) to which future generations have no direct relation, compare with a monument to the heroism of who knows what Kaiser, whose imposing statues can be seen in so many German cities? The young generation cannot relate to him, either. In terms of the indirect, difficult-to-define relationship to what one calls "history," "people," and "fate," both monuments make sense. In terms of truth, both aspects should be invoked at once—ignominy and pride, guilt and virtue.

Martin Walser seems suspicious of those German intellectuals who never tire of accusatory rhetoric where the Holocaust is concerned, believing that they will be absolved of guilt if they labor in the service of "memory"—even if it is only for a moment in which they find themselves "closer to the victims than to the perpetrators." This is certainly no grounds for irony. It is Walser's right to shield his eyes from the obsessively reiterated nightmare, although he does not specify whether it is the horror itself he is unable to bear or the manipulation of the horror to serve ends that have nothing to do with the consciousness of guilt. Both are, in a sense, understandable, and it is precisely this capacity of mine to understand which saddens me. For what we should not forget is that the only ones who no longer have a choice as to whether or not to shield their eyes are the victims themselves, who vanished from this earth with no grave or memory other than the increasingly turbulent controversies of posterity.

Germany's "shame" is also the shame of mankind. He who does not see how the Holocaust calls into question the very fabric of humanity does not, in my opinion, have any chance at all of understanding its true dimensions and meaning.

Last year the Vatican—quite rightly—announced that it had no intention of declaring itself innocent of the consequences of the age-old anti-Jewish propaganda campaign which has provided the impetus for countless fanatical crimes. The barbaric crime of the Holocaust has a certain relation, albeit not a direct one, to this past. Christian iconography functioned for centuries as more or less fanatic "mass-media" propaganda, which for two thousand years constantly emphasized the image of the crucifixion as an example and proof of the inextinguishable Jewish guilt—an untruth that, as one knows, nevertheless has had a mystifying power that was all but impossible to resist. A dangerous cultivation of the hatred of Jews, which paved the way for the atmosphere of crime and its denial. A millennium-old monumentalizing of shame?

I understand all too well that one can grow weary of the influence of the mass media, even if this cannot be compared with the threat of death under which Jews lived in constant fear for two thousand years.

Christ, with his Jewish parents, would have been marked for death at Auschwitz. Shouldn't the Christian world dare to see him in every one of the six million Jewish victims? We may recall the Nazi song: "*Wir wollen keine Christen sein, denn Christus war ein Judenschwein*" (We don't want to be Christians because Christ was a Jewish swine).

How could the world of believers forget this apocalyptic violation of the most important of the Ten Commandments? Are fifty years too long a time to remember this "shame," which in the end is far more than merely shameful? Is the "moral cudgel" of the Holocaust nothing more than an excessive invention of the media's postmodern trivial machinery? And is the truth really so difficult to distinguish from its commodification?

I wonder whether we are allowed to lose sight of this distinction, even when the banalization, ritualization, and trivialization of truth proves too much for many of us. And even when appropriate solutions are just as difficult as the debate itself. The aftermath of the truth is, after all, nothing compared to the horrible truth itself—a fact which, I hope, is news to no one.

I hope that Martin Walser and his readers agree with me that we cannot give up our memories of the past—or their burden, or their meaning—no matter how unbearable the vulgar simplifications, no matter how regrettable the inevitable distortions to which they are subject, may be.

Translated by Susan Bernofsky, 1999

BEYOND THE MOUNTAINS

(Preliminary Ascent into Posterity: Celan–Fondane)

One evening when the sun and not only the sun had set, there went out of his little hut the Yid, and off he went—a Yid and the son of a Yid—and with him went his name, his unutterable name, it went, traipsing along, suffered itself to be heard, leaning on a staff he came over boulder and stone, hearest thou me, thou dost, it's me, me, me and him, the one thou hearest or appearest to hear, me and the other, off he went therefore, as one could well hear, when certain things had set, as is their wont, off he went under the canopy of cloud, walked in the shadow, his and the stranger's—for the Yid, as one knows, what does he possess that can be truly called his own, that is not borrowed, lent and not returned—but to resume, on he went along this road, beautiful beyond compare, walk like Lenz he did, through the mountains, he who had been ordained to live down in the plains, the lowlands where he belonged, he, the Yid, walked on and on.

On he walked, indeed, along this road, this beautiful road.

And who do you think should be coming from the opposite direction? None other than his first cousin came to meet him, his own kith and kin, a quarter of a Yid's life older than himself, he came walking large as life, along the very same road, striding in the shadow, borrowed, of course—for, I ask you again and again, how could he have come with a shadow of his own when God had made him a Yid, large as life he came, he came to meet the

other, Gross neared Klein and Klein, the Yid, bade his staff be
quiet before the staff of the other Yid, Gross.
quiet, too, was the stone. And, quiet, too was the mountain
wherein they walked, the one and the other.[1]

Paul Celan's only prose text, *Gespräch im Gebirg* (*Conversation in the Mountains*),[2] from which I have cited the opening, seems to have been written after an aborted meeting with Theodor Adorno, in the summer of 1958. Celan, his wife Gisèle and their son Eric, aged four, had come to Sils-Maria in the Swiss Alps for a vacation during which the meeting between poet and philosopher was to take place. Celan returned to Paris early, however, thus missing the confrontation—as he would say, "not by chance." He had been mistaken in believing that "Professor Adorno" was Jewish. In reality, Theodor Wiesengrund had adopted the religion and name of his Catholic mother. The dialogue on the mountain between the famous Jew (Gross) and the timid, insignificant Jew (Klein), conceived by Celan *after* his departure from Sils-Maria would be, according to some, the result of the meeting that did not take place.

The staff of "the little" mountain climber Klein keeps still as he commands it in the face of the "great" interlocutor, Gross, not necessarily out of respect, as might be supposed, but probably (as Jean Pierre Lefebvre writes in his remarkable study "Parler dans la zone de combat—Sur le Dialogue dans la montagne"),[3] out of insolence. Not really so inexplicable . . . Adorno had renounced his father's name in favor of his mother's name and religion, but he had also maintained some not so very admirable relations with the Nazis in the 1930s, as Golo Mann has shown, and he was one of those *Niebelungen de gauche* who dodged the task of protecting the poet in the horrible "Goll affair" when Celan stood accused of plagiarism.

In 1959, Adorno would pronounce his famous sentence: "To write poetry after Auschwitz is barbaric," which the poet took as a personal accusation although at the time Adorno had no knowledge of Celan's celebrated *Todesfuge*. Paradoxically—and not completely so—after *Death Fugue* was published in Bucharest in 1947 (at which time it was entitled *Death Tango*), Paul Celan's entire body of poetic work would become the most expressive and revelatory proof that poetry may be written after Auschwitz, but *not in the same way as before*. The philosopher Adorno would nuance his previous position, meanwhile, as he became Celan's admirer and exegete. Adorno would reproach the poet, in fact, for having left Sils-Maria early in the summer of 1958, for, by leaving, Celan had missed his chance to meet a truly great Jew, the learned Gershom Scholem (the researcher into Jewish mysticism) whom Celan read and admired, by whom he was beginning to be influenced and who was also present at the Alpine resort.

In his ample monograph, *Paul Celan: Poet, Survivor, Jew*,[4] John Felstiner contends that Celan's way of writing *Conversation in the Mountains* creates an original and spiritual cross between the filmic and written visions of Ingmar Bergman and Samuel Beckett.

Felstiner goes on to suggest other possible sources of inspiration for Celan's *Conversation*. These include:

1. Büchner's novella *Lenz*, in which the hero loses his mind and wanders through the mountains crying: "I am the wandering Jew!"
2. *Thus Spake Zarathustra*—itself conceived by Nietzsche at Sils-Maria (Celan would note on a copy of *Conversation*: "In memory of Sils-Maria and Friedrich Nietzsche who—as you know—wanted to shoot all the anti-Semites),
3. Kafka's *Excursion in the Mountains* (which Celan translated into Romanian), as well as
4. Martin Buber's 1913 *Conversation in the Mountains*, and

5. Osip Mandelstam's essay *About the Interlocutor* which Celan had translated into German (pp. 140–41).[5]

Any one of these, Felstiner writes, might be the source—the failed meeting with Adorno, the thought of Büchner, Buber, Kafka, the Mandelstam translation. Important here, he goes on to say, is that the narration gives voice: "voices' long held concerns about language, speech, and naming, all in a talky vein."[6]

The American critic comments on the name, "unpronounceable" or unutterable under the Nazis (and not only), as well as on the Jew's dwelling place "under" the mountains, dissociated from nature, which God has made, "not for you and not for me," on Celan's use of language that lacks the Judaic "I and Thou" on which Buber comments, on the summoning of Klein by No One, as well as on the cry "hear me" inspired, evidently by God's summoning His people (*Shema Yisrael*—Hear O Israel). Central here is that the Supreme Being has become a silenced No One, both in the Vale of Tears, through which the wanderer is eternally in transit, and in the waste to which the interlocutors (both one and the other) have been sacrificed.

Felstiner refers as well to the denomination *Jud*—in the tradition of the "Yid" of the ghetto and exile—that Celan uses in place of *Jude* (Jew), to the "star" that announces Shabbat, and to the replacement of the term *Gespräch* (conversation) with *Geschwätz*, conversation that turns into blather in the aftermath of Auschwitz, rigmarole that jams the funereal, post-mortem silence.

Felstiner underlines, moreover, the borrowing of repetitions, contractions, inversions, diminutives, interrogatives, and idioms with which Yiddish furnishes the author's "Austrian" German. Most important is that he hears a "farewell to silence" in this 1958 text. The language "gains voice" in its wounded German-Yiddish, as Celan says in the *Conversation*'s final words: "I here and I there, I, accompanied now!—through the love of those unloved. I on the way toward me, myself."

Speaking to himself through the alternating voices of those two wanderers who meet when "the sun and not only the sun was nearly set," Celan maintains the role and the position of the stray, wandering in perpetual expectation of *meeting*.

Ilana Shmueli, Celan's friend, correspondent and lover—comparable, I think, to Kafka's Milena—affirms with good reason that Celan needed this "other" (a Thou) as recipient and echo of the message cast into the sea of uncertainties. "We knew already in advance that each time Celan would need a Thou in his poems, generally a feminine Thou, a versatile Thou on whom he would call and by whom he wanted to be heard."

Poets being androgynous, this Thou certainly could have been not only his "Milena" from Cernàuţi and Israel, Ilana, but also the German Adorno "believed to be Jewish," or his predecessor from Prague, Kafka, or the teacher, Buber, or his confrere, Osip, sacrificed to the Gulag, but also other survivor-scribes of the brown, green, or red horrors.

More than any other, the hypothetical interlocutor might have been and might still be, in the posterity of both, the poet Fundoianu/ Fondane.

B. Fundoianu was born in the same month (November) as Celan, twenty-two years earlier, a bit less than "a quarter" of the 120-year lifespan of the biblical Jew. Not only that: Fundoianu began life in the selfsame Romania, in the city of Iaşi, the capital of Moldavia, then full of Jews, not far from Celan's "Little Vienna," Cernàuţi," the capital of Bucovina, then full of Jews, for Romania's former neighboring province of Galicia (once part of the Habsburg Empire) had been returned to Romania in 1918 (Cernowitz becoming Cernàuţi in the transfer). It was then partially occupied by the Soviets in 1941 and reoccupied by the Romanian and German armies. After the war, the territory remained divided between Romania and the Soviet Union, where Cernowitz would become the Ukrainian city Chernivtsi.

Barely pronounceable when not simply "unpronounceable" or *un-utterable*, like a curse, Pessach Antschel's name became Paul Antschel before solidifying as Paul Celan, which made it a natural brother to Benjamin Wechsler's, which became Barbu or B. Fundoianu (a Romanization), then Benjamin Fondane (which is "French")—the name ultimately tattooed to the skin of the page by his destiny as martyr.

When Fondane disappeared into Auschwitz in 1944, Celan was 24 years old. He had lost his parents in "Trans-Tristia" (as I called Transnistria) and was dreaming of Paris as "l'endroit idéal pour rater sa vie," as Cioran would write me one day.

On the walls of Celan's room in Paris hung a reproduction of a celebrated funeral mask (known *as L'inconnue de la Seine*) belonging to a beautiful unknown woman whose face bore a mysteriously serene expression, evoked by Nabokov, Rilke, and Aragon. The body of the suicide had been recovered from the Seine at some point, the mask saved at the Parisian morgue.

In a striking parallel, it was in Paris, whence Fondane had been sent to the pyre, that Celan allowed the Seine to extinguish his terrible disquiet along with his verse.

Lost in the fire or water of catastrophe, the two poets, so different from each other, would meet only in martyrdom and through the post-mortem dialogue between each of their lyric I's. This would be the much aspired to *meeting* of one 'semblable' with the other—each a similar yet dissimilar Thou—that would take place in and through "the great fear" that struck them both like a bolt from the blue—inspired, destroyed, and immortal.

Denis J. Schmidt affirms that "Celan writes as if he would go on living after his death."[7]

The End rewound again and again in the funereal pulsation of Memory that will not let itself be pacified: this is the "black milk" Celan continues to drink "in the morning, at noon and at dusk" and in the nights belonging to the unfinished night of the nightmare. The language of poetry contracts itself; death fragments and gradually and fatally diminishes (to zero) the state of existence in nonexistence—being in nothingness. Poetry, which is to say *life*, persists as delay. Unmistakable and irrevocable. Brief scintillations of light and illusion under the dark, gloomy tutelage of the Inevitable, watched over by the damned oracle. Repeating the sentence embedded in Memory that will not let itself be betrayed, deceived or jerked around in any way. Death doesn't allow itself frivolities; it operates impeccably like a German master clockmaker, morbid and precise, whose funeral gong prolongs an infinite torture by echo, the echo prolonged in posterity and quickened again through poetry.

Celan did not himself pass through Fondane's crematorium, but he has become a martyr in the eternity of "the total combustion," and he has most especially become the unequalled martyr of death in the aftermath of survival. From which, behold, Poetry is born anew.

In the exile prior to exile of the exiles who were each marked by the premise of exile proper, Fundoianu/Fondane's biographical and spiritual course precedes and prefigures Celan's: "And there will come a night and I will leave this place" each had murmured during the successive delays of the inevitable, the alienation of the work tenacious in each. The soil, the ground beneath them, had been gradually replaced by the letter as Levinas says; spirituality now remained the only real dwelling place, poetry confirmed itself as the essential enclave, irremediable and irreplaceable. The valley in which they had been tolerated was a temporary rest stop, no more than that, a transient state, a respite where unbounded space metamorphosed into "the letter."

The Jew Klein—and perhaps even his interlocutor Gross—lives below, in the valley where he was allowed to live from one day to the next, which is how life goes, from one day to the next. Only conversation does not develop in the Vale of Tears, which is to say in the Vale of This Life, but in the mountains beyond the mountains where the exiles and wanderers tramp with staff in hand—the staff that knows so many things—in search of someone to address, of the conversation partner with whom one may yet converse, be it even after death, in the posterity of the word.

They address one another. They're Celan and Fondane. And is it no longer possible to address the Supreme Being who has become . . . a silent Nobody after the supreme devastation.

If the Supreme Being is in each of us, then He has passed away too, for the Supreme Being—by dint of the ovens in which he burned his sons and daughters, by dint of the complete combustion, of which only the ash preserves the memory—is incinerated too. Did he die *with* every one of them and *in* every one of them, or has he survived, ruined, *with* every one of us, *in* every one of us?—and consequently, in I (Klein) and in Thou (Gross).

These two speak, one to the other, and sometimes to the staff that knows them of old and accompanies them even in their post-mortem ascent. Might the staff be a book? These two exiles are poets, and even if they were prophets or priests, the book would still be a reliable staff. The book, like the staff, aids in any ascent and not only listens, like the staff, but even converses.

I do not know if the two exiles of posterity carry some book with them through the winding curves that lead one toward the other, as I am tempted to suppose. I do not know because we are not told. It would not be at all out of the question, but we do know, in any event, that we are not told everything. It would not be out of the question . . . no, it would even be probable for them each to have a book, be it visible or hidden. It is certain that they carry a book *in* themselves, and more—written by them, themselves, and by the other and by the others.

And without doubt they hold Buber's work inside themselves, in the form of his book, *I and Thou*, a volume the size of a pocketbook, known to both. It would be suitable, and not just for this reason. Definitively, this work also embodied the meeting and conversation on the mountain between I and Thou. Not at all by chance, it was and is most precisely an emblem of Judaic thought and feeling.

Sh'ma Yisrael! the sacred Hebrew prayer is an address: Hear, O Israel!

It is an appeal from I to Thou, before being an appeal from I to You (plural). *Sh'ma Yis'ra'eil Adonai Eloheinu Adonai Echad!* Hear, O Israel, the Lord our God, the Lord is One!—the Lord is the only God.

The refrain, often repeated, in *Conversation in the Mountains*— "You hear me? Do you hear me? . . . It is I" seems an echo of the sacred invocation, emptied of the sacred after the burning.

The Supreme Recipient of Our Addresses—muffled in time and as a consequence of the total combustion—survives, though, as long as He claims to be the like of us and we of Him. He too survives after death. Did God die at Auschwitz? There existing no resort "more supreme" than the Supreme, God cannot die except as a result of His own decisions and actions, through self-negation, self-demolition, and abandon: by suicide, by Himself dispossessed of immortality, and dispossessed through his own lack of power, of sacredness. He who has lived All Things and All Times would have to live this too, in the image of and likeness unto mortals, as one of them. Powerless to stop evil, did he commit suicide in each of the slain? Yet he would rise, too, in each survivor, become mortal in every new generation, in the cycle of the ephemerals, brief as mayflies, the final solution to which He has yet to bestow upon us.

"The personalization, the personification, the embodiment: I cannot, naturally, describe the nature of God," Buber warns us, but "it is permitted and necessary to say that God is, likewise, a person." Thus, "the Other" too is himself "another."

The need to address also contains the aspiration to address the unrepresentable, unpersonifiable divinity existing, nevertheless, in I and Thou, as in the potentiality of the absent *semblable* and in all that surrounds us, visibly and invisibly. The implacable authority has lost his authority at Auschwitz and in so many other sinister celebrations of death; dying with each of the martyrs, He has risen with each of the survivors, in this way becoming, like them, the mortal unworthy of immortality, in solidarity, finally, with all, like Him and like them, wandering with them in valley and mountain, and beyond valleys and mountains.

The dialogue in the mountains and beyond the mountains aspires to a greater resonance than it would have as simply the response of alterities. The poets speak to each other—one to the other—the one recently dead and the other long dead, just as Klein and Gross speak, those two yet alive, uncertain if one is heard by the other but addressing each other, *and*, perhaps before everything else, addressing themselves to the sacred Thou, which—post burning—has become profane.

"Man has addressed himself to his eternal Thou in many ways. But all the namings of God remain sacrosanct because human beings speak not only *about* God but also *to* God," Buber writes. He asks himself how the "eternal Thou" might be able to be "inclusive and exclusive" at the same time. How would it be possible, with no deviation, for the "unconditioned" relationship with God to include all man's other I–Thou relations and for them to lead to God?

God is not put into question, Buber answers, but the relationship with God: for this reason we cannot avoid speaking about "the wholly other" but also about "the wholly same." It would be *mysterium tremendum* that overwhelms us, but also the enigmatic immediate evidence, the proximity "closer to me than my own I."

The Other is God, who is in the other, as He is in me.

The transcendence of *mysterium tremendum* no longer resides in the heaven found beyond the heaven of belief but rather in the diurnal and nocturnal Word of Poetry, where the unknown, unfulfilled, and terrestrial ineffable has taken refuge. The need to address the other is the need to address me myself and, by way of me, the other in myself, and possibly an invisible eternal Authority that once dwelt in the other and that may yet persist.

Shall we understand in this sense the democratic "I" of the English language that includes the socially *high* and *low* and all the cardinal points in an imperial equalization of ephemeral beings and of the nevertheless proud affirmation of self? This is an earthly "I," imperial and imperious, but not sacred.

"How beautiful and legitimate the animated and empathic I of Socrates sounds," writes Buber. "An infinite conversation, the conversational air is everywhere present, even before the judges, and even in the last hour of imprisonment." And, Buber repeats, in the case of Jesus; "how powerful, even overwhelming is Jesus uttering I and how legitimate, up to the point of being barely a murmur, of course. An I of unconditional relations in which man summons his Thou and calls it 'Father' in a way that makes it nothing other than a son."

"In the mists of posterity beyond the mountains, the post-mortem murmur of the two wandering poets does not cease searching, even after death, for *the one addressed*, the interlocutor, the confirmation of self. I wish for a Thou to become," Buber instructs his exiles: "Becoming I, I say Thou. Real life is meeting." And the life of posterity, naturally.

The conversation in the mountains follows the meeting in the mountains. The addressing of the self by way of alterity is all that has remained of the mortal abandoned by the Divinity that has, in turn, abandoned itself, and taken refuge, like these souls, in imperfection, in the too-human humanness of humanity. The poet craved and still craves to invoke the fore-life and the afterlife of the word in this way.

Posterity does not exist outside the meeting of like and unlike—

semblable and its opposite—or outside of the act of addressing: I having become Thou.

Neither life nor Poetry exists, outside the *meeting*.

The need *for addressing*—so visible even in the most codified of Paul Celan's poems and that in *Conversation in the Mountains* has become the refrain of the association that does not associate itself—does not direct itself only toward the living, but, as Geoffrey Hartman underlines in his essential pages on 'the longest shadow and its aesthetic,'[8] it directs itself "even toward the slain." Perhaps especially toward them . . .

To quote Celan, "He speaks truly who speaks shadows"—a phrase that might be alternatively translated, "He utters the truth who gives voice to the shadow."[9] The precariousness of any attempt at dialogue after the catastrophe solicits, I would say *imposes*, the necessity for authenticity and depth. At stake is the silencing of language not only "corrupt" of the real, as Adorno says, but directly burned in the darkness of the real. The silenced souls of those incinerated haunt the morbid void the poet traverses.

"Celan's archeology is more exemplary for us than Schliemann's," Hartman writes.[10] This funereal and fecund "depth" creates, in the end, that long-awaited Thou, that *semblable* that can no longer be, after the Holocaust, anything other than . . . phantomatic. Essential as it is, the cry to the other party, the evocation of the other party, who is even to be found "on the other side," is itself the legitimization of the other. The phantomatic Celan speaks to the phantom Fondane who is beside him, alive, in the proximity of the halting place in the mountains beyond the mountains. He knows that he can speak *only* to him, even if the murmurs seem dizzy, stammered, mumbled, wounding the alpine silence of the earth, itself phantomatic yet so alive. Staff and stone speak too; the lily of the wood tempts whomsoever may be tempted. Our speakers are fractured interlocutors, and in the end they are dumbstruck in the stillness from which each has come.

Celan and Fondane are each the other's addressee. If the apocalyptic combustion ruined the chance of a language that explains the modern crematorium, precisely because language lost the innocence of voice that belonged to former times, as Blanchot believes, and "the will to speak" itself is endangered, the obligation to speak persists, as even so taciturn a being as Samuel Beckett affirmed immediately after the war. In this stuttered and confused mourning of the "aftermath," revelation is "betrayed through an unknowable" (Hartman) and, I would say, *unhearable* monologue. "Hearest thou me, thou hearest, thou really, thou, the one to whom it appears that thou hearest me?" As Hartman says, the logos no longer produces an event. Old children of the Logos, Celan and Fondane know it. Ample and heavy, crammed with unborn words, silence makes them brothers, like no one else.

Born into a family of bookish people and attracted early to Romanian, Yiddish, and French literature, prolific and insatiable, Fundoianu took his pseudonym from the Fundoaia estate (in Dorohoi), where his grandfather on his father's side was a tenant. He made his literary debut and imposed himself rapidly on the literature of his country, which he would leave in 1923, at just 25 years of age, oppressed not only by the provincialism of a colony of French culture, as he would maintain, but also by not infrequent encounters with local anti-Semitism, either in its primary, hooligan form or in forms that were both codified and elitist.

Right after his expatriation, his superb volume *Privelişti/Landscapes* (1930) appeared. It marked him as one of the major poets of his generation,

In Fundoianu's case, landscape does not heal but rather exacerbates suffering sensibility, as does as the earth-shaking premonition that follows. The volume marks "an advanced stage in a process of demystifying nature, which Romanian poetry hadn't known till then," observes the exegete Mircea Martin. It is an "experience of becoming alone, not of communion . . . the rhetoric is descendant, not ascendant . . . the withdrawing of the poetic from landscape constitutes the fundamental aesthetic initiative, while the anti-pastel is its specific way of realizing that goal." Emblematic here is the lyric memory of that Moldavian *shtetl* ("In the market it smells of rain, of autumn and cut hay") in the much-anthologized poem *Herţa*, to which the name of the poet is inseparably attached.

Compared to *the cry* that will later mark the ever more accelerated and acute writing of the exiled Fondane, what is significant here is the sedentary silence of drowsy nature in the poet's birthplace. Mircea Martin remarks on the poet's "opacity" and contrasts it with "his internal ferment." The mountain and the wood are mute, human beings are deaf, the same as beasts of burden, in women, "the cry of deaf children," silence is "long and grey," the poet perceives it as "made of glass;" he sees its spout and waits for it "to cover him with snow on a bench" in the waste over which the orgy of crime will soon rush.

Like so many of his confreres in Romania and in his adopted country, Fundoianu had naturally flirted with the iconoclastic temptations of the avant-garde; he had consumed his passions and devotions in a frenetic expansion of the I, but, like few of his close associates, he quickly understood, too, the traps of Red Revolution and the dangers of the Hooked Cross prepared by the then modern codes of "rationalism." The acute and hopeless premonition of the Holocaust, visible in the poem "Exodus" (and in other poems as well) submits the verse to a planetary extension, dilates the call to uprising and resistance to the whole body of apathetic and complicit humanity, and thereby intensifies the millennial lament of the oppressed people. Poetry, which has now become the "cry" in the wilderness, is the solitude that does not wish to be conquered.

Verses like this from *L'Exode/Exodus*—

Vous n'êtes pas nés sur les routes,	You were not born on the roads,
personne n'a jeté à l'égout vos petits	your little ones weren't taken
comme des chats encore sans yeux,	like kittens still blind and flung in sewers,
vous n'avez pas erré de cité en cité	you have not wandered from town to town
traqués par les polices,	hounded by cops
vous n'avez pas connu les désastres à	you've not known the disasters at daybreak
l'aube,	the cattle cars
les wagons de bestiaux	you haven't known the bitter sobs
et le sanglot amer de l'humiliation,	of humiliation,
accusés d'un délit que vous n'avez pas fait,	or paid in expiation for
d'un meurtre dont il manque encore le	a crime not done by you,
cadavre,	for a murder with a corpse yet lacking
changeant de nom et de visage,	changing your name and your face
pour ne pas emporter un nom qu'on a hué	to escape your name uttered
un visage qui avait servi à tout le monde	with endless loathing and you face
de crachoir!	the whole world used as a spittoon.

—have a resonance surprisingly similar to the motto Primo Levi affixed to his memories of Auschwitz ("You who live in the safety / of warm houses / You who find, on coming home, / at dusk / warm food and the faces of friendship"[11]). Those at home are summoned to ask themselves if the one sacrificed isn't "still a human being." The poets' attempts to escape the names Wechsler and Antschel, uttered with disgust and spat upon, manifests the same *mise-en-question* and *mise-en-abîme* (putting so many values into question in a way that creates a story within a story as well as the sensation of infinite depth one has in the presence of one mirror reflecting another) for the generic (Jewish) human being considered as inhuman.

Fondane's Parisian exile in the existentialism and frenzy of the convulsive moment before the Nazi storm had deepened the poet's dramatic recovery and restitution of his Jewishness. The "Jewish Ulysses" (as the poet called himself) had finalized his old Chestovian Athens–Jerusalem obsession, as well as his moving fraternization with the wanderers and the refused of the world: "An unseen hand rips out my lids / I cannot close an eye / And I must raise my ceaseless cry / Until the end of the world."

Fondane's death may be considered a suicide, as well, if we keep in view his decision to refuse the salvation he had been offered so as to assume his sister Lina and the other martyrs' fate. Among these would have to be counted the death of his confrere, Celan, who committed suicide in the Seine two decades later.

If Iaşi was the starting place for Goldfaden's Yiddish theater and A.I. Cuza's anti-Semitism, Cernauţi was the place where the International Jewish Congress of 1908 took place. That Congress decided the apparently definitive (but in reality utterly temporary) victory of Yiddish in its long fratricidal war with Hebrew. Despite the regeneration of Romanian nationalism that flowered after the restitution of Bukovina to the mother country in 1918, the city's cosmopolitan character and its Habsburg tradition of multinational cooperation would maintain the atmosphere of intense cultural stimulation. In "the last Alexandria of Europe," as Zbigniew Herbert would call the capital of Bukovina, that eastern enclave of German-Austrian language and culture irradiated Romanian, Jewish (Yiddish and Hebrew), Ukrainian and Polish cultures, which re-experienced in their turn the inevitable influence of the Habsburg mentality.

In Iaşi, the Jewish community met with a rich Romanian culture (Fondane's mother frequented the famous Junimea literary circle, the classic Romanian writer Ion Creanga was a guest of the family, the "Viaţa Romaneasca"—Romanian Life—circle hosted the poet in a truly friendly way) and with a marked French influence. In Cernauţi, eyes were fixed on Vienna and Berlin.

"Die Landschaft aus der ich zu Ihnen komme, dürfte den meisten von Ihnen unbekannt sein"—The landscape from which I come must be unknown to the majority of you, Celan told the audience present at the granting of the Bremen City Prize for Literature. "Es war eine Gegend, in der Menschen und Bücher lebten" —It was a province where people and books lived.

It was a definition of belonging that Fondane would have been able to pronounce facing his Parisian or Argentine hosts or, at the last moment, when he was thrown on the pyre, as in the hypothetical post-mortem dialogue "in the mountains" with the Bukovinian Celan.

To write in "the language of the executioners" means much more than the contradiction it announces with such vehemence. This possible impossibility conveys the history of centuries of persecution and their convergence in "the Final Solution" as well as the cultural venom that the national creative geniuses conveyed— not just once—with guilty ease and which (an ever repeated and incomprehensible paradox) those sent away carried on—in their case, however, to maintain the admiration of readers and apprenticed writers. The poet can only write in the language of his poetry, even when, as Celan says, "the language is German and the writer a Jew." Here, there is an "impossibility" that art makes possible, necessary, and miraculous.

Why does "the unpronounceable name" remain a handicap? Both in Iaşi, which hosted the oldest Romanian university and which was an effervescent center of culture and creativity, and in the cosmopolitan big-little metropolises: Cernăuţi–Vienna–Berlin–Paris? Let's leave the question to the ideologues of "multiculturalism" today.

Was Celan's pseudonym only an anagram of his own name, as is often said, or was it the larkish invention of the student of Romance languages at the University of Cernăuţi who had recently discovered Thomas Celano, the Italian poet and philosopher of the thirteenth century and biographer of Francis of Assisi, as Israel Chalfen suggests? From the friend of his youth, Edith Silberman, we learn that the suggestion for the anagram came, in fact, from a whisper on the part of Frau Jessica Margul-Sperber, the wife of Celan's literary mentor.

Celan passed through Romanian schools ("with regard to anti-Semitism in our school, I could write a book of around three hundred pages," he wrote in a letter to his family) and Jewish and German schools as well. He began to study medicine in France and "came back home" to study Romance languages. He let Nazism and anti-Semitism push him toward communism. Confronted with the "Soviet liberators," he emigrated from Ukrainian, Soviet Cernăuți to Bucharest after the war where his unbearable retrospection (his mother having been killed in Transnistria would remain an obsessive guilty memory even in maturity) found much anticipated solace: the "Latin" joyfulness of his pals, reading and writing, contact with the Romanian Surrealists and with Alfred Margul-Sperber and the translations that he began from Russian literature. This was a happy period for the Pun, as Celan would call himself, and it blessed him with an affectionate and lasting memory.

He made his literary debut—"scandalous" for the dogmatic Stalinist period—with 'Death Fugue'/'*Todesfuge*' in *Contemporanul* (The Contemporary) in 1947, an appearance that was largely due to able maneuvers in the wings by literary critic and historian Ovid. S. Crohmălniceanu (born Moise Cohen). This poem was translated into Romanian by his close friend Peter Solomon. It would become the perennial centerpiece of his later celebrity.

The exile of the two poets, joined for posterity in a conversation of silences, is both an eclipse and a liberation, as it was and is, too, for so many of their confreres before and after them. Debacle and drive (disorientation and springboard), exile offers an initial stimulating shock and then a state of persistent ambivalence in the face of the indeterminate and the unknown.

Aggressed in exile by upsets, mischances, and stupefaction, the center of being loses the ability to articulate within the premises of the time before. For Fondane and Celan, "the privileged trauma" of exile, as I once called it, was more privilege than trauma, though tragic endings hastened toward them. The long-awaited time when they freed themselves from the limitations and hostilities of their native environment signified for them the chance to become situated in a beneficent, "metropolitan" way in essential questions as well, for in their case alienation had destabilized the conventions of identity, reduced them to the solitary "entity" of the pilgrim to nowhere, and it turned each of them, more than once, toward the millenial exile of their ancestors. Even with the linguistic advantage of immigrating into a known language, Fondane did not become really French, or Celan German.

Through exile, Judaism gains another weight as a regenerating valence, something like a stable, residual magnetism with new vibrations. In exile, Fondane extends himself in a typically Judaic cry and call to awakening and universal brotherhood in the face of the cataclysm; Celan gathers himself into himself and into the neurotic imagination of memory.

Old and new accents strengthen the Jewishness of peregrination. Their distant star, "the grandfather between the flames of the Sabbath candlesticks praying: 'let my right hand forget her skill!/ If I do not remember you,/ let my tongue cleave to the roof of my mouth/ if ever I take thee in vain, O Jerusalem!'" This is how Fundoianu/ Fondane evokes the diaspora of the exiles: "The soldier in the marshes of Masada/ makes himself a fatherland/ unflinching/ against all the barbs in the wire/ toward me/ he came/ with wakened name/ hand wakened, for ever/ from that which couldn't be buried," with his eyes set on the new Jerusalem. Lyric expression becomes, in one, the almost biblical invocation of a prophet, treated to violence and vulnerable, while in the other it is a continuous, fragmented undertone aspiring to the tumult of silence where the whispers and groans of the banished ghetto may occasionally be deciphered, sacrificed, and codified into an almost cabalistic austerity of language.

Both refusing the limiting label *Jewish poet*, Celan and Fondane remain poets of the languages in which they wrote: the German poet and the Romanian-French poet, each the most expressive of Jewishness in the first half of the twentieth century: the ferocious, bloody anti-Jewish half that gave them birth, inspired them, and killed them.

Belonging to the literature to which they added and were added, and thus to the world, they form a singular, revelatory, and urgent imprint at once Jewish, lyric, and universal.

There they are in the mountains beyond the mountains of posterity: Gross the Great, tall and ardent, with long hair and dreams taken by the wind, rash, contradictory, and contrarian, with rapid changes of humor, vital, full of verve, rebellious, wrinkled, and rugged, and little Klein, short, delicate, fragile, enclosed in silences, in premature and persistent melancholy, a charming pilgrim and fugitive from the pages of Trakl and Rilke.

How would the dialogue unfold between the voluble, frenetic Fondane and the silent Celan who had walked through Paris a whole night long with Zbigniew Herbert without either one letting out a word in agreement, which they both considered sublime? It's hard to know if in the meeting "in the hereafter" our interlocutors would continue to be the same or the opposite of those they had been—or completely beyond our poor earthly imaginations. What we know is that suddenly the crutches—the staves—of those blinded by tragedy had grown silent, stilled. The same for the stones around them. The Jew has before his eyes, or rather beneath his gaze, a veil that does not impede his sight but which keeps it from being *only* sight, without, however, impeding "the always radical immediacy of sight," to quote Jean-Pierre Lefebvre. Complete peace and quiet in the mountains: the phantoms are alive and walk on beside each other as they had never done in life.

Still, too, was the stone. And still too was the mountain wherein they walked, the one and the other.

So it was quiet, quiet up there in the mountains. But it was not quiet for long, because when a Jew comes along and meets another, silence cannot last, even in the mountains. Because the Jew and nature are strangers to each other, have always been and still are today, even here.

So there they are, the cousins. On the left, the turk's cap lily blooms, blooms wild, blooms like nowhere else. And on the right, corn-salad, and dianthus superbus, the maiden-pink, not far off. But they, those cousins, have no eyes, but a veil hanging in front of them, no, not in front, behind them, a moveable veil. No sooner does an image enter than it gets caught in the web, and a thread starts spinning, spinning itself around the image, a veil-thread; spins itself around the image and begets a child, half image, half veil.

Poor lily, poor corn-salad. So there they stand, the cousins on a road in the mountains, the stick silent, the stones silent, and the silence no silence at all. No word has come to an end and no phrase, it is nothing but a pause, an empty space between the words, a blank— you see all the syllables stand around, waiting. They are tongue and mouth as before, these two, and over their eyes there hangs a veil, and you, poor flowers, are not even there, are not blooming, you do not exist, and July is not July.

The windbags!

They would have so much to say! Everything that Gross had endured and foresaw and burned and everything that Klein had lived through, and foresaw and took upon himself, gripped in the claw of guilty memory. Each would remember his Shulamith—"hair of ash" evoked by Celan and her "red" bloodied hair by Fondane—and the black milk of the condemned and survivors in *Death Tango*, as *Death Fugue* was called in a Romanian translation of 1947, and the ashen snow under the pyre of Fondanian verse, the wine and blood in the lyric of each. And definitely Iţcani (pronounced *Itscan*), "the border to the world" ("A Itzkani voici un post—frontière dans le monde," Fondane had written), the small town in Bukovina not far from Celan's Cernăuti. Iţcani was only 3 kilometres from Burdujeni, the small Moldavian town itself bordering on Romanian Moldova and not further from Iaşi than from Herţa, both belonging to Fondane's world and his poetry.

Whatever you say though, in the time *after*, the post-time, all this is just babble, chat, the shamelessness of the palaverers who insult the silence, the supreme, single, absolute definitive silence that only itself might be capable of measuring up to the annihilation of the wanderers.

There are no more words, effectively, and those that there are don't reach the intangible horror—its poisoned and glacial, tenebrous, hypnotic magic. Gross and Klein know this. Yet they must speak; the cousins have met for this reason. This is the way of the Jew, even when nothing remains to him but the ultimate crumbs of words, crumbs, fractures, interrupted whispers, indistinct codified moans, he still needs a Thou, to whom he may address his muteness. It is a feature of the first, infantile landscape of Bukovina and Herţa where "The girls await in the dirty alley deepening/ the silence that falls every evening/ and the peace and quiet in long molding things./ In houses of the simple, Yiddish springs"—there but also in the *allegro* of Little Oriental Paris, as Bucharest was called, as well as in Paris the great herself, City of Lights, with those one thousand incomparable nights and the suave Seine of the drowned.

About all these things . . . at least they might speak about all these things if it were still possible to speak, if there might still exist words that the death before death and the death after hadn't silenced.

The windbags! Even now, when their tongues stumble dumbly against their teeth and their lips won't round themselves, they have something to say to each other. All right then, let them talk . . .

"You've come a long way, have come all the way here . . ."

"I have. I've come, like you."

"*I know.*"

"*You know. You know and see: The earth folded up here, folded once and twice and three times, and opened up in the middle, and in the middle there is water, and the water is green and the green is white, and the white comes from even farther up, from the glaciers, and one could say, but one shouldn't, that this is the language that counts here, the green with the white in it, a language not for you and not for me—because, I ask you, for whom is it meant, the earth, not for you, I say, is it meant, and not for me—a language, well, without I and without You nothing but He, nothing but It, you understand, and She, nothing but that.*"

"*I understand, I do. After all, I've come a long way, like you.*"

"*I know.*"

"*You know and you want to ask: And even so you've come all the way, come here even so—why and what for?*"

"*Why, and what for . . . Because I had to speak, maybe, to myself or to you, speak with my mouth and tongue, not just with my stick. Because to whom does it speak, my stick. It talks to the stones and the stones—to whom do they speak?*"

"*To whom should they talk, cousin? They do not talk, they speak, and who speaks does not talk to anyone, cousin, he speaks because nobody hears him, nobody and Nobody, and then he says, him- self, not his mouth or his tongue, he, and only he, says: Do you hear me?*"

In the "undeserved" hour of survival, the phantomatic Celan meets his cousin from the East, he too having escaped somehow to the West and been sent back from there to the Eastern land of death. Celan is targeted, struck, penetrated, "stricken" to his depths and forever, although he had not been reached physically like his pre- decessor Fondane. *Sh'ma Yisrael, Here, O Israel!*" repeats the echo Klein or perhaps the echo Gross. Their voices no longer distinguish one from the other, nor have they any reason to separate, although one of them was "struck" and the other, who hadn't the opportunity, was stricken too.

These two search for each other, cry one unto the other in the wasteland, the solitude beyond death and the mountains. They call each other reciprocally: it is I, I the one it seems you hear, or that you seem to hear. They have so much to tell each other, the Jew Klein and the Jew Gross! "Do you hear me, do you hear me" becomes a repeated and empty echo; the palaverer's nickname, "Do you hear me" is the code or the nickname for one and the other in the empty space of the absolute silence belonging to *the time after*. "Do you hear me" babbles senselessly and endlessly, here and now *after* the end, *after* sunset when Klein and Gross, and Celan and Fondane, and their cousins and their cousins' cousins are dead and the "peace and quiet" of the "purification" has settled at last in the mountains where there no longer exist I and Thou. Peace and quiet has descended, finally, desecrated and forever. The sun has gone down and peace and quiet—serenity—with it. I and Thou no longer exist, and eternity seems eternal, a crafty, malicious, voracious eternity.

They stand, Klein and Gross. The beautiful path does not belong to them, and they don't belong to it. They are from the Valley of Death, in the dark of beyond and of afterwards, where only the white crutches—like the bones burned at Oświeçim* in the East and washed in the West, in the morbid Seine—illuminate the road that is not a road on which they have climbed, one toward the other, one beside the other. Everything has set, like the sun and not only the sun and its light—not only the sun.

"On the stone I lay prostrate," Fondane recounts at the beginning of the end. Or maybe it was Celan among the captives aligned at the place where they quarry funeral slabs. Or maybe Gross and Klein recount in turn and simultaneously, as happens among those like them, among condemned cousins that slept and slept not, dreamed

*Auschwitz.

and dreamed not, as happens also to our interlocutors, Antschel and Wechsler (the real Jewish names of Celan and Fondane), in the darkness of hereafter and afterwards.

They lay prostrate, yes, together on the funeral stones, the one and the other, among the unloved, and the one and the other had a sense of their being different. They were many and who should love the like that's unlike? The One. Only the Single, the Supreme, the Invisible, the Great Anonymous whose unpronounceable name is forbidden by the holy laws, as is His invisible image forbidden, hidden in the sunset that has swallowed the mountains, and not only the mountains, our unpronounceable name, like His name, and our images made after His image and so forbidden.

It is not easy to love yourself in the mirror of the many. Mirroring multiplied, dilated, twisted, contorted: disfiguring. Brotherhood was becoming a hindrance with access to too much—too full—too superlative and too little and with the breakdown of everything. They knew this: Celan and Fondane as well as Gross and Klein. The *semblables*, converted into a mass, into an implacable anonymization (like death itself), no longer permit the potential I and the potential Thou—both pre-existent outside and inside ourselves— equally annulled in the collective identity, and condemned without likeness and without escape. We cannot love ourselves too much in this deformed mirror of pluralities, not when it's a matter of being converted into a mass prior to nothingness.

The mothers do not disappear, however, not even in the fog of massification; they enchain us beyond their life and death and ours and give us birth again every instant in the corner where the candle sustains the memory and the chance of *meeting* and of love, until the last flicker. Mother's face did not disappear for Pesach, nor for Benjamin, the one who could not let go of his sister's and mother's hands, even to save himself. Beyond the sacred and profane is precisely the face of that innate Thou that accompanies us and which, when it is absent, keeps watch beyond life.

The murmur of Jewish mothers among the flames of the candle-sticks: the candles protected by trembling hands cannot be forgotten, however, nor the salt mine silence of the room, nor can the father of the Jewish mother be forgotten; even today Grandfather Abraham, the unforgotten, burns the sacred candle in all the houses where the coming Day is celebrated, the seventh, after which follows the first again, if it weren't to be the last. The poets—both the one and the other, the prodigal sons serving the word that is still searching for the same eternal Thou in the lyric charade of silence —have both remained forever near the biblical mother lighting candles and protecting the flame with her hands and the murmur of verses, the love that cannot be repeated.

"*Do you hear me, he says—I know, cousin, I know . . . do you hear me, he says, I'm here. I am here, I've come. I've come with my stick, me and no other, me and not him, me with my hour, my undeserved hour, he who has been hit, who has not been hit, me with my memory, with my lack of memory, me, me, me . . .*"

"*He says, he says . . . Do you hear me, he says . . . And Do-you-hear-me, of course, Do-you-hear-me does not say anything, does not answer, because Do-you-hear-me is one with the glaciers, is three in one, and not for men . . . the green-and-white there, with the turk's cap lily, with the corn-salad . . . But I cousin, I who stand here on this road, here where I do not belong, today, now that it has set, the sun and its light, I, here with the shadow, my own and not my own, I—I who can tell you:*

I lay on the stones, back then, you know, on the stone tiles; and next to me the others who were like me, the others who were different yet like me, my cousins. They lay there sleeping and not sleeping, dreaming and not dreaming, and they did not love me, and I did not love them, because I was one, and who wants to love One when there are many, even more than those lying near me, and who wants to be able to love all, and I don't hide it from you, I did not love them who could not love me, I loved the candle which burned in the left corner, I loved it because it burned down, not because it burned down, because it was his candle, the candle he had lit, our mother's father, because on that evening there had begun a day, a particular day, the seventh: the seventh to be followed by the first, the seventh and not the last, cousin, I did not love it, I loved its burning down and, you know, I haven't loved anything since."

No, nothing could be as it was back then, long ago. The candle burns toward its end and above it, the biblical mother watches, praying.

Ashen memory: our mother's Father, the Grandfather of us all, among the flames of the candlestick and the pyre, goes on praying, still had time to spare before the seventh day, the last, when Klein and Gross disappeared, each borne up by the staff that was speaking, murmuring Fondane's and Celan's mortuary verses.

The staff fell silent in the end like the stone on which the one and the other had lain prostrate, the funeral slabs under which the one and the other would have to lie. The star announces the wedding celebration, the holiday of rest and of prayers for the biblical mother and her biblical Father. The wedding ceremony before sunset, bloodied before setting, before the dark that spread over the sunset and beyond sunset, when they finally met—Celan and Fondane and the white crutches of their books—and they were able to speak for the first time at length about themselves and about us, the ones who have climbed with them, toward them, near them and their bloodied shadows.

Chat, barren hum, idle words! There could not be conversation after their setting and ours, *beyond* the mountains and sunset . . .

There could only be idle speech, babble, stammering, with Gross and Klein, with "I" Do-you-hear-me, and "thou" Do-you-hear-me, the inebriation of the Earth not made for us, tongue and language are no longer ours, the flowers and their fruit were never for us, the ones with the forbidden name, wavering shadows, foreign, borrowed, crutches that speak without our understanding their matter or their silence and that light our steps and those of strangers without our seeing, under the distant, painful star, "I" here and "thou" here. We come from the Vale of Tears where they tolerate us, sometimes, for a while, to draw behind us our souls emptied of soul for a new funereal ascension, another hallucination from which we will be hurled into the tumult of the shades.

No, nothing. Or maybe whatever burned down like that candle on that day, the seventh, not the last; not on the last day, no, because here I am, here on this road which they say is beautiful; here I am by the turk's cap lily and the corn-salad, and a hundred yards over, over there where I could go, the larch gives way to the stone-pine. I see it, I see it and don't see it, and my stick which talked to the stones, my stick is silent now, and the stones you say can speak, and over my eyes there is that moveable veil, there are veils, moveable veils, you lift one, and there hangs another, and the star there—yes, it is up there now, above the mountains—if it wants to enter it will have to wed and soon it won't be itself, but half veil and half star, and I know, I know, cousin, I know I've met you here, and we talked a lot, a lot, and those folds there, you know they are not for men, and not for us who went off and met here, under the star, we the Jews who came like Lenz through the mountains, you Gross and me Klein, you, the windbag, and me the windbag, with our sticks, with our unpronounceable names, with our shadows, our own and not our own, you here and me here—

In the murmur and babble of the dialogue and of the memory in which the flame of love from *back then* still flickers and with which nothing can compare, the staff has grown still, intimidated by the undertone with which Buber tries to halt the two interlocutors, as if back then, long ago, when each of the wanderers had been instructed under the flickering of the Friday night candle.

Buber would try again to turn them from their pilgrimage so that he might join them, but they would no longer heed him.

"The spirit in its human manifestation is man's response to his

Thou . . . the response toward that Thou that appears out of the mystery and that addresses us from the mystery. Spirit means word," Buber whispers to the two who have long known that spirit is word. "The Spirit resides not in I but between I and Thou," he repeats to the poets who have known this for a long time and who have learned it again with every step of their meeting, because "then when we follow the road and meet with a person who comes toward us following his own way, we know only our own road, not his, which he only reveals to us through meeting. The other party, his side happens to us through meeting," Buber had whispered long ago, *back then*, under the flickering of the guttering candle and whispers to the wayfarers again, now, in the undertone of meeting and conversation in the mountains.

Something and more than something was setting, was declining, was guttering out: then, thereafter, this minute. The two poets do not hear the shadow of back then; only the staff hears and absorbs the high, clear peace and quiet, more eloquent than words.

The interlocutors are now witnesses too, witnesses to the dying out of a world of which only the meeting in posterity reminds them. They keep silent, and silence is kept by the staff, and the mountains of stone and the woods . . . "a pause, an empty space, a blank—you see all the syllables stand around, waiting."

This is the silence that culminates in all the silences prior to addressing, to meeting and conversation. "Only the keeping silent before the Thou, the silence of all languages, the taciturn expectation in the unformed, undifferentiated, pre-linguistic word liberates that Thou that stands in reserve, there where the spirit does not manifest itself but is." They keep silent but they are beside each other in the undying that is only granted to the dead that resurrect in speech and meeting. The staff stands between them absorbing the silence and the shades of the land of hereafter and afterwards, absorbing the spirit of *between*: mutuality, the space of relationship, of the appeals in which the two have animated destiny.

As a child Buber spent his summer vacations in Bucovina, in a village near Sadagura, near Cernăuți and not far from Herța, gazing at the Hasidim, who were no more than diminished surrogates of their forebears in whom, once flickered—back then, like a candle ready to gutter out, like sunset lowering its nocturnal mantle over the pilgrim's wanderings—the *word*: the word of Rabbi Eleazar, "the word created for the sake of the perfect man."

For the sake of... "for the sake of the imperfect man" the poets of the word would irritatedly reply—the one from Cernăuți the other from Herța—"for the sake of the imperfect man, but in his perfection." *That* is how the poets would reply if they heard the whispers of the declining shadow.

"Any living being is a meeting," the *melamed*, the children's teacher, would murmur, unheard, "And so is posterity. One only resurrects through meeting," the wanderers would repeat with a single, unheard voice like fraternal shadows.

The day burned down to its end, the love they could neither give nor receive from those flung under the selfsame slabs, now after sundown, after ash, after their uniting like brothers, recalls and reclaims those unloved. Now on the eve of departure from here when the sun and not only the sun is nearly set, Celan and Fondane have united in brotherly love with the forever unloved, on the final road toward themselves, up there in the eternal and non-eternal depths:

"me here, me, who could tell you all this could have and don't and didn't tell you; me with a turk's cap lily on my left, me with corn-salad, me with my burned candle, me with the day, me with the days, me here and me there, me, maybe accompanied—now by the love of those I didn't love, me on the way to myself, up here."

The frail, the silent, the short one who hides beneath the undulating dusk of the Seine goes on speaking to the lofty one, with long locks and lofty shadow, smoky, smoking, diffusing smoke. Klein speaks to Gross, without being able to tell him the too much that would be told in the unspoken language that Celan tries again, overwhelmed, in the *Con-Versation (or Speaking With) in the Mountains*. Black parody: the conversation is not conversation and the mountains are not mountains. Carefully, Paul Celan, the author—like Rilke and Trakl, among the flowers and flora that are not for Gross or Klein, nor are they for him, Paul Celan—is turned toward the candle that neither he, nor Klein or Gross, nor Fondane have forgotten and toward the Day burned down to its end.

Love: they have not been able to give and receive as they would have wished. Hurled under the same wandering shadow, on the eve of departure, of the ultimate exile, when the sun and not only the sun is going down, Celan and Fondane have met and been brothers, finally with the forever unloved, now in the hour of ash, in their ascension toward themselves.

Translated by Jean Harris, September 2011

Notes

1. From Paul Celan, *Conversation in the Mountains*, 1959. Translated from the German by Florin Bican, 2011.

2. In the manuscript version the text was named *Gespräch im Graubünden* after the Swiss canton Grissons (Ger. *Graubünden*) in which it was written.

3. *Europe*, 861–862 (January–February, 2001).

4. Yale University Press, 1995.

5. "A prototype for 'Gespräch im Gebirg' was the novella *Lenz*, by Georg Buchner . . . Celan felt some sympathy with Nietzsche and inscribed a copy of his story 'In memory of Sils Maria and Friedrich Nietzsche, who—as you know—wanted to have all anti-Semites shot.' . . . Also hovering behind 'Conversation in the Mountains' was Franz Kafka, whose *Excursion into the Mountains* Celan translated into Romanian after the war. . . . Above all, 'Gespräch im Gebirg' owes to Martin Buber, whose philosophical writings and retellings

of Hasidic tales Celan was reading during the late 1950s. . . . A visceral presence in the 'Conversation' must surely be Mandelshtam." Felstiner, pp. 140–41.

6. Felstiner, p. 144.

7. *Readings of Paul Celan*, ed. Aris Fioretos (Baltimore, MD: Johns Hopkins University Press, 1994), p. 124.

8. Geoffrey Hartman, *The Longest Shadow* (New York: Palgrave Macmillan, 2002).

9. Paul Celan, *Selected Works*, Vol. 1., p. 135 (Berlin: Suhrkamp, 1983).

10. *The Longest Shadow*, p. 54.

11. From Primo Levi, *Survival in Auschwitz: the Nazi Assault on Humanity*, translated by Stuart Woolf (New York: Macmillan, 1961), p. 8.

SOME THOUGHTS ON SAUL BELLOW

I

Often novels provoke readers to believe that they can best be understood as thinly veiled arguments, responses to topical, controversial issues. Reviewers "translate" fictional events into their "real-life" foundations and unmask characters by identifying the actual "models" on whom they are based. Some years ago, when Saul Bellow's final novel, *Ravelstein*, appeared, I was shocked at the book's reception, not only in the United States, but in my native country, Romania, where reviewers prattled incessantly about issues such as "political correctness" and "the Holocaust industry" as if Bellow's novel had been written mainly to instruct us on such matters. And I was struck, too, by the confidence with which these reviewers speculated about the real-life counterparts of characters, as if there was little question about Bellow's sentiments and intentions.

Of course there was reason for Romanians to be interested in Bellow, and not merely because he was a very great writer. *The Dean's December* is partly set in Romania, and though *Ravelstein* has relatively little to do with events in Romania, the peripheral figure Radu Grielescu somewhat resembles Mircea Eliade, and the novel alludes in passing to E.M. Cioran, among other Romanian characters. American readers, noting these elements, may have paid them little attention, but in Romania, as also in the Romanian diaspora, it seemed that these were the most important aspects of those novels.

In the United States, to be sure, *Ravelstein* was also much discussed as a *roman-à-clef*. Debate focused on Bellow's relations with his friend Allan Bloom, who was, apparently, the model for Ravelstein himself. Was the elitist ideologue and acerbic cultural critic *in fact* the figure portrayed in Bellow's novel? Were the frailties and frivolities depicted in the novel invented, or did they belong to Bloom himself? Was the portrait a "betrayal" of a long friendship? These were the questions most insistently directed at the novel by many American reviewers, who were, in their own way, as obsessed with Bellow's motives and the politics of the novel as were Romanian readers. The media's tendency to look for scandal and secrets was something Bellow understood all too well, and he surely recognized all of the familiar signs in the responses inspired by *Ravelstein* and earlier books.

Cynthia Ozick offered a necessary corrective to this tendency when she wrote: "When it comes to novels, the author's life is nobody's business. A novel, even when it is autobiographical, is not an autobiography. If the writer himself breaks the news that such-and-such character is actually so-and-so in real life, readers still have an obligation—fiction's enchanted obligation—to shut their ears and turn away. . . . Fiction is subterranean, not terrestrial. Or it is like Tao: say what it is, and that is what it is not. . . . The originals vanish; their simulacra, powerful marvels, endure." The statement is informed by characteristic good sense, and if it is not always possible to follow the terms of the "enchanted obligation," we can surely understand that it is important for us, as readers, to do our best with it, if only to prevent ourselves from indulging the penchant for gossip and oversimplification promoted in the mainstream literary press.

Of course there are other reasons to be wary of readings that move more or less effortlessly from fiction to "reality." Probably the most significant of these is that, in yielding to such readings, we swallow misleading "information" about the so-called historical record and ignore the contradictory signals and ambiguities that are essential features of the novelistic text. In *Ravelstein*, Bellow includes dates and facts that support the connection between Radu and Eliade, but he also provides other information that flagrantly contradicts that presumed connection. Accusations leveled against Radu in the novel usually come not from the narrator, Chick, but from his wife, Rosamund, and from Ravelstein. At times, the narrator timidly defends Radu against the charges, though the defense soon comes to seem increasingly ambiguous and ironic. "Grielescu was a follower of Nae Ionescu, who founded the Iron Guard," announces Ravelstein emphatically, as if he were comfortably familiar with names and organizations most sophisticated American readers wouldn't know at all. Nor, for that matter, will the reader know that Nae Ionescu did *not* found the Iron Guard. Are we to believe that there is some intention here to overwhelm Chick with false information? And does any of this material count for very much in the framework of the novel as a whole? Ravelstein isn't a historian in the novel that bears his name, and there are several absurdities he scatters among his frothy paradoxical digressions.

In fact, as readers, we can know only what the novel tells us to make of the assorted bits and pieces of "fact." We understand that Chick has a weakness for Radu, for his encyclopedic conversation, and even for his high society comic slips into vaudeville routines. When Ravelstein wants "to know just what Grielescu's line was like," Chick tells him "that at dinner he lectured about archaic history, he stuffed his pipe, and lit lots of matches." Does this settle anything about his purported relations with the Iron Guard or his sentiments toward Jews? Obviously the account is not intended to settle such matters, and our understanding of the character Radu may be most powerfully shaped by the image of him gripping his pipe "to keep it from shaking, and then the fingers with the match [trembling] twice as hard. He kept stuffing the pipe with the rebellious tobacco. When it didn't stay stuffed, he didn't have enough thumb-power to pack it down. How could such a person be politically dangerous?"

That concluding question is by no means conclusive, but it does perfectly indicate the kinds of "information" that readers of novels must process. When Chick sarcastically evokes the courtly manners of Grielescu, who remembers every birthday, wedding date, and other tender anniversary, we must note that these "facts," and the sarcasm with which they are delivered, have something to do with Yela, Chick's former wife, who was sensitive, he tells us, to these trifles. But we also understand that an American like Chick would be typically suspicious of such European acts of gallantry and it is not surprising to hear him reflect, "I suppose I said to myself that this was some Frenchy-Balkan absurdity. Somehow I couldn't take Balkan fascists seriously." The reflection does not, to be sure, prevent a reader from taking this fascist, or fascism in general, seriously, but the novelistic treatment of things demands that we do not read *Ravelstein* as a one-dimensional indictment written for a simple purpose. Bellow has Chick reflect on the fact that the Jews were "Hitler's ticket to power," but he goes on to say, "I don't think he [Grielescu] was a malevolent Jew-hater." In some novels, perhaps, that might serve to close the issue and move on to something else, but Bellow wants at least so suggest that there is more to be said. Perhaps, Chick goes on, Grielescu was not malevolent in his Jew-hatred, "but when he was called upon to declare himself, he declared himself. He had a vote and he voted."

To think of Mircea Eliade in all of this is to think of someone whose activities, however much they inspired the depiction of Grielescu, cannot be adequately assessed on the basis of Bellow's account. Debates that swirled around *Ravelstein* in Romania were so often fruitless and misleading because they were based upon a futile effort to establish one-to-one correspondences between the novel and the so-called historical record, a part of which I wrote about myself years ago in a long essay, "Happy Guilt," included here (pp. 92–118 above). But even without offering a portrait of the actual Eliade, Bellow's novel invites us to think about a phenomenon all too familiar. The image of the intellectual who in decisive moments "voices" for evil isn't, as well we know, limited to Eliade or Nae Ionescu, or Romania, or the right's extremism. Here is a better reason for meditation than the simple confrontation between biographical and historical facts and the "reality" the novel offers us. And, just as we would expect from a writer like Bellow, the very idea of thinking about the intellectual who votes for evil is made to seem both irresistible and difficult. As Ravelstein sees it, "thinking it all through" is "unpleasant work," and a man like Chick has "a Jewish life to lead in the American language, and that's not a language that's helpful with dark thoughts. . . . But then, from left field, or do I mean right field, Ravelstein urges everyone to read Céline. Well, by all means. Céline was widely gifted, but he was also a wild lunatic, and before the war he published his *Bagatelles pour un massacre*. In this pamphlet Céline cried out against and denounced the Jews who had occupied and raped France . . . *Un Iupanar Juif—Bordel de Dieu*. The Dreyfus Case was brought back again . . . I agreed with Ravelstein that Céline wouldn't pretend that he took no part in Hitler's Final Solution." As for the Romanian scholar: "Nor would I trade the short-stop Grielescu for the right-fielder Céline. When you put it in baseball lingo you can see how insane it was."

Unable quite to let go of Grielescu, who, as a sort of generic Romanian (and Eastern European) intellectual, slides frequently into caricature, Bellow nimbly contrasts him and Céline and thereby opens up further questions, as for example the perhaps irrelevant consideration about a writer's honesty in acknowledging guilt and responsibility. Does it matter really that Grielescu, or for that matter Eliade, pretended, when Céline did not? Surely it is a question worth considering in the moral universe constructed by Bellow's novel, if not elsewhere.

II

I first met Saul Bellow in the late 1970s in Bucharest at a small official gathering at the Romanian Writers' Union. Our socialist democracy needed a few Romanian-Jewish writers to greet the famous American Jewish writer.

I already knew Saul Bellow's books in their Romanian and French translations, and I had even written on the forceful originality of his urban world, in which the Jewish spirit finds its new, free, American voice, its new serenity and its new restlessness, a new humor, and a new sadness, and finally, an unprecedented way of posing life's unanswerable questions. The gloom of that Romanian period, acutely described by Saul Bellow in *The Dean's December*, quickly became apparent in the large, elegant official meeting room. The Romanian publisher, who had published the translation of *Humboldt's Gift*, rose with the joyous energy of a man half his age to resurrect the ancient topic: "Who is behind you, Mr. Bellow?" The sunny lightness of the spring day was all at once overwhelmed by that "darkness at noon" which we all knew so well. Nobody in the audience had any difficulty in grasping the implication of the not overly subtle question about the invisible but ubiquitous conspiracy of the chosen (and inevitably Jewish) demons. And yet our guest, with his skeptical, gentle smile and his elegant courtesy, appeared not to have noticed the interrogator's aggression. "Who gave you the Big Prize, Mr Bellow? Who is behind you, Saul Bellow?" the Romanian intellectual repeated. But Bellow maintained the smile and courtesy and, in his own sweet time, told us two little stories about the personal consequences of winning the Nobel Prize.

The first was about a Chicago policeman who, for many years, had greeted Bellow daily at the corner of his street and who, unaware of the Nobel Prize Universal Literary Event that had already taken place, offered the same simple, friendly, and conventional greeting that he always had. "Good morning." "Good morning."

The second incident pertained to a high school friend of the writer's, whom he hadn't seen for decades. Unexpectedly bumping into him on a Chicago street—again after returning from Stockholm—Bellow was pleased to hear news from him about their schoolmates and hear about the friend himself. At last, the friend remembered to exhibit some curiosity of his own. "And you, Saul, what do you do for a living? How do you make a buck?"

Hammered by unpleasant questions, the elegant, cordial, and detached Saul Bellow didn't display the unease he felt in the course of his visit, but he discussed it with some Romanian acquaintances. "He lived through a kind of psychosis . . . He believed he was always followed on the street, that there were microphones everywhere," Antoaneta Ralian, his Romanian translator, wrote in *Observatorul Cultural*, an important Romanian cultural weekly, in 2000. "When he saw that at the residence where he was staying they put pillows on the telephone and that the radio was turned up all the way, so that the conversation couldn't be recorded by police listening devices, he was completely shocked."

I had my first conversation with Saul Bellow not in Bucharest but in Newark in 1992, at the writers' conference on Eastern Europe organized by *Partisan Review*, the magazine that Bellow had been associated with in the 1950s and 1960s, and was partially associated with later on. To me, he seemed distant and troubled. I suppose that my Romanian identity wasn't a favorable recommendation, nor did my essay "Happy Guilt," on Mircea Eliade, recommend me to him, for there I opened up troubling questions about a man who had been a good friend of his.

At any rate, because our breakfast was limited to conventional matters, I didn't use the telephone number he had given me as we said goodbye, and our closeness grew slowly, little by little over the following years, owing, I suppose, to some mutual friends.

We got to know each other better in the first two consecutive summers he invited us, that is Cella and me, to his summer home in Vermont. In the mornings he wore a T-shirt and jeans with many pockets, a baseball cap with a long, blue visor; in the evenings, at the restaurant Le Petit Chef where he was a kind of celebrity guest, he was elegant and eccentric, with pink or red shirts, and bow-ties in unusual designs. He had a natural, open manner, without pretentiousness or affectation. He seemed to be a farmer, or an old aristocrat, or an artist on vacation.

He asked me about Bard College, where he had taught in his younger days and where he'd lived together with his friend Ralph Ellison, a sort of literary "aristocrat" himself, and, like Bellow, of modest social origins. He knew that Hannah Arendt was buried at Bard, but be didn't admire her. "She had one foot in Nazism with Heidegger," Bellow recalled, "the other in communism with her second husband Bleicher, a philosophy professor at Bard. He's been in the leadership of the German communists, I believe. She never talked about this. She knew too much; she fled from confessions."

When he came as a young writer to teach at Bard, Bellow entered quickly into conflict with the old guard of literature professors, fervent guardians of "great literature" and skeptical of modern writers. The prevailing Great Lady was Irma Brandeis, the head of the Italian department, a translator, and a former virgin lover, people said, of Montale. A strong personality, formed by "classic" convictions, and intellectually aggressive. The young Bellow naturally found himself on the side of the rebels, but after only a few years he came to understand that youth "revolutions" rarely live up to their promise.

After a few decades, preparing to evoke his outworn sentiments in the story "Him with His Foot in His Mouth," Bellow called Leon Botstein, the president of Bard, complaining that he couldn't remember Irma Brandeis' voice anymore. Leon invited him to a special dinner where Irma would be present, too. An amicable, pleasant evening full of amusing recollections. In the end, Bellow declared that he had returned to Bard not just to remember the atmosphere of another time but to ask in public for Mrs. Irma Brandeis' forgiveness over their conflict in which, as he had learned over time, he was on the wrong side.

I had already lived at Bard for more than ten years myself, housed in Irma Brandeis' former bungalow, Casa Minima. I knew by now in what way novels like *Herzog* and *Henderson the Rain King* were tied to the space and time the author knew at the college that hosted me; I discovered local anecdotes about his life in the region that had become so familiar to me as sometimes to resemble my own lost Bukovina.

I didn't insist, however, on our rehearsing the old Bard days during our dialogue in Vermont. I was more interested to know what the novelist thought about the present. According to Bellow, the modern era seemed to have confirmed at least one of the Marxist predictions: the victory of man over nature. Bellow didn't seem at all enchanted by this "progress." Of course, he conceded, there have been enormous improvements in medicine, feeding the poor, instant communication, the ease of moving from one place to another. Inevitably certain values are lost, they change; new values and criteria appear. But Bellow routinely referred to something essential that seemed to be lost, something not only alluded to but obsessively emphasized in his novels. What is said to sink the heart in Bellow's fiction is the reliance on brutal pragmatism in American society, the banality of ordinary discourse and the appetite for scandal. These matters were often brought up in his conversation as well. Who would have suspected, he said, that a writer like himself would sometimes be categorized as "reactionary"?

All the same, he assured me, his books sold, even in today's market, 60,000–70,000 copies with each new American edition. He continued to receive many letters from readers, some of them anti-

Semitic. In spite of this, and the banality, and the scandal, Bellow kept up a moderate optimism. He hoped that American common sense might resist the idiocies of present public and political life. He considered himself lucky to be by disposition a skeptic and to have maintained a clear distance from his daily environment. He had even found himself, at last, in old age, a young and ideal partner. Intelligent, refined, and totally devoted to her husband.

"My own future wife will be a Jew from Little Tokyo," I told him as I said goodbye, looking at Janis and her almost Japanese, Semitic face.

Bellow's affectionate wit was seductive, and you knew unmistakably when he had accepted you as an intimate. His sentiment was discernible in all the small courtesies we enjoyed in his Vermont home, where he prepared for us roasted French coffee in the morning, showed me the library and the nearby lake, discoursed on the flowers and the tomcat, and told me about the course he taught at Boston University.

I noted—it was impossible not to notice—his courteous manner around women, that of a conqueror once famous for amorous adventure and for numerous marriages and divorces. With women he became again the easily eternal cavalier, mastering the special idiom of direct, American, affable courtship, the charm, the seductiveness impressive, though obviously tame by comparison with what it had been in earlier years.

I spent time with Bellow also in the tense period before the appearance of a biography about him. He showed me, at a certain moment, the passport that his mother used to leave tsarist Russia. "Am I charged with falsifying my origins? In order to deny my Jewishness, that is? My family name in Russian is Belìi, meaning white. White. It's just like that. Look: Liza Belia. It became Bellow here, but not somewhere else. But what, really, does this mean for people who are looking for scandal? Does it mean anything?"

Reviewing the James Atlas biography, the critic James Wood remarked that it wasn't "the biography of a freedom-loving mind, of an imagination, but of a seducer, a bad husband, and money-earner who also happened to write some good books." The critic remembered a remark from Bellow's speech upon receiving the Nobel Prize: "There is another reality, the genuine one, which we lose sight of. This other reality is always sending us hints, which, without art, we can't receive."

I saw how sensitive Bellow was at the prospect of new attacks in the press and how detached he nevertheless remained. "Everything hurts him and nothing touches him," I told myself then and I said it to some of our mutual friends. They agreed; they had rediscovered and recognized "The Prince" of their literary youth.

But the Prince was not always at ease, and in our casual conversations, as in a long formal interview I conducted with him some years back, he very much disliked talking about things Romanian. He didn't like the subject, I sensed immediately. Nor the memory of his former wife, nor that of Eliade. Not even a question about Eugen Ionescu, whom he understood that I admired, could get him to talk.

It became clear why in all these years he hadn't ever discussed my article about Eliade with me; in fact, he never warned me that he was writing the novel *Ravelstein*, which in December 1999 must have been on the road to print, precisely when we were conducting our six-hour videotaped interview for the Jerusalem Cultural Project.* In 1997, when, uneasily, I prepared for a visit to Romania, he advised me to follow my instincts and avoid the trip. Not because it would be dangerous, as others maintained, but because I would only torture myself unnecessarily. "You have enough to torture yourself with here. You don't need a supplement. You'll feel miser-

*This is a non-profit Israeli organization that sponsored a series of interviews with important Jewish writers.

able. I just read another book about another celebrated Romanian. The manners, the culture, you know. But what's underneath . . . No, don't go. Profit from the distance."

When I met him at the Romanian Writers' Union in 1978, I asked Bellow if he would choose between Herzog and Humboldt. Between the intellectual, rationalist, humanist, contemplative, on the one hand, and the genius artist, damned, excessive in everything, on the other. "Difficult question," he had responded, adding that he felt tied to both characters.

In 1999, I asked the question again in America, reminding him of the meeting in Bucharest. I added that I had the impression that in the intervening years he had become closer to the artist, that he had developed a basic distrust of the intellectual.

"Maybe. I hadn't thought of this. I'm not used to thinking about such questions. These are questions of a theoretical interest, but something else drives you. To define who you are: an intellectual or an artist? It leads to thinking about who is actually more naïve, the intellectual or the artist. I've never reached a conclusion. I'm not even sure that being naïve is a sin. Maybe the question leads to something much more serious."

In our last meetings Saul could seem tired or apathetic and suddenly awaken, spring to life at some slight provocation or piece of wit. Before a reading he was to give in 2002 at the 92nd Street Y, we sat with him in a luxurious Central Park West apartment, at a party given in his honor. But most of the other guests were unconcerned with him, absorbed by the day's gossip. Bellow lay absently, alone on the sofa, like an aged grandfather that no one paid attention to anymore, and he watched, amused, from time to time, his two-and-a-half-year-old daughter, who ran tirelessly from corner to corner. When Philip Roth appeared and greeted him with classic Middle English verses, however, he woke up promptly. He responded in turn with other verses from *The Canterbury Tales*. For about ten minutes, an amazing, merry contest was pursued, with poems recited from memory. Neither of the competitors could be defeated. I was astonished.

"It's nothing special. Clever boys always," Philip said. "Didn't you learn important Romanian poetry by heart?"

Yes, in high school I had won a sort of unofficial contest for the memorization of Romanian poetry.

III

The incident reminded me of a dinner we had in the summer of 2001 at Le Petit Chef in Vermont. Saul woke up abruptly from his dreamy absence when his editor asked him, as she had asked everyone else, what he thought about the decadence of American culture and his own relation to it. Bellow looked at her for a long time and responded, somewhat obliquely: "When I decided my way in life, I knew that society would be against me. I also knew that I would win. . . . And that it would be a small victory."

He had been completely blank until that moment, and it was difficult for us to believe that he could be brought back from his amnesia. His appealing response woke us up too, and I took it also as an answer to the many questions I had put to him—in Bucharest, in Boston and Vermont. And I pursue him still, with my questions, to this very day.

Translated by Carrie Messenger, fall, 2005

A STROLL WITH NATHAN*

The last time I met Nathan Zuckerman was July 2006, when he came to Bard College for the birthday party celebrating the end of my puberty.

That evening I found myself reflecting upon our nearly twenty years of friendship, during which Nathan has served as an unconventional and invaluable guide to American life, psyche, and art. And I was struck yet again by what a privilege it has been, as a newcomer to this country, to have someone like Nathan decoding for me this unknown, new territory.

We live today in a time when nothing is seen, heard, or read if it's not scandalous and nothing seems scandalous enough to be memorable. Yet, in his triple role—as author, character, and narrator, a quite unusual literary performance—Nathan has proven, over a long and extraordinary career, to be, and to remain, memorable.

How does a writer who declares himself preoccupied with "introspection and subjectivity" become a master chronicler of the American twentieth century? By using the individual—the real subject of literature—as the focal point for introspection in a nation that doesn't have time for introspection and doesn't like it too much. Suspicious of parochial thinking or habits, Nathan has nevertheless established himself as a deep and knowledgeable observer of communal and community manners, Jewish, black, feminist and even political correctness. For him, "running away" from our narrow, little routines

*This text was read at the festive evening at Queens College, New York, Tuesday April 28, 2009, honoring "50 years of fiction" by Philip Roth.

means a necessary flight from bigotry, feuds, social hypocrisy and other constrictions in order to acquire references larger, as he says, "than the kitchen table in Newark." Yet he also understands, painfully well, not only the liberating but the taxing power of such an essential and risky enterprise.

A reviewer once called Nathan's work "the comedy of entrapment." As someone who comes from a place and a biography where the tragicomedy of entrapment was daily, unavoidable and for everybody, I can understand what my American interlocutor means when he says: "As an artist the nuance is your task and the intrinsic nature of the particular is to fail to conform." Or when he confesses: "Disillusionment is a way of caring for one's country." Or when he warns us: "About a man everything is believable." What essentially fuels his battles and his successes is the uncompromising courage, humor, intelligence, and talent evident in all his writing. His creed has persistently been the same: "My mind is my church—my laughs are the core of my faith." This may be one very good reason why his readers have not parted from him.

Nathan has always been an independent and solitary thinker, using himself as a guinea pig for daring artistic experiments. He is an artist who works from a model (reality being his constant model), which he accesses through avid curiosity, irony, skepticism, and free play. He doesn't hesitate to put himself in the often disturbing position of being a target of his own sarcasm; the same sarcasm that he levels at society as a whole. Even when he focuses on the most intimate and elemental of all human desires, the erotic, he is searching for layers of nuance, the individual confronting itself, as well as confronting those outside the self. Perhaps the guiding principle for such an unsettling search for trouble is to be found in Kierkegaard: "The opposite of sin isn't virtue, but freedom." Freedom to think and feel and speak out, in order to face up to your true self, has been the main obsession of Nathan's comedy of manners. His linguistic range, and the immediacy and charm of his style, have always served to conflate the personal and political, the inner and outer world, in a relentless scrutiny of the traps set for all of us by our centrifugal, challenging, rapidly changing and disconcerting modernity.

I hadn't seen Nathan since our Bard meeting in 2006, but the following year I received a copy of *Exit Ghost*, along with some nice words of friendship. I tried to call, he never answered. Still, over the past couple of years, I've had some news about him. During a trip to Berlin, I read in an important German daily an article entitled "Where is Nathan Zuckerman?" In the name of his readers, the journalist deplored Nathan's disappearance from the literary news. This claim was recently contradicted, even if not entirely, by a blog entitled "Nathan Zuckerman as Presidential Adviser," in which we learn that President Obama's intellectual formation is due to Jewish scholars and writers, including none other than Nathan himself. And now, in the current issue of the *New Republic*, an article entitled "English anti-Semitism on the March" starts with this quote from Nathan, *circa* 1987: "England's made a Jew of me in only eight weeks." Obviously, because of its open and hidden anti-Semitism. The article continues: "Twenty years on, it is difficult to imagine Nathan Zuckerman lasting eight days in England, let alone eight weeks."

In *Exit Ghost*, Nathan reaffirms a concern we first see in *The Ghost Writer* in 1979; that is, a concern to protect his former mentor, E. I. Lonoff against the new cannibalism of the mass media, its vulgar and cynical exploitation of a writer's private life.

It was in Lonoff's Berkshire home that, many years before, Nathan had first encountered the charming Amy Bellette, the young mistress of the old man. Thirty years later Amy writes, in a letter to the editor of a prestigious newspaper:

> During the decades of the Cold War, in the Soviet Union and in Eastern Europe satellites, it was serious writers who were

expelled from literature; now, in America, it is literature that has been expelled as a serious influence on how life is perceived . . . As soon as one enters into ideological simplifications and the biographical reductivism of cultural journalism, the essence of the artifact is lost. Your cultural journalism is tabloid gossip disguised as an interest in "the arts," and everything that it touches is contracted into what it is not. Who is the celebrity, what is the price, what is the scandal? What transgression has the writer committed, and not against the exigencies of literary aesthetics but against his or her daughter, son, mother, father, spouse, lover, friend, publisher or pet?

Amy's letter was, in fact, Lonoff's letter, which was Nathan's letter, and, in the very end, the letter of the master being celebrated here this evening. Reading it, I was thinking, unavoidably, about Nathan's many appearances as a character and narrator in Philip's great books. And I was thinking, of course, about Nathan's last meeting after so many years with Amy Bellette, that inspiration of amorous fantasies past, that former mesmerizing embodiment of mystery and attraction and passion (including a passion for literature), now a dying old woman. Nathan meets her, this time in New York, at the same time as he meets Jamie Logan, the new mesmerizing young woman, the new embodiment of mystery, sensuality and literature, for the now old and sick and not totally tamed Nathan.

The crashing exit of this last, virtual lover, and of love itself, is an extraordinary moment of perplexity where the classic and obsolete literary confrontation between passion and duty is replaced by the much more authentic and actual confrontation between excitement and extinction, desire and dullness, youth and old age, life and death. Should Nathan give in to the unforgotten crazy needs and dreams of youth still contained in old age? What does he want? Sex, of course. The impotent man wants frenetic abandonment and

fulfillment, the incontinent old man wants tender and savage inter-
course, its urges and hypnosis, the solitary man wants life and light
and intensity, he wants time past in time present. Melancholy and
vitality, weakness and resilience, bitterness, desperation and pride
and sadness are accomplices in one of the most moving literary
moments in contemporary prose.

After so many books and battles, we may ask ourselves what makes
Nathan Zuckerman a hero of our time in such different places as
Newark and Chicago and New York and Sarah Palin's Alaska, in
post-Nazi Germany and post-communist Romania and postmodern
France and in so many other places.

Nathan is quite an original, and very contemporary, cerebral
magician, a tireless and appealing explorer of his and our environment, its vigor and void, its dynamism and dread. He is also a
burlesque and incisive explorer of eroticism, a profound experiment
in social knowledge. He achieves a unique and paradoxical breakthrough in modern literature as a trustworthy seismograph of the
shifting tectonics of American political life during the Roosevelt era,
the era of the Vietnam war, the time of Nixon, Martin Luther King,
Bobby Kennedy, Bill Clinton, and George Bush, as well as the
post-9/11 period, all the way up to the present moment.

Through his fresh, funny, and ferocious scrutiny of intimacy and
subjectivity, we are offered a revealing portrait of America over the
past fifty years, its scandals and prejudices, its shallowness and energy, its clichés, candor, and rebellions. The turbulence of the individual is always seen in connection with the taboos, treachery, and
tragicomedy of the common culture. I don't know of any witness to
the drastic changes and the stable aberrations of this country who
has been able to express its contrasts with such wit, irony, and imagination, with such rich and meaningful ambiguities and contradictions. Nathan enters through his self-made secret door into the
history of American literature, but also perhaps into the history of

America itself, just as *Don Quixote* could be seen as part of Spanish history and Gogol's *Dead Souls* as part of Russian history.

Surprisingly, a few days ago, I received a phone call from Nathan. I knew why he was calling. "Are you coming to the celebration?" I said. "What celebration?" "Five decades of fiction, three decades of Nathan Zuckerman! You should come, you're part of it." He kept silent. "Everybody will be there, Sabbath, the puppeteer, Coleman Silk, the whitened black, Seymour Levov, the Swede and his brother Jerry, the doctor, and the women, Miss New Jersey and Faunia Farley and Consuela Castillo." Nathan was silent. I understood that he preferred to stay in his cave in the Berkshires. But he spoke, finally. He whispered, in fact, like an old man. "Mister So-and-So, published another book. I'm not in it. Another one is coming out. I'm not in it. And one is already on his table, I'm not in it, either. Tell him I know everything. Even here, in the woods, I can find out everything."

Then silence, then again a whisper. "Yes, I know, you'll speak there. About me, I heard, about me. It's fine, I don't care. It's fine because I don't care anymore. It's OK. Be brief and careful with your accent and with your Romanian Dada irony. That's it. Adios muchachos." Silence. Schluss. Konetz filma.

Nathan has fooled me in the past. And I'm quite sure he will fool me again in the not too distant future. I'm sure he will be back. He returned after his farewell in *The Prague Orgy*, he returned after his hiatus in the 1990s. So I'm sure he is hiding somewhere, watching us and taking notes.

When we last spoke, he repeated his former mentor Lonoff's last words with an exaggerated satisfaction: "Reading/writing people, we are finished, we are ghosts witnessing the end of the literary era."

He said this, I'm sure, because he knows that our festive gathering contradicts such a dramatic statement. Or perhaps not. He has always liked contradictions and questioning, is stimulated by them. So I'm sure he is here, taking notes, as he should be.

THE EXILED LANGUAGE

In the beginning was the Word, the ancients told us. In the beginning for me, the word was Romanian. The doctor and all those who assisted at my difficult birth spoke Romanian. Romanian was spoken in my home, where I spent most of my time with Maria, the lovely young peasant woman who took care of me and spoiled me, in Romanian. Of course these were not the only sounds around me. German, Yiddish, Ukrainian, and Polish were spoken in Bukovina, as was a peculiar dialect, a Slavic mixture typical of the Ruthenians. It is notable that the family quarrel between Yiddish, the earthly-plebeian language of exile, and Hebrew, the holy-chosen language, peaked at the 1908 Czernowitz conference when the celebrated triumph of Yiddish ("The Jews are one people, their language is Yiddish") gave no sign of the spectacular and definitive domination that Hebrew would attain with the founding, four decades later, of the State of Israel. When my grandfather asked at my birth if the newborn had nails, trying to gauge my chances of survival, he presumably asked in Yiddish, although he knew Hebrew and spoke fluent Romanian. The books sold in his bookshop were, in fact, Romanian. At five, when I was deported to the Transnistria concentration camp, along with the rest of Bukovina's Jewish population, I spoke only Romanian. With my first expulsion beyond the Dniester, the Romanian language was also banished.

The Yiddish poet Itzik Manger once said: "When the great calamity overwhelmed the German-assimilated Jew, when a brutal sergeant-major roared: 'Out, Jew!' the German Jew woke from his self-justifying dream, from his trance of German culture, and began to run. But in himself, and with himself, he carried a bastard: a foreign language; a foreign body."[1] In my case, a brutal Romanian, not German, sergeant-major roared: "Out, Jew," but the Romanian language I carried wasn't a bastard or a foreign body; it was my only language. It was also, of course, the language of that brutal sergeant-major, and this I was already aware of at too early an age.

In the camp I learned Yiddish from the elderly captives and Ukrainian from native children in the neighborhood. After liberation by the Red Army I attended a Russian school for one year. When we returned to Romania in 1945, I enrolled in a Romanian school, but my parents soon arranged for me to be privately tutored —in German. What we experienced during those years of terror in "Trans-tristia" had originated, they knew quite well, in Hitler's Berlin, but they were also aware of, even though they were not particularly well educated in, the difference between recent horror and the longer view, between hatred and culture. I studied Hebrew for only one year, when I was roughly 13, in order to be formally accepted among the "men" of the tribe. Surprisingly, traces resurface, even today, when I least expect them. In high school I learned French and Russian, but none of the languages I had taken up ever became fully internalized. Echoes of my subconscious "cosmopolitanism" sound only occasionally these days when, suddenly and without effort on my part, the proper turn of phrase occurs to me in a conversation held in one of these half-familiar, still foreign, languages, even when I have access to them.

In the end, I feel at home in only one language.

Writing seems a childish pursuit, as we well know, even when done with the excessive seriousness to which children are prone.

My long road to this immaturity began one July day in 1945, several months after our return from the camps. An Edenic summer in a small Moldavian town. The enchanted banality of the normal, the overwhelming joy of finally feeling secure. A perfect afternoon: sun and stillness. In the room's half-light, I listened to a voice that was mine and yet not my own. The green book of Romanian folktales I had been given just before I reached the solemn age of nine spoke directly to me. It was then, I think, that I experienced the wonder of the word, the magic of literature: both wound and balm, disease and therapy. The language to which I had been subjected in the Transnistria camps was a cacophony that mingled despair with barked orders from the guards, that brutal sergeant-major roaring. Yiddish, German, Ukrainian, Russian: all the camp's idioms rushed into the chasm it had rent in my life.

In 1945, the survivors and their nomadic language were repatriated. An impoverished language, anemic, hesitant, and confused, it needed, as I did, the nutrients of normality. I made all sorts of rediscoveries: food, games, school, clothing, relatives, but above all I was mad for books, newspapers, magazines, posters. I discovered new words and new meanings, my language absorbed them quickly and with great excitement. Early, too early, I dreamed of joining the clan of word wizards, the secret sect I had just discovered.

My first literary attempt was, of course, an "amorous discourse," as Roland Barthes would say. In 1947, in the lowest high school class at the Jewish Lyceum in Suceava—a private school that was to be banned a year later—I dedicated my childish rhetoric to the blond girl whose name followed mine in the class registry: Manea, Norman; Norman, Bronya. I read that solemn declaration, full of pathos, to Bronya and a small group of bewildered classmates. And then, in the first year of the "Dictatorship of the Proletariat," I continued with the same childish enthusiasm to write poems in honor of the Revolution, of Stalin, of world peace—terrible poems, of course, which may compete, I would say, with the terrible poems written at that time by mature and renowned poets all around the world. Yet, I was already searching for something "different," something that would transcend daily trivialities, eager as I was to uncover my true self among all the individuals who inhabited me. The one-party system of the socialist dictatorship took over, gradually, any private ownership: land and banks, industry and schools, farms and hospitals and newspapers, apartments and kindergartens, stadiums and pharmacies and libraries, agriculture and culture—everything. All of us were owned by the state, and the official language of the Party dominated our daily life, sometimes our nightlife, too. Some people could still find a shelter in their family library. That was not my case. Coming back from our nomadic ordeal, we didn't have much of anything. The bookstore of my grandfather was gone, as was he himself, buried in a nameless grave in the Ukraine. Hunting for books took many useless detours and traps before I could find, finally, after a great waste of time and energy, the authors I was looking for. Yet, reading saved me from the deadening effect of the dictatorship's wooden language. My imagination was inflamed by German Romanticism; I immersed myself in English and French realism; but above all I was mesmerized by the great Russian literature, at the time extensively and superbly translated in Romania. Tolstoy and Goncharov, Gogol and Pushkin, Chekhov and many others. It was not until the "liberalization" period of the 1960s that I would experience the true Dostoyevky and the great modernists, Joyce, Proust, Faulkner, the Latin Americans, and the Surrealists, as well as modern Romanian writers who had finally been republished after years of a stupid ban. Reading preserved me from ideological idiocy and grotesque opportunism, first as an unhappy student at the polytechnic and then as an unhappy engineer. The naïve illusion that a solid, practical profession might save me from socialist demagogy and terror was soon dispelled.

My first story, "Pressing Love," published in 1966 in a small avant-garde literary journal banned after six issues, was filled with coded erotic anxiety. I had timidly tried to re-establish a thematic and linguistic normality. The official press immediately condemned the text as apolitical, absurd, aestheticizing, and cosmopolitan.

Soon after, I finally heard my voice in my own book, which coincidentally also had a cover as green as that of the folktale book I discovered on my return, in 1945, from my first exile.

I found the refuge I had so long desired. I was finally at home. I had protected my language as well as I could from the pressures of official speech; now I had to defend it from suspicious and hostile censors who would massacre or eliminate sentences, paragraphs, and chapters in the books that followed. In that period, the tedious jargon of power that had reigned for years gradually opened the floodgates to the dictator's endless stream of a new-old nationalism. Everything was oriented toward the head clown: television, the press, laws, the Party "debates," preschool education, cheering and athletic events, philatelist conferences.

Twenty years after my first published story, an apolitical, strictly literary text, and before my flight to the West, in 1986, my allegorical novel *The Black Envelope* gave strong political accents to daily life under socialist misery and terror at a time when the propagandists and censors were encouraging the "aesthetical" approach to writing in order to abandon daily reality for a more magnificent one.

I left the socialist "penal colony" much too late, because I was childish enough to believe that I did not live in a country, but in a language. Liberation, I knew, entailed a malignant curtailing of freedom itself. In December 1986, I boarded a flight to Berlin knowing full well that I might have traded my tongue for a passport. But I didn't feel, even in this extreme situation, that my language was "the usurpation of an alien property," as Kafka thought. It was, in fact, my only property, and the willingness to accept this loss speaks volumes about the "flaming brothel," as Cioran called the region he himself left behind, not suspecting the horrors the socialist combination of brothel, circus, and prison would bring.

For the writer, language is a placenta. Language is not only a sweet and glorious conquest, but legitimization, a home.

Being driven out of this essential lair, his creativity is burned to the core.

My second exile (this time at the age of 50 instead of 5) gave expropriation and delegitimization new meaning. The honor of being expelled was inseparable from being silenced as a writer. Nonetheless, I did take my nomadic language with me, like a snail its house.

The sacred text was, as we know, the instrument of exilic Jewish survival. In my case, it was not the old, sacred text of the Bible that accompanied me in exile. It was a secular language, my very inner language, the language of writing.

Is the Jew in exile "restored" to his nativity of dispersal, as George Steiner says? Does this "chosen foreignness" become "ontological," as Hegel argues? The house I was carrying was my language, and my language happened to be Romanian. Nazism and then communism robbed me of connections to a real Jewish tradition, yet I was what I am always told I am: not only a Jew but "the Jew," housed not in place but in time and, as usual, in a not very hospitable time. I would have liked to have believed that my case proves again that "truth is homeless," as Steiner kept repeating, that exile is the only realm of truth, but I wasn't yet sure about this.

At the time of my first exiled year in Berlin when I was overwhelmed with this and many other questions, I didn't know Steiner's essay "Our Homeland the Text." I only recently discovered that I was then putting to myself the same questions he was asking at precisely that period. "Plato records the hunter's halloo when a truth is cornered—even if this hunt should lead to his own destruction or that of his community. It is here that the creed of Spinoza and of Kafka meets with the conduct of Socrates," Steiner says.

> A true thinker, a truth-thinker . . . must know that no nation,
> no body politic, no creed, no moral ideal and necessity, be it

that of human survival, is worth falsehood, a willed self-deception or the manipulation of a text. This knowledge and observance *are* his homeland. It is the false reading, the erratum that make him homeless. . . . The man or woman at home in the text is, by definition, a conscientious objector: to the vulgar mystique of the flag and the anthem, to the sleep of reason which proclaims "my country, right or wrong," to the pathos and eloquence of collective mendacities on which the nation-state—be it a mass-consumer mercantile technocracy or a totalitarian oligarchy—builds its power and aggressions. The locus of truth is always extraterritorial; its diffusion is made clandestine by the barbed wire and watch-towers of national dogma.[2]

Paradoxically, German was soon to become my first linguistic asylum in the West. In 1987, during my fellowship in West Berlin, my first translated book, *Composite Biography*, was published as *A Robot Biography* by Steidl Verlag. My familiarity with the German language eased the trauma of uprooting, which was fraught with discouragement and confusion. German, spoken by my friends and my parents' friends, had survived the decades of socialism in Bukovina, once part of the Habsburg realm. In 1987, I was overjoyed to discover that the German language, so long dormant in me, was ready to be resurrected.

When I arrived in Göttingen for the final editing of my German book, my editor and I knocked our heads together over the manuscript until midnight. He tried to console me. "I assure you, we can translate anything. In Goethe's language there are equivalents for everything! Absolutely everything! Even the most unusual, astonishing turns of phrase. All you need is talent, dedication, and work. Hard work and then more work. And, of course, money."

Yes, translation is badly paid in the capitalist markets. Unlike

Günter Grass, not every author can offer his translators the extended working visits that can help circumvent the semantic obstacles that arise in moving from one language to another.

My first public appearance in New York in the fall of 1989, when the East's implosion gripped the world's attention, was as one of a panel on Romanian literature sponsored by the American chapter of PEN on "The Word as Weapon." Suspicious of the topic's belligerence, I chose to speak about "The Word as Miracle." Naturally I evoked that July afternoon in 1945 when I discovered the marvelous Romanian folktale by Ion Creangă. A few days later I received a letter from a distinguished writer and translator of Romanian descent who had attended the event. She mentioned Ion Creangă's anti-Semitic writings and comments.

I knew that German was not only the language of Schiller and Goethe but of Hitler and the SS; that the Romanian of Caragiale and Bacovia was also that of Zelea Codreanu. It is unfortunate and very disturbing when great writers and intellectuals become accomplices of the ideology and language of hatred; but, again, Romanian was for me also the language of love and friendship and literary apprenticeship, the language my parents and grandparents speak to me even though they are dead.

Jewish authors have often been reproached for writing in the "executioner's language," African writers for serving the "colonialists' language." Language cultivates and preserves the poison of hatred just as it gives rise to love or innovative art. It encompasses both indolence of mind and lashes of brilliant creativity, majesty and monstrosity. Baudelaire's French *Les Fleurs du mal* (Flowers of Evil) and Tudor Arghezi's Romanian *Flori de mucegai* (Mouldy Flowers) broach this ambivalence even in their titles.

When I spoke of the wonder of the word in New York in 1989, I referred to my native, nomadic language and not to the language to which I had emigrated. Its wonders were not accessible to this shipwrecked latecomer. Could it have been? Could I have relived in English the enchantment I had first encountered as a nine-year-old and then my subsequent adventure of self-discovery through Romanian words?

During a stay at the Ledig House writers' colony in Switzerland some years ago, I asked a renowned German translator of Russian what age one had to start learning another language well enough to become a writer in it. Nabokov had learned foreign languages as a child. Conrad had sailed between ports and languages when still young enough to adapt. I knew that the usual examples did not fit. "Twelve," the expert announced. "Too bad," I said, "I'm already thirteen." By then I had more than doubled the double of that age.

Yet the uprooting and dispossession of exile are a trauma with some positive aspects. They only become apparent once one understands the advantage of relinquishing the idea of one's own importance. Impermanence and insecurity can be liberating. Exile is also a challenging pedagogical experience. There is much to learn when one is forced to begin again at an advanced age, to enter into the world anew and to prove one's abilities again like an old child whose past has been wiped out but who has been offered a "second chance" to rebuild his life from scratch, even if without one's former energy and vigor.

At the age of 26, the Romanian writer E. M. Cioran began appropriating the wealth of the French language like a greedy pirate. He called this metamorphosis of linguistic identity "the greatest, most dramatic event that can befall a writer." "Historical catastrophes are nothing compared to this," he later claimed. "When I wrote in Romanian, words were not *independent* of me. As soon as I began to write in French, I consciously chose each word. I had them before me, outside of me, each in its place. And I chose them: now I'll take you, then you." The break to which Cioran had aspired in leaving Romania was more than linguistic. "When I changed my language,

I annihilated my past. I changed my entire life." Is this true? As a famous French author and brilliant stylist in his adopted language, Cioran was constantly haunted by ghosts of the past, which he found oppressive and humiliating. "My country! I wanted to hang on to it at any cost—but there was nothing to hang on," he wrote in the 1950s. Cioran's glorious linguistic transmutation, however, was not completely triumphant after all. "Today again it seems that I am writing in a language that does not fit me at all, that has no roots: a hot-house language. French does not suit any temperament. I need a *savage*, drunken language," he told Fernando Savater in 1977. On his deathbed, he rediscovered Romanian, but not himself. He experienced the ecstasy of Alzheimer amnesia. The greatest joy, the highest penalty. The End.

My reasons for severing my ties were perhaps stronger than Cioran's, but still I hung on to my native tongue, and, since I could not turn back the clock, I could not aspire to the transfiguration and profound, radical change toward which Cioran struggled during his decades in exile.

Ultimately the question concerning writers is related not only to their linguistic identity but also to their individual drive and destiny. Compared to collective historical disasters, their worries seem childish. Many artists and writers collapse in exile or at home before the problem of a change in their linguistic identity arises. And yet, historical catastrophes may pale beside the dark forces that destroy their language.

I was almost completely at sea in English. To my fright, I found myself to be like Nabokov's Professor Pnin, who thought *Hamlet* sounded better in his native Russian than in English. In my first decade here, I became terribly anxious when invited to speak at conferences. Not only because of my accent, but also because I constantly feared I would lose or forget my script. I still remember arriving in Turin in 1991 and finding that my bags were missing. I was to give my lecture in English the next morning and, in despair, I tried to convince the conference's organizers to move it to the afternoon. In the meantime, my suitcases arrived and my luck increased: several Italian–Romanian interpreters were attending so that I could speak off the cuff. This epilogue was much happier than the story of the poor Pnin, who misses his train to the conference and even brings the wrong lecture.

The legitimization that translation confers when one lives in one's own country changes when one has left. "At home," translations are welcome gifts from the unknown. An author who is translated into several languages cannot evaluate all these translations. He lives in his own language, in which he has found his voice and character. The foreign travesties do not disturb his essential creativity; the alien codes in which his writing has been encrypted and which he himself often cannot decipher are nothing but flattering gifts.

For an author who has been uprooted, translation becomes a sort of entry visa into the land where he now resides (as well as into other lands and realms). Along with citizenship, it ensures he has a literary ID, an entry into a new and fully ambivalent sense of belonging to a community he has joined as an "alien." Translated, he is better expressed than in his daily speech, and it my open up opportunities for more communication with his fellow citizens and with his fellow writers.

Yes it all remains hopelessly indefinite for an exiled writer, who, although translated into another linguistic territory, still writes in his native and now nomadic language. Such a frustrating working hypothesis merely spreads uncertainty. The heteronymous, as Fernando Pessoa called his contradictory and complementary creative valences, are replaced by one and the same orthonym that appears wearing the masks of different languages.

A writer's integrity and his inner self are inseparable from his language. They become variable and indefinably foggy when he is robbed of his native tongue. The doubts he has always had to rein in can gain the upper hand in the ambiguity and uncertainty of his new situation.

"My infallible method of determining whether a sentence is good or bad is to imagine I am in the middle of the Sahara without any books. In my pocket I find a note with one sentence. If it suddenly illuminates the desert's meaning and I no longer wish to leave, then I know the sentence is a good one." The words of a Romanian writer and friend. In the Sahara of exile, in the desert that Levinas believed to be the root of the spirit, able to replace the ground with the letter, I have often had to repeat these words. For a moment they lent this desert meaning and offered the refuge I had sought for so long. And yet . . . In New York, a "good" Romanian sentence would have to be channeled through contortions and convolutions, metamorphoses and mutilations in order to be translated into the language in which my identity is now clothed.

The years had flowed by like water and I knew quite well how unreceptive I was to the illusion of imperviousness, but I also knew how much I depended on that illusion. My dilemma became much clearer in the summer of 1991 than it had been in Germany in 1987 during my apprenticeship in Göttingen. My New York publisher, Grove Press, planned a collection of short stories and a collection of essays for my American debut. Various translators had taken on the short stories, and, together with my editor, I tried to improve their English versions. The Romanian text lay on the table next to the French and Italian translations. Fortunately for me, the American editor spoke both those languages. Together, we jumped from one language to the next and reworked the English version. *How* each sentence tried to express something became less important than *what* it tried to say. It was a logical, "Aristotelian" reduction to erasure, a kind of Darwinian struggle for existence in which originality could prove to be the greatest disadvantage. As Walter

Benjamin said, "any translation which intends to perform a transmitting function cannot transmit anything but information—hence, something inessential."

My book finally appeared in a version that had been cobbled together from many sources but sounded reasonable in English. Despite my three months in purgatory, I was delighted to hold the book in my hand. Seeing it displayed in the bookstore's windows and reading the flattering reviews, I was forced to remind myself that the ordeal of translation is a privilege many gifted authors, at home or in exile, never receive.

Was I accepting a surrogate, an impostor, a shallow impersonator? I reminded myself that I had read Spanish, French, Russian, Italian, and German literature mostly in translation and how important it proved to be in such an encounter with great masters. In translation, of course, always so or mostly so.

The first sentence of my 1984 collection of essays, *On the Contour*, goes like this: "The unity of a people is, above all, one of language." I truly believed that language was the matrix, the fundamental, formative factor of communication between the individual and community. During that period, I was attacked in the socialist press as "extraterritorial." That is, foreign, cosmopolitan, antinationalist, antiparty.

In the end, as we can see, I could not avoid becoming a true extraterritorial, expatriate, exile. Yet, as Wittgenstein says, "The boundaries of my language are the boundaries of my world." Common sense, or the not quite tender age in which my exile occurred, should have been cause enough to disabuse myself of the chimera of writing. Still, I have continued the adventure begun in the difficult political conditions of my own country and language.

An author's exile is a terrible trauma for the writer, skinned and unsouled, forced to replace the internal organs of his linguistic being. It has proven, more than once, to be his suicide.

The simulacrum offered by translation, although just a substitute, a surrogate, a double, can provide some unexpected relief. It has similarities with exile itself; it's a textual migration, a process of migrating from a place (a language) of *departure* to a place (a language) of *destination*. In the same way, it is a process of rebirth and adaptation of the nomadic text to a new context.

Assimilation entails the translation of the ego into another language and culture, where it tries to find its place and its expression. Aggressive "distortions" (to recall, again, dispossession and dependence) bring with them incentives of uncertainty. Conscious or unconscious mimesis often marks the childishness inherent in the spectacle of assimilation.

The exile has new, particular themes for reflection. He is, in the end, a hybrid, a compromise between what he brought with him and what he acquires later.

Translation provides a new linguistic form for the old content. We find, in the process of linguistic relocation, many of the modulations that the exile experiences himself. The text is a living body, a being. The final product must belong entirely to the new language, to the target language, as they say, and not to the old language. The transformation takes a defined period of time and the result is already beached on the new shore, in the new linguistic territory, the new textual residence. In contrast, the exile often swings, for a long time, if not forever between the past and the present. Between formation–deformation–reformation, between different possible egos until, gradually, *the double* appears to represent him on the new social stage. It is an osmosis: loss and gain, wound and revitalization, the fracture of the old and the nutrition of the new, an intense exchange of energies.

Exile is also an extraordinary process of education and re-education, especially for those who come to the new land as adults. Where one begins and where one ends are poles of a privileged existential adventure, with intense suffering and exaltation. The great school of pointlessness, of dispossession, and in the end, of death, the ultimate dispossession, does not exclude scenes of exhilarating jubilation. Feelings of rebirth are gifts of inestimable worth to our ephemerality.

As with everything human, the extreme condition of exile contains both loss and gain, hopelessness and hope. The trauma of translation also has positive effects. It has happened more than once that in checking even an imperfect translation, I have discovered certain word choices I like better than in the original. I have then changed the original Romanian to a word translated from English. Translation may sometimes be, as the Romantics said, the best literary criticism. You are forced to see where the text is clumsy.

We should remind ourselves that Proust only found himself through Ruskin's translations. In translation, in writing as translation, he found a model and a voice. "I have two more Ruskins to finish," he wrote in 1904, "and after that I will try to translate my poor heart, if I haven't died by then" We can never emphasize the importance of translations enough, for the expansion of knowledge, for dialogue among nations. Especially, though, for the individual discovery of unforeseen, great friends. More important friends than those we meet in the morning for a coffee.

I am connected to Paul Celan by more than Bukovina and the camps of Transnistria, which marked our fates in different ways. Celan's German, from the beginning a language of exile, came to the Habsburgian province of Bukovina from Vienna and not from Berlin. He called his brief, carefree youth in Bucharest a time of word games and puns. He believed his German gave him an unfair advantage over his friends who wrote in Romanian. Eugen Ionescu claimed that he himself would probably have been a better writer in Romania than the more important one he became in France. My Romanian biography and language were not just episodes in my youth. My "word games" have lasted throughout the greater part of my life, as an alternation between horror and joy, danger and re-birth, apathy and creativity, back to drama, humiliation, uprooting.

It was in Paris, and not in Vienna or Berlin or Zurich, that Celan settled and continued to write in his exiled, nomadic German. No wonder he considered language to be the poet's homeland, even when the language is German and the poet a Jew. Even when the language is Romanian and the writer a Jew, I would add . . .

Had Paul Celan won his well-deserved Nobel Prize, which country could have claimed him? The prize is explicitly awarded to an individual and not a country. I was not surprised when V. S. Naipaul responded to the news from Stockholm by saying that he did not belong to any particular country. He should have added, I think, that he does indeed belong to a language. And so should Elias Canetti, Isaac Bashevis Singer, and Kafka, too, for that matter, had his marvelous, nocturnal cryptograms managed to reach that du-bious committee of world glory.

One of the most interesting debates at the 1998 Conference of Jewish writers in San Francisco concerned the hypothesis that the greatest Israeli writer in Hebrew in the twenty-first century may not be Jewish. In recent decades, as world events have followed their bloody course, Israel took in immigrants from Vietnam and Chile. Their children have been Israelis for more than twenty years and are "grounded" in the Hebrew language. Today many Romanian work-ers and cleaning ladies from the Philippines and Thailand are living in Israel. What if the next inspired bard of Hebrew is a Chilean-Israeli, or the child of a Romanian worker, or a Filipino, and not a Jew? Most of the conference participants, including the Israeli dele-gation, composed of Jews from Iraq, Morocco, Romania, and Ger-many, responded enthusiastically. Quite a paradox for a state that believes itself to be the solution to the insoluble question of Jewish exile. It is not impossible that this new century will also see a great

German poet of Turkish descent, or French-Algerian or Japanese-Australian.

In New York I still live in the Romanian language, as in Paris Paul Celan lived in German. Despite the fact that I also publish now in Romania, my literary message is no longer sent in a bottle to someone on a distant shore but in an ephemeral capsule that floats through a dream in which—and only in this dream, under lucky circumstances—it will have to invent its own legitimization, its own recipient.

The structural differences between Romanian and English are more difficult to bridge than those between Romanian and the Latin languages. Romanian is, in fact, a mix of Latin and oriental languages. My volume *Compulsory Happiness* came into English through a French translation; some other stories and essays were translated into English from German translations. It seems difficult for a relatively inexperienced translator to find English equivalents for vagueness, metaphors, wordplay, lacunae, equivocal allusions, ironies, intertextual blurrings, as they are practiced in Romanian literature. To embrace the American idiom, the text has often to be retailored; incompatibilities must be eliminated and all that is too obscure or specific has to be altered. Naturally, a great translator, with the necessary time and dedication, can find brilliant equivalents for anything. Intermediaries of genius, unfortunately, are not found on every corner. As my first German editor pointed out, some twenty years ago, translations require persistence and talent, effort and money. And he was not even considering today's ever decreasing literary standards, the increasingly rushed tempo of reading and editing, the growing aversion to oddities or eccentricities within other literary traditions in favor of what can easily be understood and sold. Books have become simple products that should be as readily bought and used as any other market product.

Should one simplify one's thinking or expression in order to ease the task of the translator before easing the task of the publisher and the reader? I sometimes tried this compulsive distortion in order to avoid being caught in a dead end. The result didn't resemble Kafka's "white" style but was a vacant account of absence with no digression, enchantment, or mystery. Avoiding stylistic risks, difficulty, or subtlety, picturesque or idiomatic expression, I myself became simpler, so pale as to disappear completely into the blank page.

The writer's block underscores the insanity necessary to pursue this venture, an absurdity that exile only heightens. It was difficult to weather this crisis, if I have indeed done so. When I am occasionally asked in New York in which language I write, I answer, only half in jest, in the language of the birds.

Hannah Arendt, herself an exile, once said: "What remains? The mother tongue remains." No one can take away the language in which one has been formed and deformed. The Romanian I hear in my thoughts or that I speak with my wife, and the English of the newspapers, television, and banking forms, of my American friends, of the college where I teach, or of my doctor, are not easily divided into public and private realms. Their interaction cannot be compared merely to that between an individual entity and social identity. The tension is not simply linguistic but also geographic, historic, and psychological in origin.

My English is a rented tongue, borrowed by this Robinson Crusoe for the social interaction needed to fit with those harboring him. Far from its natural sphere, my "old" language now exists only for me; I alone reign over its nomadic magic.

The language of life after exile accosts me from all sides. Those nearby who speak to each other or even to me have started, gradually, even if timidly, to reach corners of my inner language. The tension between my two languages of today eventually creates fruitful synergies and interferences. Misunderstandings and misrepresentations are only the unavoidable negative aside of an exchange that also brings insights when the languages mirror and enrich each other. At times, I am rewarded with sudden inspiration when I return to a chapter in the original Romanian text after the simplifications of the English version. A therapeutic spirit helps me recover the way back into myself, heals the cramping undergone in the foreign text that is mine but, strictly speaking, also not my own. Marvelous, untranslatable Romanian words and expressions I had never thoroughly examined before suddenly reveal their uniqueness, incisiveness, and originality.

If separated from the land and the people who rejuvenate it every day, one's mother tongue, one's language "with roots," risks petrifying into an artifact. When transmuted into another linguistic medium, however, it may reveal beauties buried by routine. Yet, the relationship between one's native and now nomadic tongue and its homeland, left ever further behind, does not become any simpler.

The fact that one belongs to a language in no way heals the wounds that the homeland has inflicted on one's life; and however incurable the wounds, they do not lessen the priceless gift, language, which we inhabit.

When my first translated stories were published in 1970 in Israel in a Hebrew anthology called *Jewish Writers in Romanian*, I was annoyed by the title. I considered myself, quite simply, a Romanian writer. My "ethnicity" was my burden and my wealth and my history, but it was no one else's business. I didn't consider the language a "tormenting usurpation of an alien property," as Kafka said.

Since then, I have learned that writers are often classified by other categories than the "essential" one of language: black writers, gay writers, Catholic writers, women writers, and, of course, Jewish writers. They are all claimed by subgroups according to particular identities and not according to their intrinsic "entity," their language.

My own biography is a reminder that history and personal history cannot be ignored. A biography marked by Holocaust, communism, and exile points to a certain identity, independent of the language of its owner.

Do we eventually grow into the identities that are repeatedly assigned to us? Do we finally become what we're always told we are? Am I an American writer in the Romanian nomadic language or an American Jewish/Jewish American writer in the Romanian language? Or am I, simply, a Romanian writer in America? An exiled writer, as I was even before exile? Or a Jewish writer in the Romanian language, as I was labeled by fellow sympathizers and by many enemies?

These seemingly futile questions became more confusing when the alien in his homeland was forced again to become an exile and his language became, again, a nomadic one. I couldn't avoid, in the last twenty years, wondering if the annoying title of that Israeli anthology wasn't—despite my irritation at that time—an accurate premonition: the correct assessment of my destiny.

In one of the dreams Antonio Tabucchi describes in his picaresque novel *Requiem: A Hallucination*, a dream expedition in search of Fernando Pessoa, the narrator meets his dead father. The father is young and, surprisingly, does not speak Italian, the only language he knew, but Portuguese. Is that because the hallucination takes place in Portugal or because the Italian writer did not write his book in his native tongue but in his second language, Portuguese? "What are you doing in a sailor's uniform here in the Pension Pensao?" the son asks. "It's 1932," the father answers. "I'm doing my military service, and our ship, a frigate, dropped anchor in Lisbon." He wants to know from his son, who is older than he and knows more, how he will die. The son tells his father of the cancer which has, in reality, already killed him.

Not only in the beginning was the word. Before the final silence, we often end our existence with the Word. Chekhov spoke his last words, "Ich sterbe" ("I'm dying") not in the language of his life and works but in that of the land where he ended his earthly adventure. In the rare dreams in which I see my parents, they speak Romanian. And yet, I cannot foresee in which language I will take my leave of this world. Death's language sometimes differs from that of the life to which it is putting an end.

From fragments translated by Alexandru Vlad,
Tess Lewis and Sean Cotter

Notes

1. Itzik Manger, *The World According to Itzik* (New Haven and London: Yale University Press, 2002), p. 237.

2. George Steiner, *No Passion Spent* (New Haven and London: Yale University Press, 1996), p. 321.

CASA MINIMA

"The besieged man had finally escaped from the Colony of Rhino." Those were the words I used in my 1999 essay on Eugen Ionescu, entitled "Berenger at Bard" (see pp. 157–75). The Rhino colony, of course, stands for the penal colony of socialism administered by the ultimate Rhino leader: president Nicolae Ceauşescu. July 9, 1989 was another crucial watermark in the life of the wanderer I had since become. Now at Bard, an American college, I found myself right in the middle of Herman Hesse's Glass Bead game, transposed to the end-of-the-twentieth-century New World.

I began my life at Bard first living in the house of a professor of chemistry gone on sabbatical, then in the house formerly belonging to Mary McCarthy, which comprised several spacious, sunny rooms on the first floor and three tiny bedrooms upstairs, haunted at night by strange distortions of the daily academic games. At the beginning of my third year, I moved into a shack away from the beaten track, which had instantly caught my fancy with its basic utilitarian charms. It might well have been designed as a cabin for deer or wild turkey hunters, as it stood surrounded by hospitable woods that sheltered, indiscriminately, teachers and students alike along with squirrels and stags and rabbits and birds of all colors and sizes. The doorway opened unobtrusively into a large living room sporting one huge window facing the forest. This wall of glass imposed no boundaries to the surrounding landscape and brought its soothing presence right into the middle of the room. One minimalist bedroom and a bathroom to match, as well as a den, were part of the house that some of my acquaintances called with congenial irony "The Unabomber's

House." The label stuck not only on account of the cabin's secluded location, but also because of its inhabitant, the eccentric East European refugee. Neither Berenger nor myself, the solitary exile, were in any way connected to the notorious Theodore John Kaczynski, the brilliant Harvard graduate turned recluse, who had compiled his "Manifesto" against an industrial society in his own hut and who had mailed it along with his bombs to various universities and airline companies (Unabomber stands for University and Airline Bomber). Even though this champion in the struggle against modernity had ended up killing three people, wounding twenty-three more, and eventually getting a life sentence, the label that graced my abode seemed neither hostile nor unpleasant to me. Rather than claiming the right to rebel, my self-imposed isolation and withdrawal was a quest for peacefulness. I needed a haven.

Almost fifty years had passed since another similar autumn, no less enchanting than the ones I was enjoying at Bard. I recall the day when I was forced to leave my birthplace in Bukovina and was shipped along with other sinners of the same ethnicity, to the extermination camp. The world of my childhood with its sweet scents and colors had lost its ability to protect me. When we were ordered to leave our home, my parents took along the money they had been saving for their very first house, a house they would never live to acquire.

The Red Army eventually freed us, so we were able to return to Romania after the war was over. Eastern Europe was sizzling now in the light of a utopian and oppressive Soviet sun. THE LIGHT COMES FROM THE EAST. This exalted formula was repeated ad nauseam in all possible keys . . . Private property had been abolished: factories, banks, farms, movie halls, flocks of sheep, private homes, stadiums, hospitals, buses, and hotels, they had all become state property and so had all of us associated with them. In what came to be known as Romania's multifaceted socialism, "the housing norms" had come to allocate a scant 8 square meters (less than

100 square feet) per person. An extra room was a rare privilege, assigned by draconian laws and obscure byzantine practices. The notion of an "enclosed town" was beginning to take root: only those born within its confines were permitted to remain there, with the few exceptions of those allowed to do so by the fiat of a Higher Authority. The secret police undersigned all passports for traveling abroad and the few beneficiaries were those who were ready to reciprocate and serve its shady purposes. The public space became the stage for political masquerades while private space dwindled under the watchful eye and keen ears of secret police informers. It was hardly a paradox that the common citizens struggled to erect additional walls to protect their privacy within this restrictive, mistrustful space. The results, similar to Kafka's Chinese Wall, thickened progressively the boundaries of the enclosure, keeping a threatening environment at bay, until the living space within dwindled to the point of smothering its occupants. Time itself had become state property by way of countless impositions: political meetings, demonstrations and parades, and sundry civic duties in the service of the Party. As a young man, I seemed to live out of a suitcase, always on the move from one temporary apartment to another, in a continuous succession of stages. I felt like a larva perpetually and hopelessly waiting for the time of a final metamorphosis.

At long last came the moment when I broke away from the Rhino Colony. As an exile, I felt that the future opened itself up to puzzling uncertainties written in a new code of probabilities that I could not read clearly. The Unknown appeared boundless, to be sure, and the frantic sense of a newly acquired freedom was overwhelming. Liberty came at a price, too: feeling dislocated and dispossessed has always marked the life of the wanderer. Mutability was the actual "physical" foreign space of freedom, and time became the remaining and transcendental property of the homeless. My only refuge and possession was my native language, the language into which I was born, that has shaped and misshaped my very being. I yearned to reacquaint myself with my own fractured self.

I enjoyed looking at the old buildings at Bard designed to house Protestant seminaries, admiring the way the stern, Anglo-Saxon Gothic style blends with the "nouveau style" of the more recent dorms, with the library built in the fashion of a Greek temple, and the newer, postmodern wing, with the chapel for sacred and profane services, with the institute for curatorial studies and the museum, rendered more modern by the recent acquisitions, with the impos-ing building of the Levy institute, its plateau reminiscent of the deserted park scene in Antonioni's *Blow-Up*. One could see the Hudson from this site. Far in the distance, the faint blue mountains reminded me of the mountains of my native Bukovina, in north-eastern Romania. *Bukovina on the Hudson*—just like in the title of an interview I gave here in New York. Having missed a "sense of nature" all my life, I ended up here in its turbulent splendor, intan-gible and meaningful.

My cabin I liked to call—imagine that!—CASA MINIMA—*The Minimal House*. It had belonged to Irma Brandeis, whose grave is next to Hanna Arendt's, another legendary lover guilty for having fallen in love with a word craftsman. Casa Minima was incompara-bly larger, brighter, and more hospitable than the monastic cell Kafka had rented close to the castle in Prague in order to protect his solitude and writing. The woody Bard College muffled the darker overtones of an East European past, offering a rejuvenating new homeland to a suspicious stranger who had never enjoyed one be-fore. Eventually, the exile no longer came to see his estrangement as a handicap, but rather as beneficial uprooting.

This little independent Liberal Arts College was becoming ever more cosmopolitan via the international students who came from thirty different countries, along with staff joining its faculty from the most exotic corners of the planet. Saul Bellow, Toni Morrison, Roy Lichtenstein, Ralph Ellison, Arthur Penn, Isaac Bashevis Singer,

Philip Roth, Danniel Mendelsohn, Ismail Kadare, Orhan Pamuk, Mario Vargas Llosa, Claudio Magris, Antonio Tabucchi, Antonio Muñoz Molina, Edna O'Brien, Peter Sloterdijk, and Cynthia Ozick, have all been here. Chinua Achebe, the great master and mentor of its academic Glass Bead games Leon Botstein, John Ashbery, Ann Lauterbach, Ian Buruma, Mary Caponegro, Robert Kelly, David Kettler, Elizabeth Murray, Stephen Shore, Francine Prose, William Tucker, Peter Hutton, Brad Morrow, and Joan Tower were in my proximity.

The campus itself has changed over the past twenty years, sprouting many new buildings that establish a dynamic and provocative dialogue between the present and the past. The history of American architectural styles over the past two centuries can be viewed in the array of buildings with their artful features set in stone and wood, as well as in steel and glass. Earlier examples include the fanciful Gate House. Today housing the Institute for International Education, it was designed in the first half of the nineteenth century by Alexander Jackson Davis, the architect and thinker who first promoted the Romantic idea of dwelling in close harmony with nature. The Protestant chapel was built around 1860 by Frank Wills who is also responsible for the Episcopalian Cathedral in Montreal. The Ludlow building that houses administrative offices today, along with the edifices in its immediate vicinity, was designed by Richard Upjohn, architect of the famous Trinity Church that stood next to the ill-fated Trade Center in New York. The architect's trademark can easily be seen in the cloistered austerity of the Anglican colleges built before the Civil War. The Library building, completed at the end of the nineteenth century, is named after Charles F. Hoffman, a major patron. As the college's Parthenon, it is naturally situated on top of the hill, Greek-fashion. Architect Venturi's more recent enhancements, especially the fanciful arabesques of its front windows, have added a contrasting postmodern touch to this classic temple of knowledge. A temple of music has sprung up at the edge of the campus in the past few years, whose walls of concrete and glass designed by Frank Gehry make it comparable with Bilbao's Guggenheim Museum. Recently I saw the completion of a state-of-the-art Science Center based on architect Rafael Vinoly's plans, with glass walls reminiscent of the giant window in Irma Brandeis' little house, which both separated me from, and drew me closer to, the forest.

To me, the day of 9 July 1989 feels like yesterday, yet it is already in a past millennium. Since my arrival here almost twenty years ago, the spectacular changes on campus have proudly reinforced its modernity. As I was beginning to "settle into" this new world, time itself seemed to moderate its fluctuations in a benevolent, accommodating complicity—that is, until 2006, a year of a landmark birthday that ought to have granted me the mark of wisdom. But this is not what happened; time suddenly grew restless, and very unwisely so. When the college decided to rebuild and extend my place of refuge in order to bring it up to date to match the standards of the new millennium along with those of the freshly minted American citizen that I had recently become, I went through a severe cardiac shock. It came as a warning that coincided with and was in sharp contrast to the beneficial changes meant to turn my improvised home into a real residency.

A convoluted personal history has accustomed me to accept the strange ways in which fate has played itself out in space and in time. The wanderer has now come to tick off the days on his sedentary calendar in a permanent, optimal dwelling place, fully aware of how ironic this late accomplishment may be, yet accepting gratefully every moment of his reprieve.

Translated from the Italian by Abitare, *October 8, 2007*

MONUMENTS OF SHAME:

TWENTY YEARS AFTER THE BERLIN WALL*

When asked to evaluate the French Revolution, a Chinese dignitary famously said: "it's too early to judge." Twenty years may be a much shorter period in history but I don't think we risk sounding presumptuous if we deem the events of 1989 the crossroads in the development of contemporary Europe.

Some historians consider the year 1989 as the de facto end of World War II; others see the events of that year as actually marking the end of the twentieth century, with our twenty-first century starting out, in fact, on September 11, 2001. If the bleak and bloody twentieth century did indeed end in 1989, a brief look back may be in order.

On August 2, 1914, Franz Kafka wrote in his *Diaries:* "Germany declared war against Russia. In the afternoon, swimming." Despite his apparent detachment from the immediate unreality of that day, the reclusive and visionary Central European writer is the man who gave the name "Kafkaesque" to his century.

World War I, the Russian Revolution, the Nazification of Germany, the Spanish Civil War, World War II, the atomic bomb, the proclamation of the State of Israel, the Cold War, India's Independence, the Chinese Revolution, the Korean and Vietnam wars, the decolonization of Africa and Asia, the Hungarian Revolution, the

*This is the text of a lecture delivered at the Centre de Cutura Contemporània de Barcelona in the spring of 2009 and at the New School for Social Research, New York, in November 2009.

Prague Spring and the Solidarity Movement, Mao's Cultural Revolution and the Cambodian genocide, the Soviet invasion of Afghanistan, and finally the fall of the Berlin Wall—a kind of Chinese wall around the penal colony of the Soviet bloc. Each of these historic dates, and all of them together, marked significant changes in the world and new phases of the modern age. But they also announced today's postmodern, centrifugal present time, where the supremacy of the computer, the speedy and depersonalized daily life, the deterioration of the environment, the globalization of exile, as well as the spread of religious, political, and even cultural terrorism have assumed an unpredictable shape and intensity.

World War II replaced the most important European power, Nazi Germany, with the communist Soviet Union. It was a war inscribed in the cruel history of humanity with its horror symbol called Holocaust, a terrible, eternal emblem and a frightening point of reference for all the other genocides that have happened or may yet happen.

If the year 1989 marked the postponed end of World War II, it obviously belatedly redefined the victors and losers of that horrendous bloody act.

I had the undesirable privilege of experiencing the traumas of that nightmare and of its East European aftermath, but I do not claim this as a reason to extol my judgment. Instead, I would prefer to consider myself as one of too many exiles floating in our contemporary world, identifiable as such in all the corners of our troubled planet.

It's not by chance, probably, that I have lived these last twenty years in New York, the Dada capital of exiles, and that age has brought me peace with my new home and homeland.

Central and Eastern Europe weren't, of course, only the places of right and left dictatorships, of provincial ethnocentrism and xenophobia, of perpetual and frozen conflicts, of explosive contradictions. They were also the birthplace of a spiritual heritage, of thinkers and artists, of a specific mode of creativity and of a persistent search for meaning, beyond pragmatic negotiations with the daily chaos of life. It's an old and vital part of our European culture, defined by some as the tense and fruitful spiritual bond and borderland between Athens and Jerusalem.

In 1989 these nations returned to the broad European civilization from the desert and storms of utopia and terror. That natural and irreplaceable part of the continent carried in its return to Europe its spiritual diversity and richness, its vivacity and mysteries, its potential as an active contributor to our common destiny.

And it brought with it its memory, of course, as well as its old and new aspirations.

My fellow exiles, who had evaded totalitarian Eastern Europe, experienced first hand the shocking transition that their homelands went through after 1989. On arriving in the West, we saw that we had missed out not only on decades of economic evolution, but also an evolution of the mind, of public debates, of a new approach to human rights and acceptance of otherness—political, religious, ethnic, sexual otherness.

We saw the truth of what Thomas Mann once said: "Freedom is more complicated than power." Moving from a closed society to an open and free one isn't an easy task. It's even more difficult when that closed society is locked within itself, which meant, in the case of real socialism, total censorship, a ban on private property, the impossibility of leaving the country or even of traveling freely outside it, the state as the only employer, a fierce owner of our social and even our private lives. From a political point of view, it seems obvious that it is easier to exercise state power over an electorate of frightened opportunists who vote 99.9 percent for the Supreme Leader and the only one party in existence than over a diverse, divergent electorate in which the winners obtain only 4 percent more votes than the losers.

Easier and simpler, but that doesn't mean that our life under the oppressive, omnipresent power of a police state was simple or easy. It only emphasizes the great difference in the choices we had to make, their frame and substance; it means another realm for individual and collective responsibility, the contrast between initiative and apathy, between enterprise and obedience, between competition and total dependency on the master state, embodying a kind of unshakable fate.

Soon after the ecstatic moment of liberation, the former socialist states of Eastern and Central Europe went through a difficult and turbulent transition, with many new tensions, economical and political, but also psychological and moral. As slavery has to be learned, step by step, if one is to survive its terror and tricks, freedom must also be learned, step by step, if one is to face up to its chances and competitions, its rewards and restrictions. The turmoil of 1989 brought hope and happiness, but it also revealed nasty secrets that destroyed families and friendships and a common sense of togetherness; it shattered our kind of social stability, however insecure or falsified it was; it enhanced resentments and a desire for revenge. Sometimes it even replaced the old hypocrisy and opportunism with new ones. The truth is that what came to be known as the "post-communist transition" shattered more than families, friendships, biographies, and even language; it also, and rightly, shattered cultural borders that had been closed for too long. A free press and an incomparably more diverse publishing industry, freed from censorship, became the new channels for information, entertainment, and debate. Books and authors banned for decades arose from the dead. Great books and mediocre books and garbage books, religious books and cookbooks and pornographic books, and forgotten masters of free thinking and of superb artistry.

I still recall the excitement of the late 1970s, when the Genius of the Carpathians, our Romanian buffoonish leader, had one of his sudden bizarre inspirations and decided that the socialist conscience of his socialist citizens had reached such a level that censorship was no longer necessary. It had to be replaced by committees of brave citizens in every institution who would check every little sentence destined to go into print. But this thaw soon proved to be a chaotic exercise in cowardice and conformity. Soon everybody started to want the restoration of the old state institution of censorship.

It happened that I was participating in a literary colloquium in Belgrade, in the early 1980s, when an official representative of the Romanian State Publishing Industry delivered a pathetic speech praising the wise and luminous initiative of banning censorship in Socialist Romania. Asked if it were possible to publish religious or pornographic books in Romania he was quick to answer that it might be possible, but that nobody in Romania wanted such books.

Today, of course, porn and smut do seem to be wanted, as a quick glance at any Bucharest kiosk will show. To move from a society based on mendacity and self-deception to one founded on money is to adjust to a different vision and a different speed of life. At that still fluid border between old and new, people craved what they didn't have before: freedom of thought and expression, prosperity, information, the right to be an individual not a sleepy part of a sleepy mass, the right to pursue happiness as they saw fit, even to look at pornography. Here was Happiness not as defined by the state and the Party but as defined by one's own will and wishes, in whatever way you dreamt of them being fulfilled.

My dream throughout my postwar life was to find an inner resistance against the ubiquitous external pressure. Living within yourself, it turned out, was for me the mode of resistance; it formed a center for the moral being, a means of separating from a corrupt and corrupting environment, a hope, however uncertain, of maintaining one's conscience with integrity. Reading and writing were a shelter, even if menaced, and the best therapy against the poisonous spread of lies and hypocrisy.

Forced to leave, once again, in 1986, as I had been more than fifty years before, when I was deported as a child to a concentration camp, I found myself leaving my place and my language—the only forms of wealth that really mattered. In 1986 my exile began in Berlin. The name of that city was a frightening word in my child-hood and yet West Berlin became my first happy shelter in the Free World, two years before that joyful November of 1989. I used to take long walks with a French writer and neighbor. Our western side of the Wall was full of funny, amusing graffiti; the eastern side of the Wall wasn't approachable, guarded by armed soldiers defending the socialist paradise. My French friend always complained about West Berlin as an artificial and closed enclave, one populated with spies and artists, and everywhere that oppressive Wall that kept us impris-oned and separated from the outside world snaking past. Even the train from East to West Germany, which passed through West Berlin, was completely locked, so that no one could escape it. But for me the Wall was a blessed protection against the poisonous environment that lay behind it—the German Democratic Republic and beyond that, the Soviet bloc of the so-called socialist countries.

The autumn of 1989 found me already in the United States of Exiles, where I happily watched the collapse of the Berlin Wall and the gradual collapse of the many other walls and iron curtains that separated the closed societies of the Eastern bloc from the open societies of the West. I also followed with great emotion the violent changes in my own country, the overthrow of the dynastic dictator-ship of our Great Clown and the rushed and improvised execution of that much-hated supreme couple.

The events of 1989 in Eastern Europe marked the demise of a decayed system, after a long agony charged by mendacity, apathy, complacency, oppression, and corruption. The big project of "com-pulsory happiness" promoted utopia as a cover-up for terror, hu-manism as a trap and a rhetorical diversion.

Germany offered the best-case scenario for a post-communist transition from that captive universe of perverted revolutionary slo-gans to democracy. The reunification of Germany, which followed fast on the disappearance of the Berlin Wall, was a crucial, though much-debated, step towards today's European Union. Unlike all the other socialist countries, East Germany benefited a great deal from the support and assistance of the prosperous and democratic West Germany in the reconstruction of its institutions, industry, and judicial system. Yet, even there the situation was far from ideal.

I returned to Berlin frequently after 1989 and discovered odd surprises each time. The reunification of the two parts of Germany didn't reunify the people on the two sides of the old Wall. The "Ossies" (the Easterners) were frustrated to discover themselves second-rate citizens in a capitalist state. They were enraged by the cynicism of what they perceived as a selfish and vulgar society, with big and painful social gaps, and with everyone obsessed with comfort and domesticity. The "Wessies" (the Westerners) saw their former brothers as a financial burden, because they were forced to pay for the professional and social training of these new and maldeveloped citizens, whom they saw as seething with prejudices and resentments, as well as being lazy and demanding. Both sides were far from the much-hoped-for brotherhood.

For a visitor with my background it was ironical to see that the Germans were experiencing a social conflict provoked not by some inferior foreign race, but by sons and daughters of their own people, with the same language and religion, with the same historical and cultural heritage, and with a long common past, for which the last forty years proved to be more than an ignorable misfortune. I took all this as yet another paradoxical and sardonic lesson of history on human nature and its dynamics.

The situation in other Eastern countries has proved to be even more complicated since the wall came down. This should not come as a surprise, yet many people were caught off guard as the new post-communist societies became breeding grounds for a revived nationalism, the return of the old slogans of Nation and Land, the obsolete pastoral ideal of a sheltered homogeneous and heroic community facing the hostility and misunderstanding of a corrupt and degenerate outside world.

A cheap and manipulated populism invaded the public discourse of the new "democratic" politicians in some of these countries, many of whom found their support by backing a new kind of cheap and profitable Bolshevik anticommunism in the game for power.

Those who fought for a democratic future, for a new solidarity among all citizens, confronted a political landscape often obsessed with revenge and resentment, with the fierce fight for social status and the spoils of power. Ethnocentricity, xenophobia, and anti-Semitism flourished. Darwinian competition for enrichment stimulated corruption, nepotism, underground and illegal schemes, and a new demagogy in the public arena.

In this chaotic burst of freedom, some of the former *nomen-klatura* activists and secret police employees became the new political parvenus and nouveau riche—well aware that the power of money was much more efficient than the unstable privileges given by the omnipotent Party.

One of the most outrageous examples of this sort of quick-change act occurred in Romania, where a former court poet of the Ceauşescu clan, a fierce nationalist and anti-Semite, Comrade Corneliu Vadim Tudor became the leader of a new extreme-right party called, no surprise, Great Romania. Barely changing his old slogans, this noisy old-new agitator was elected a member of Romania's Parliament, even becoming at one point a serious candidate for the presidency. Today, Comrade Corneliu is a member of the European Parliament. Nobody can say that the afterlife isn't interesting . . .

Soon after the fall of the Berlin Wall, public debates in Eastern Europe started to exhibit a fierce and quite astonishing confrontation between two different hidden memories, memories that were impossible to discuss openly during the communist era: the memory of the Holocaust and that of the communist terror and crimes. A rhetorical and stupid competition in suffering quickly sprang up between these two nightmares, the Holocaust and Gulag, totalitarian Nazism and totalitarian communism.

During the first turbulent years after 1989, some people looked with a kind of nostalgia to the idealized pre-communist period of their countries. The Christian orthodox countries of Eastern Europe seemed to face much greater difficulties than the Catholic or Protestant ones in adjusting to the modernity of the end of the twentieth century. But even countries that, historically, were more connected to Western civilization displayed many of the same prejudices and resentment as those situated beyond the religious border in the east of Eastern Europe.

It became obvious during this time that the contradiction between two different memories was also alive in the relationship between East and West. Both Holocaust and Gulag happened mainly in the East. After the war, the West European countries debated the Holocaust repeatedly, recognized their complicity and guilt in this horrible crime and so educated a new generation in the spirit of cordiality and responsibility. The Gulag was less of a preoccupation in public debate, not only because it didn't involve Western participation, but because it also shamed the great rhetoric of "progress," constantly manipulated by communist propaganda in the East as well as in the West. To this day, the huge crimes of the communist dictatorships, from the Soviet Union to Cambodia and China, from Romania to Albania and Afghanistan, have yet to become a central topic for discussion.

The post-communist turmoil of Eastern Europe was followed by the dismembering of the Soviet Union, the war and ethnic atrocities of Yugoslavia, the Chechnya nightmare, the Kosovo deadlock, the divorce in Czechoslovakia, Putin's authoritarian rule in Russia with its energy policy of blackmail and old imperial bullying, the stumbling Velvet Revolution in Ukraine and the conflict in Georgia, and xenophobia everywhere toward the new Gypsy scapegoat. These are only a few of the tense additions to the big central issues of immigration and terrorism which are dangers to Europe and the world.

In the face of all this, Europe cannot afford to remain an idyllic venue for spas and museums, a great historical monument of culture and art for global tourism. It cannot afford to be complacent about new totalitarian ideologies and fanaticisms, as happened in the past with Nazism and communism. Europe must defend itself courageously and lucidly against the new dangers of our time and of the future.

We must disappoint those who believe that the end of some totalitarian states meant the end of totalitarianism, or that the happy rupture of 1989 marked the beginning of perfect cooperation by the people and for the people. The great religious or secular dreams of a New Man and of a happy utopian society have been brutally compromised by bloody, extreme ideologies and totalitarian systems of governing.

Yet the consumer capitalist society has also become compromised through its vulgarity and illiteracy; its self-centered ignorance; its ever more mediocre political leaders; its political debates; its TV shows with the same rules of entertainment and mass approval as a rap diva or a skating competition. Nothing seems perceptible in this cacophony unless it's scandalous and the scandals are soon forgotten.

In 1989, at the end of World War II and its heir, the Cold War, new hopeful and utopian predictions were filling the public arena: the end of history, the end of ideologies. Many people bought into these hollow thoughts.

Soon after the start of our new century and millennium, the religious terrorists of September 11, 2001 proved, with their murderous spectacle of fanaticism, that we are still far from a serene earthly paradise beyond history and ideologies. The human story and mankind's history go on, as before, through ideas and conflicts, through new–old projects of happiness, and through cruel unhappiness and disasters in daily reality.

The blinded pilots of sacred barbarism of September 11 were fulfilling, paradoxically, the prediction that the twenty-first century would be religious or it would not be at all. But such a prophesy went only so far. It forgot to tell us what would happen if our century did, indeed, become religious. The loudest answer to this question seems to come from the new *chevaliers de la mort*, crying "God is great!" Not the God of all people, of course, only their God who is fighting all other gods and all the followers of other gods and all the godless sinners of the world as well. Paradoxically, this God becomes the supreme counter-argument against the most important commandment of all religions: thou shall not kill!

Frightened, repelled by so nightmarish an Apocalypse in the name of happiness, should we perhaps give up forever on our need for transcendence? Should we resign ourselves to the narrow pragmatism of our domestic, limited, and trivial happiness and unhappiness, to our modest, ephemeral struggle to just go on, from one day to the next? All historical periods have faced similar unsolvable questions, paying the heavy price of hope without hope.

Modernity has accelerated, more than any other human epoch, history's centrifugal dynamics. Yet, even modernity, perhaps more than the traditional past, left the individual alone, robbed of any other center than his own self. This clouded, convoluted, and pulsating SELF has proved to be insufficient and frustrating for too many people.

Does anyone seriously believe that mankind is prepared to renounce the great enterprise of crime and killing? A deep skepticism, if not bitterness and despair, seems unavoidable.

Some ten years ago I proposed something very much non-utopian, and I would like to revisit that proposal today. It was in an intervention I made in the famous Walser Debate of 1998 in Germany (see above, pp. 193–201). As some of you may recall, the esteemed German writer Martin Walser, in his acceptance speech on receiving the Peace Prize of the German Booksellers Association at the Frankfurt Book Fair warned against the "permanent represen-tation" and the "monumentalizing of German shame."

My response was to suggest that every country—and I emphasize again *every country* and *every people*—should complement its monu-ments of heroism with monuments of shame. This would mean recalling a nation's wrongdoings towards other countries, other peo-ple and also to its own people. To love our neighbors as ourselves may imply scrutinizing ourselves with the same objectivity as our neighbor; and not doing to others what we don't like to suffer our-selves. It is probably good therapy to look at ourselves with the same exigency as we look at others, to put ourselves in the shoes of others in order to understand their otherness. Aren't modesty and humility and self-questioning a desirable and sound exercise for being truly human?

But if we really want to return to a more hopeful perspective, we need to return to the individual, the frail, sinful, and heroic con-queror of nature and sometimes of his own nature, to his rich and resourceful imperfection, to his struggle to be more than he suc-ceeded to be, to find a meaning in his often meaningless environ-ment, to be a creator who adds to what is already spread around him.

Despite the great scientific and technical achievements of mo-dernity, despite prosperity and the visible improvement in human rights, the loneliness and estrangement of the individual has not disappeared. Indeed, the opposite is true. The multi-colored and noisy void around us has not made life more meaningful. The mod-ern world is a centrifugal world, and few people can live without a center, whatever that center may be. The lonely wanderer encom-passes all of us, he remains our lonely, fraternal companion, torn between solitude and solidarity, a lucid, compassionate, indepen-dent, and selfless fellow who deserves our confidence. A lot of peo-ple have today a kind of mystical belief in *identity*—as a magical potion for curing any illness. *Identity* is what connects us to others: gender, language, wealth, habits, convictions, and aspirations, even physical or psychological features. *Identity* has, undoubtedly, its place and its importance in social and private life. But the core of humanness is, in the end, the individual *entity*: what remains when we are alone in an empty room before or after we connect to a collective identity. Without such a lucid, soulful, conscientious *entity, identity* remains an empty association of empty terms.

Montaigne says in a kind of avalanche of aphorisms: "A wise man never loses anything, if he has himself. Every man bears the whole stamp of the human condition. We must reserve a back shop all our own, entirely free, in which to establish our real liberty and our principal retreat and solitude." And he never forgets to warn us: "Even on the most exalted throne in the world we are only sitting on our own ass." Something we should not forget when we stand up, ready to meet our peers.

The Silence of the Eastern Bloc

In the sound and fury unleashed worldwide by the Rushdie affair, we might take note of a significant silence from the Socialist East. I do not refer only to the authorities' "tactical" silence, to those always in search of advantage in the game of power, I refer also to the silence of the organized groups of artists, writers, and intellectuals, and, above all, to the absent voices of individuals, for whom it is impossible to speak out.

I am saddened but not surprised by this silence. I know the complexities of the process of regeneration and social normalization now under way there and I know, too, the attitudes that not only writers but ordinary citizens have to an event with so many implications for their own historical predicament.

I myself still remember vividly the agitation and dark premonitions I felt when Khrushchev stipulated that Pasternak could travel to Stockholm for his Nobel Prize only if he did not return, or when Brezhnev exiled Solzhenitsyn. At such moments, one feels acutely the danger to one's position as a citizen and, more simply, as a human being. I have endured more than once, in my turbulent past, the violent impact of this kind of danger: as a child in a Nazi concentration camp, as an adolescent in the Stalinist regime of postwar Romania, as a writer in the bankrupt, ambiguous socialism of recent decades.

The burning of *The Satanic Verses* in public squares reminds us of those who, when they heard the word culture, put their hands on their guns. Yet, however fragile books may be, they nonetheless endure and are reprinted, and the important ones have their posterity assured; the life of a man, however, is unrecoverable. The death of Salman Rushdie has not just been publicly demanded (and we know of enough authors who have been killed in secret, because of their books or political convictions) but is to be rewarded by a huge sum of money, in the style of the tempting bounties once placed on the heads of notorious malefactors.

The Rushdie case is, thus, entirely different from that of Pasternak or Solzhenitsyn. Even in the worst crimes of Stalinism, in the demonic assassination of so many artists and thinkers (always performed in the dark and camouflaged by the authorities) there was generally a certain prudence exhibited, a hint of embarrassment displayed; in short, a fear of publicity. The order to assassinate Rushdie was public, repeated, relentless, addressed to thousands of potential avengers, and, despite its obvious political motivation, it was decreed in the name of religion.

The threat against the life of Salman Rushdie, proclaimed openly, unequivocally, awakens memories of Nazi rites but it is also reminiscent of Stalinist justice; the accusation cannot be scrutinized, the faithful millions called on to repudiate the book are also forbidden to read it. As under Nazism or Stalinism, what is asked of the followers is blind obedience to a decision taken by the leaders on their behalf.

We need not necessarily admire *The Satanic Verses* or subscribe to its author's polemic in order to support his right to create and to express his opinion. (This statement may sound pedestrian to Western readers; in great parts of the socialist East, however, readers and writers are still longing for this simple, banal reality.) This is imperative, especially for those who have not been seduced by the novelist's art, or who reject his ideas. To side with Salman Rushdie *despite* the feeling of irritation that his work may have aroused in us is an elementary obligation, just as it is an elementary obligation not to escape into puerile comparisons or frivolous relativism when a life is at stake.

The Nazi crimes were a precise execution of Nazi ideology, which openly professed hatred and murder. The Stalinist crimes, we are told today, were actually in contradiction to Marxist ideology, which claims humanistic values at its roots. (Marx: "Man is the most precious capital.") If Salman Rushdie's book has truly offended the sensitivities of the Muslim faithful, is it then necessary to burn the book and to kill the author? Is such a decision in accordance with the deep beliefs of the Islamic religion or is it, in fact, an aberration, a desecration of the Muslim faith? Is this the decision of a dictator who is courageously executing the inherent, irreducible tenets of his faith, or of a dictator who is criminally subverting his own ideology?

The answer to these questions shouldn't be proposed, I think, by Christians, Jews, or atheists; they must come from Muslims themselves, from Egyptians, Pakistanis, Turks, Moroccans, Yemenites, Palestinians, Jordanians, Iraqis, Yugoslavian and Soviet Muslims. In answering, Islam will unveil itself to the world. That answer has become important not only for Muslims but for the sake of international peace.

In recent weeks, not a few people have found the strength and common sense to repeat, even for those who do not want to hear, that: a work of fiction is to be judged by its spiritual and literary values, no matter how irritating or enraging it may be, whereas a society—as well as a secular ideology or a religion—is to be judged by the manner in which it tolerates the challenge of a work of fiction.

In the silence that comes from the socialist East, I think I also discern this message.

The Cuban Shipwreck

Reading the García Márquez article, datelined "Havana," in the *New York Times* a few days ago, I took away a more vivid image of the tragedy that has overtaken Elian Gonzalez than I had previously culled from the American papers. With the powerful storytelling talent that distinguishes all his work, Márquez conveys to the reader, in less than one of four newspaper columns, the biography of the troubled marriage of an amiable Cuban couple and of their amiable divorce, and also reveals in the deliberate misapplication of a single word in his final paragraph—the word "shipwreck"—his own distinctive ideological slant on the constitutional realities of American life.

In the article, we find out about Elizabeth Brotons, "an amiable and hard-working chief housekeeper at a hotel," who fell in love at 14 with Juan Miguel Gonzalez, whom she married at 18, and from whom she separated finally on "the most amicable terms." Everything, according to Márquez, seemed to have been as perfectly amiable in the aftermath of the couple's divorce as it had been during their marriage—until, that is, the mother, without the father's knowledge or permission, decided to take their son out of Cuba.

As Márquez writes, "An infallible formula for being well-received as an immigrant in the United States is to be shipwrecked in her territorial waters." So Elian's 28-year-old mother, who wishes to defect to America with her son, starts to prepare just such a shipwreck. And so here begins Elian's tragedy—not on American soil but *on the Cuban shore.* Foolishly, Elian's mother undertook the illegal voyage on an illegal boat—no other means of escape was available to her—in order to bid goodbye forever to amiable Cuba. She is helped by the leader of this risky adventure, her lover—according to Márquez, not at all amiable, but in fact a neighborhood "tough"—Lazaro Munero, who takes fourteen people in his improvised aluminum boat, including his younger brother, his aged father, a convalescing mother, as well as his partner's entire family. The trip was plagued with mechanical mishaps from the start, and ended abruptly in "an inferno of panic" at sea, when the boat capsized after the failing motor was thrown overboard by the captain. Among those who drowned was Elian's mother.

Had the adventure succeeded without incident, mother and son would, of course, have settled in Miami, and Elian would no longer have lived more or less between two divorced parents as he did in Cuba but would have remained solely in the mother's household on American soil. For Elian and his mother, this would have constituted a solution to their Cuban problem—surely a drastic problem, in the mother's estimation, if it required the drastic solution of this dangerous journey by sea. But instead, remarkably, Elian survived and was received in Miami by eager relatives, who had themselves found an American solution to their own Cuban problem some decades earlier.

From the start, American public opinion was heavily in favor of the boy being returned promptly to his father, who appeared to love him, who immediately claimed him, and who, without hesitation, asked for his return. After considering the family situation in Cuba, the American legal authorities swiftly decided in favor of Elian's father's claim and against the claim being made by Elian's Cuban relatives in Florida. The Florida relatives, as was their right, then utilized whatever legitimate legal channels were available to challenge the judgment of the authorities and to seek to have that judgment overthrown. Their stubbornness was fortified both by their ferocious hatred of the Cuban communist system and by their exuberant exploitation of rights as free citizens in a free country. Despite their legal efforts, however, and despite the pressure from right-wing American politicians in Washington—and also despite the cliché-ridden, noisy demonstrations (complete with schoolchildren making canned speeches) *against* America staged by the Cuban government throughout Cuba—the American judicial system, coolly, common-sensically, in accordance with the law, without an explosion of vile propaganda or stupid political rhetoric, continued to confirm its initial decision to return the boy to Cuba. All of these details are missing from the painstakingly detailed account of Elian's tragedy as narrated by García Márquez.

Márquez concludes his account by saying, "the real shipwreck of Elian did not take place on the high seas but when he set foot on American soil." Is this really so? Is this a proper conclusion to draw from the story Márquez himself tells? Of course it isn't. Didn't the shipwreck—to accept Márquez' metaphorical touch—begin on Cuban soil when his mother decided to leave her country and was without the legal means to do so? Didn't the shipwreck begin when, in lieu of any other, she accepted the risks for herself and her child of this crazily hazardous solution? Didn't the shipwreck begin in her persistence, in her desperation, in her determination to reach the other shore with her child for whatever reason, good or bad?

And isn't this shipwreck part of a larger shipwreck, the shipwreck of communist Cuban society? Isn't it because of the larger ship-wreck—one known to the entire world—that the Cubans in Miami who are now so enraged wound up in Miami in the first place, and that the Cubans who continue to flee Cuba wind up coming to the United States to live? And in the fanatical zeal of Miami's Cuban community to keep Elian in America, militant, misguided, narrow, propagandistic, and politically driven though that zeal may be, isn't this community responding to the equally militant, misguided, nar-row, propagandistic, and politically driven zeal that has, for decades now, marked the undemocratic, one-party, one-man, rule of the island across from Florida?

Whatever the ending may be of this sad and convoluted story "on American soil," it will not be a "shipwreck" in any sense of that word. It will end on American soil as it began with Elian's arrival on American soil: as a case for the courts. The conflict will be resolved through the orderly workings of the judicial system of a free country, which, as Márquez fails to note in his thorough documentation of the Gonzalez case, Cuba is not.

New York, March 31, 2000

A Lasting Poison

Next year [2009] will mark the twentieth anniversary of the collapse of communism in Europe. Liberated from the complexity of knowing too much about the cruel past, the young people of Eastern Europe's post-communist generation seem uninterested in what their parents and grandparents endured.

Yet the recent revelation of the Czech writer Milan Kundera's presumed complicity in the face of Stalinism is but the latest of the long half-life of a toxic past. Other examples come to mind: the accusations of collaboration with the secret police raised against Lech Wałesa, Romania's public controversies surrounding Mircea Eliade's fascist past, and the attacks on the alleged "Jewish monopoly of suffering" which equate the Holocaust with the Soviet Gulag.

Friedrich Nietzsche said that if you look in the eye of the Devil for too long, you risk becoming a devil yourself. A Bolshevik anti-communism, similar in its dogmatism to communism itself, has from time to time run riot in parts of Eastern Europe. In country after country, that Manichean mindset, with its oversimplifications and manipulations, was merely refashioned to serve the new people in power.

Opportunism has had its share in this, of course. In 1945, when the Red Army occupied Romania, the Communist Party had no more than 1,000 members; in 1989, it had almost four million. One day after Nicolae Ceaușescu's execution, most of these people suddenly became fierce anti-communists and victims of the system they had served for decades. Residual traces of totalitarian thinking can also be found in the hostility to former dissidents such as Adam Michnik or Václav Havel, both of whom argued that the new democracies should not exploit resentments or seek revenge, as the totalitarian state did, but instead build a new national consensus to structure and empower a genuine civil society. Former generals of the secret police and members of the communist *nomenklatura*, untouchable in their comfortable villas and retirement, must derive great pleasure from watching today's witch hunts and manipulation of old files for immediate political purposes.

But the case of Kundera appears different—though no less disturbing. In 1950, Kundera, then a 20-year-old communist, reportedly denounced to the criminal police as a Western spy a man he had never met—a friend of his friend's girlfriend. The man was later brutally interrogated in a former Gestapo torture facility and spent fourteen years in prison. Kundera's name was contained in the investigating officer's report, which was authenticated after a respected historian discovered it in a dusty Prague archive.

The reclusive Kundera, who immigrated to Paris in 1975, has declared that "it never happened." Moreover, Czechoslovakia's fearsome secret police, who had every interest in silencing or compromising the famous dissident writer, never used the incident to blackmail or expose him. Until more information is forthcoming, both from Kundera and from the authorities, the case will not be solved "beyond reasonable doubt." But *if that happens*, the case will call for deeper reflection.

As far as we know, Kundera never was an informer, either before or after this incident, and we cannot ignore the fact that he later freed himself from the compulsory totalitarian happiness that communism propagated. Indeed, his case also serves as a reminder that the early 1950s was the most brutal period of "proletarian dictatorship" in Eastern Europe—a period of great enthusiasm and terrible fear that poisoned the minds and souls of devoted believers, fierce opponents, and apathetic bystanders alike. Moreover, Kundera's case is hardly unique. In 2006, the Nobel-Prize-winning German author Günter Grass disclosed that, sixty years earlier, he was, as a teenager, a member of the Waffen-SS. Similarly, a few years ago, the world was shocked to learn that the famous Italian writer Ignazio Silone had, in his youth, collaborated with the fascist police. Daily life under totalitarianism, be it communist or fascist, was routinely based on a deep duplicity the effects of which are longstanding.

I don't agree with those who say we should not be interested in the dark episodes in the life of a great writer. Why not? We should be interested not for prosecutorial purposes, but in order to gain a more profound understanding of a bloody, demagogical, and tyrannical utopia—and of human weakness and vulnerability. We may even consider it a rewarding testament to an artist's ability to overcome his past mistakes and still produce priceless work. But can we justifiably defend morally compromised artists and intellectuals on the basis of their work's merit, yet condemn ordinary people for often less grave offenses? An egregious example of this was the way followers of Romanian philosopher Constantin Noica defended his support for the fascist Iron Guard and his later collaboration with the communists, while at the same time condemning even a generic cleaning woman for mopping the floors in the offices of the secret police. Shouldn't that cleaner's drudgery to support her family, children, and her own survival be taken equally into account?

Life under totalitarianism was an extreme situation that requires us to apply special, nuanced rules to *all* the captives of that ordeal. To understand that epoch, we have to know and judge carefully often ambiguous and overwhelming circumstances, never simplifying a multilayered daily reality for the sake of current political goals. If nothing else, in order to forgive, we have to know what we are forgiving.

Crime and Punishment, Refugee Style

The horrible murder of Giovanna Reggiani that took place near a Romanian refugee camp in the suburb of Tor di Quinto in Rome shocked both Italy and Romania. The case gained significance by adding fuel to the fiery public debates now under way not only in Italy but across Europe on the status of refugees and foreign residents.

Some Italians responded violently; some Italian and Romanian politicians, eager to offer quick and tough solutions, made scandalous statements that echoed the xenophobic and totalitarian slogans of the past. We are encountering, not without irony, a grotesque reverse of the "national pride" seen when cultural and sporting stars are appropriated by the state and presented as part of the collective patrimony.

The murder was an individual crime and to compound the tragedy of a crime through measures that target an entire minority is irresponsible and will have grave moral and social consequences both for the unjustly punished and for the punishers. No minority is, after all, homogeneous, as was demonstrated by the fact that the person who alerted the police was a compatriot of the killer and from the same camp of refugees. Collective punishment also means a type of amnesia by Italians and Romanians, not only about what happened under Fascism, Nazism, and communism, but also about their own national histories. Italians, after all, migrated not only from Italy's south to its north, but to other countries looking for a better life. They, too, know what it is like to be a refugee, an exile, a stranger.

Romania, for its part, has a history not at all admirable in regard to its "Roma" minority, whose shortcomings and deeds always attract blame but never any real action by the state to improve their condition. The Roma minority first appeared in Romania in the fourteenth century, but only in 1856 was its slavery abolished!

Nowadays, Romanian society is dealing with the consequences of decades of terror and lies, of demagogy and poverty that have scarred several generations. These wounds cannot be instantly healed. Communism's fall unleashed a huge surge of human energy, but this started with a bizarre and cynical transfer of privileges and assets within the old *"nomenklatura,"* and with a new general Darwinian struggle.

Although economic progress is visible across Romania, and a gradual renewal of a civil conscience with the arrival of democracy has appeared, Romania's burlesque of a political life—despite its European Union membership—shows how persistent its bad old habits of duplicity, inconsistency, fatalism, inertia, and corruption are. Corruption, indeed, now seems to be the society's engine. There remain in Romania today disadvantaged and neglected groups who are pushed to society's sordid margins. In fact, of the Roma population 41 percent are seasonal workers, 33.5 percent lack any professional skills, and 38.7 percent are illiterate. This is a Romanian problem, but it has also become a problem for all of Europe.

Nicolae Romulus Mailat, the young man of 25 accused of Giovanna Reggiani's murder, had been interned at age 14 in a school for re-education. He was later condemned for theft, but was pardoned a year before arriving in Italy.

Was poverty the cause of his juvenile offenses in Romania and his crime in Italy? In Dostoyevsky's great novel *Crime and Punishment*, Raskolnikov is pushed to commit his crime by his nihilism and rebelliousness, but also by poverty. His social identity is not the same as Mailat's, his spiritual "entity" is drastically different, but his double crime is no less abominable.

For now, there is no reason to hope that Mailat will find through his crime a new start towards salvation through suffering and spiritual renewal. But perhaps we should listen again to the words of one of Raskolnikov's interlocutors when he speaks about the "disgusting Sodom" in which he wanders and says that poverty is not a vice, but misery. In poverty one still has a kind of "innate noble sentiment," while in misery moral collapse is inherent and disastrous.

Maillat sought escape from his Romanian misery and his Romanian past, but could not imagine that he would find in an Italian refugee camp as much misery as before; that the image in his mirror of his daily new life would be that of a killer. People who know the frightening neighborhood of Tor di Quinto, where Giovanna Reggiani was killed have harsh words to say about the neglect and indifference of Rome's city government. This isn't, of course, an excuse for this or any other crime, but it cannot be ignored.

Although we cannot expect a miraculous reincarnation of the criminal Mailat, we can and must ask for a radical review of the situation faced by such marginalized people. That review must be carried out by Romanian and Italian states, by the Roma community in Romania and Italy, and also by the European Community itself. For the perpetrator is a member of all these communities.

We hear voices now that are exasperated by the EU's enlargement and the social tensions it has provoked. Increased migration is, indeed, a daily fact in our centrifugal and global modernity, but it isn't only a negative one. The free movement of people doesn't only mean more social conflict and criminality. It also means a gradual and beneficial cohabitation that began immediately after World War II as a common effort to help out the defeated countries and enhance their chances for democracy and prosperity.

When I visited Barcelona and Madrid last year, I was delighted to receive enthusiastic news about the successes of the growing Romanian community in these cities. Some Romanian refugees were already candidates for the local elections, praised for their hard work and honesty. It will happen, I hope, in other places too and not only with Romanians but with all the people ready to face the provocations of our time. For these are not only examples of individual success, but also victories for the community as well.

Europe deserves to prove that it is a real community, one that is diverse, democratic, spiritual, free, and prosperous.

Revolutionary Shadows

What happens after the euphoria of revolution fades? Today's Eastern Europe, some two decades after the revolutions of 1989, may offer a salutary warning for today's defiant and jubilant Arab youth that they must remain vigilant.

Ever since I left Romania for exile in 1986, my returns have been rare and tense. Although the schedule for my most recent trip was overwhelming, and offered little real contact with ordinary people, I could still grasp—from daily newspapers, TV programs, and conversations with friends—the profound economic, political, and moral crisis engulfing the country. Mistrust and anger at a corrupt and inefficient political class, coupled with skepticism about democracy —even nostalgia for communism—is to be found nowadays, not only in Romania but also in some other parts of Eastern Europe.

Some 70 percent of Romanians reportedly now claim to regret the death of Comrade Nicolae Ceauşescu, whose summary execution in 1989 elicited general enthusiasm. Of course, the source of such an astonishing finding is difficult to trust, like everything else in Romanian politics, but the vulgar and radical coarsening of public discourse—now peppered with old-new xenophobic elements— is clear enough.

I was offered a taste of this as a guest on a well-respected TV cultural program. I was amused that the debate focused not on my books, but on issues such as the "Jewish cultural mafia" and the "exaggerated" anti-Semitism of past and present Romania. My interviewer was kinetic, taking over the dialogue with insinuations and personal interventions. I assumed that I was supposed to be provoked into unguarded comments, a method that fashionable TV journalists everywhere use nowadays. But I faced a new surprise the following week, when, on the same TV program, the hostess was rather passive toward her guest, a militant journalist turned mercenary journalist, as he confessed his admiration for Corneliu Zelea Codreanu, the "Captain" of the Iron Guard. The journalist considered Codreanu a "Romantic hero."

A group of Romanian intellectuals, including me, protested in an Open Letter against this effort to rehabilitate a murderer and propagandist of hate and xenophobia. Romanian TV answered promptly that it understood that victims of anti-Semitic crimes might feel hurt by such a program, but that the program had not promoted this kind of propaganda, offering the bizarre interview with me the previous week as proof of the channel's good faith.

The debate didn't end there. Soon after, the national committee for the media condemned the program. And soon after that, some leading intellectuals condemned the national committee's condemnation as an affront to freedom of speech. No one mentioned the danger of inciting an already radicalized audience. In fact, the responses from members of the public to these controversies were mostly of a vulgar nationalistic and anti-Semitic tone.

Romania is not alone, of course, in reliving this dark comedy. Revitalization of the extreme right in Hungary and the rise of "National Bolshevism" in Russia, where Tolstoy is now re-condemned by the Orthodox Church as a proto-communist, suggest a deeper and more pervasive atavistic longing.

I was reminded of my last class at Bard College before my trip to Romania. We were discussing Thomas Mann's *Death in Venice*. Commenting on the moment when "Asiatic cholera" kills the great and troubled writer Gustav von Aschenbach, a brilliant Asian student pointed out that Mann related the disease to the "pestilence" of the Ganges delta, which traverses China and Afghanistan, Persia and Astrakhan, and "even Moscow," before reaching Europe through the "city of the lagoon." She noted with gravity today's migrations from poor to prosperous countries, the globalization of evil, the contradictions and conflicts of modernity, the angry terrorist response to it, and the contrast between a rational, pragmatic West and a more idealistic and superstitious East, prone to religious fanaticism and political extremism.

It was a relief to listen to my student's well-articulated opinions and to see in her the hope of a new, cosmopolitan generation. But her example was also an unavoidable reminder of the great dangers of our time.

I needed that hope, for what I saw in Eastern Europe had depressed me as much as what I was seeing in the United States, my adopted homeland. For someone who has lived through two totalitarian systems, it is almost unbearable to contemplate America's decline. Although we refugees, immigrants, exiles, and outcasts do not boast ad infinitum that "we are the best," as many Americans do, we still believe that the US remains a powerful guarantor of freedom and democracy, and we consider its incoherence part of its liberty.

For far different reasons, the US, and the entire world, seems condemned to simplification of thought, action, and feeling in the service of immediate, quotidian efficiency. Of course, art and culture can offer a respite from the oversimplifications of our age—a respite that we need more than ever if we are to reckon with the destiny behind and before us. But we also need modesty about ourselves and our societies.

Against Simplification

It is said that Americans have a genius for simplification. Gradually, however, the quest for it has become a global trend, one that continues to conquer new territories, just as blue jeans once did. The speed of our daily life is visibly increased—and not for the better—by this unstoppable evolution. The tyranny of pragmatism seems to mark all of the complex dilemmas of our time. Too many valid choices are either ignored or skirted through the routine of short cuts.

Nowhere is this trend more damaging than in today's mercantile approach to art. Even the much-praised notion of competition seems fake and cynically manipulated by the "corporate" mentality that now pervades the world of culture—by the financial pre-selection that determines what publishers, producers, and other impresarios will support. Just imagine what might have happened to the works of, say, Proust, Kafka, Musil, Faulkner, or Borges had they been subjected to mass-market competition like shoes or cosmetics.

Culture is a necessary pause from the daily rat race, from our chaotic and often vulgar political surroundings, and it is a chance to recover our spiritual energy. Great books, music, and paintings are not only an extraordinary school of beauty, truth, and good, but also a way of discovering our own beauty, truth, and good—the potential for change, for bettering ourselves and even some of our interlocutors. If this respite and refuge is gradually narrowed and invaded by the same kind of "products" as those that dominate the mass market, we are condemned to be perpetual captives of the same stunted universe of "practicalities," the ordinary agglomeration of clichés packaged in advertisements.

I was thinking again about these old and seemingly unsolvable questions during my rereading of a quite challenging novel by a close friend and a great writer, not very present in the vivid landscape of American letters of today. The theme, style, and echo of his work says a lot, I think, about our simplified world.

The novel is *Blinding*, by Claudio Magris. Hailed in Europe as one of the great novels of the twentieth century, *Blinding* arrived in America after a great delay, and never received the attention it deserved. Unfortunately, that is no surprise. The number of literary translations undertaken nowadays in the United States is, according to a United Nations report, equal to that of Greece, a country one-tenth the size. Imported books are thought to be too "complicated," which is another way of saying that literature should deal with simple issues in a simple way, obeying the rules of the mass market, with its tricks of packaging, accessibility, advertisement, and comfort.

At the core of Magris' book is the destiny of a group of Italian communists who travel to Yugoslavia after World War II to contribute to the construction of a socialist society, only to be caught in the conflict between Stalin and Tito. They are imprisoned for their Stalinist allegiance; when they are finally allowed to return to Italy, their old comrades refuse to accept them.

The book's plot spans two centuries of revolution. Then, suddenly, "the party vanished, overnight, as if all of a sudden a giant sponge had drained the entire sea, Adriatic and Austral, leaving litter and clots of mud, and all the boats stranded. How can you go home again if the sea has been sucked down a vast drain that opened up beneath it, emptying it who knows where, into a void? The earth is arid and dead, but there won't be another one, nor another heaven."

The solitude of the individual facing his faith alone, without collective illusions, and forced to do something with himself in the arid, noisy world tells us something important about the exiled world of modernity and its complex and contradictory problems.

Magris' novel is not only an important literary achievement; it also has a deep connection to the dangers that we face now, particularly the wave of fanaticism, from Mumbai to Oslo, in the name of a holy war against the "other." Are all the extremists searching for a new coherence, for a lost illusion of togetherness and a new hope of resurrection?

Can we ever forget September 11, 2001, the start of a bloody century in which the mystical force of hatred and destruction has recovered its strength? Are Osama Bin Laden's minions, the bloody Hamas-Hezbollah battalions, or troubled loners like Timothy McVeigh, Theodore Kaczysnki, and Anders Behring Breivik, the "heroes" of our contemporary nightmare? Is this the "rebel" response to an overly globalized, incoherent, and ultimately disturbing reality?

If so, their barbarism demands scrutiny—in relation to both historical precedent and to our modernity—rather than merely being labeled "monstrous" (though it certainly is that). The new religious militants, fighting in the name of their particular and peculiar God, seem as fanaticized as the Fascists, Nazis, and communists of earlier decades.

Magris' main character is a rebel in more than one embodiment: as Salvatore Cipico, one of the inmates in the communist concentration camp in Yugoslavia; as Jurgen Jurgensen, ephemeral king of Iceland and a convict forced to build his own jail; and as Jason, the mythic adventurer searching for the volatile truth.

A multilayered and complex chronicle of the devastating tragedies of the twentieth century, *Blinding* is an insistent, informed, and irreplaceable incursion into the moving landscape of the human soul, its wounds and voids, its vitality and versatility, its deep distortions and its unpredictable dynamics. It is a fascinating story about the conflict between ideals and reality, or utopia and humanness; about being faithful to a cause and betraying it; and about sacrifice and solidarity. It is also a rich and original literary achievement that challenges today's consumerist ethic. By renouncing simplicity, it repudiates today's prevailing confusion of information with literature, of facts with creativity, and bestselling products with true works of art.

Another Genealogy

It seems that the notion of "identity"—with its many meanings and connotations—has evolved rapidly in our current environment into a slogan that, not only in public and political life but also in private, is used and abused as a miraculous key to solve any and all the difficulties of daily toil. Have you discovered your identity? Then you're a forceful owner of a flag, a poster, if not an anthem too, with an invincible card of membership, obviously equipped to confront the far too many barriers in the competition for happiness, prosperity, self-esteem or many, again too many, other issues of the dreamlike project of achievements.

In fact, identity is too profound a topic to be transformed into a simple pretext for slogans, however justified they may be. It deserves a scrutiny of our history and the history of "others" in the realm of the national and international past and present. The much-dreamt-of "melting pot" of global, modern society is often confronted by an obsessive, nostalgic need for tribal togetherness, where communal memories and impulses gain a combative, sometimes vehement, nature. What we should never forget is that the "other" isn't evil because he might be from another party or race or faith; evil is the "man in uniform", among the others and among ourselves, the fierce believer in unanimity, homogeneity, uniformity and uniform obedience.

The most recent example of the unsolvable conflict between "politicians in uniform" in a free, democratic country was, unfortunately, the deplorable show in the American Congress about the late 2000s financial default.

It seems the right moment to remember how the American writer Gertrude Stein referred to the difference between *identity* and *entity*. She saw identity as connecting us to a certain social group. This means by gender, ethnicity, race, language, sexual orientation—as well as perhaps by some specific physical or psychological features, trivial preferences, etc. In a more frivolous way, the social group with whom we identify can even be the fat and/or myopic people, baseball lovers, handicapped people, stamp collectors, followers of a certain diet, etc.

By contrast, entity is what is left when we are alone. Even in such a solitary situation the connection to other people isn't totally annulled, of course; it only becomes implicit rather than explicit.

In any case, with both identity and entity, the particular premise or the main imprint of our biography (family, religion, persecution, victimhood, professional distinction, etc.) plays an important role. For we are not only the product of a family, religion, country, community, school, profession, etc. Are we not, in the end, the result of our readings, the product of our bibliography as well as our biography? I don't necessarily mean political-ideological books such as the Little Red Book of Mao or the green one by Gaddafi or Bin Laden's terrorist commandments or even Hitler's *Mein Kampf*—although they undeniably have their readers and even followers. Rather I have in mind books rightly considered the canon of our Western culture, from the Bible to Aristotle, from Cervantes to Darwin, from Einstein to Shakespeare, from Spinoza to Whitman. It's an artificial but important genealogy that competes as well as cooperates with the natural one in structuring our personality, in shaping our options, our beliefs and projects. It expresses our need for something beyond our too-human limitations, our family, religion, territorial, linguistical narrowness, something that exposes us to the vast uncertainties and togetherness of the world.

It's odd to speak about such "esoteric" questions in a time of increased mass-media dominance, and instant communication through Facebook, mobile phones, Twitter, etc., with its cheap oversimplifications, replacement of readers with TV fans, of the word with the image, of increasing illiteracy and lowering of standards of education among young people. But just because of such an acute and worsening situation it may be worth reminding people that the consequences of a too "pragmatic", simplified, and speedy approach to life may have significant consequences in the choices people make for their own lives and for the lives of their communities, what principles they respect, what kind of representatives they select, what type of coexistence they wish to have with their close neighbours and with far-away neighbours on our endangered planet.

Books and art and culture provide a necessary and instructive break from our daily rush, from the tyranny of excessively trivial details in the daily odyssey we embody. Books often play a second, intimate yet essential role in our being. Our "bookish genealogy" might sometimes be even more important than the one found in the archives of heredity. In the adventure through the printed page we may find relatives who are closer and who go even further back than those in the family lineage, however extensive it may be. The appealing companions we discover in the library shelves in fact form another kind of world population. As interlocutors, models, advisors, friends, challengers, these fictitious individuals tell us about the mind and soul of the planet's real population, things that are more important than the daily news and scandals. They are for some of us the real formative and trustworthy comrades with whom we share the hopes and disappointments of our spiritual selves, of our "thinking" biography, with its solitude and inner landscapes and intensity.

Phylon of Alexandria dared to say that the Word (*Logos*) was the very first image of Divinity, the first representation of God, that the intellect conveys, in fact, His and man's real image. He argued that the *spiritual* connection is the real human factor of cohesion, not the genetic or ritualistic one. The intellectual nature of *Logos* means, Phylon said, the spiritual affinity amongst us, and it represents "the image of the divine."

In the difficult years of Eastern Europe's socialist dictatorship, under the ubiquitous eye of the censor and of police informers, my generation persisted in a dangerous hunt for banned and "illegal" books; despite the great risk, it fueled our survival, our fight for freedom, our hopes and our revival. Not only Solzhenitsyn's *Archipelago* but books of "decadent" poetry and prose, prison diaries, the UN

Declaration of Human Rights, the American and French Constitution, books on the Inquisition and religious reformers and martyrs, books by Erasmus and St Augustine, books by Raymond Aron and Koestler, Nadezhda Mandelstam and Pasternak and Nietsche and many others.

When I returned, after the war, from the concentration camps, I read whatever I could lay my hands on. In my student years in Bucharest I took advantage of the great public libraries to discover the banned Romanian modern literature, and in the following years, during the so-called "liberalization" period, I finally had access to Proust and Kafka, Joyce and Babel, Sabato and Virginia Woolf.

When I eventually put my own library together, I had to leave the country, due to the hysterical evolution of our harsh political system. Expelled again, at fifty, as I had been at five, this time by another dictator and another ideology, I gradually came to consider it a great honor, not a repeated misfortune.

In the first tough years of displacement and dispossession that accompanied my forced exile, I tried to regain, step by step, the familiar companionship of my author-friends, still alive on the library shelves, even if dressed now in other languages. I recalled again, as I did in many other difficult moments, that during the terrible blockade of Leningrad in World War II when its citizens were dying of hunger and cold, the survivors were stubborn readers of Tolstoy and Dostoyevsky, who had been provided with spiritual food and warmth of another sort.

Old and new books formed again, in my intense effort of adjustment, a protective "lair" where I could hide from the unknown, from outside chaos, so different in its shape and dynamics from that in my previous life.

The word is replaced more and more today by image; literacy is diminishing although printed matter can be accessed rapidly and multiplied, with no risk, and the huge amount of the human mind's achievement is available instantly to anybody who is interested. The speedy and practical approach to life make the intellectual endeavor appear less "divine" than before; also less appealing and praiseworthy.

Yet, it's always worth reminding ourselves of its potential and of its glorious past.

September 2011

Rich People of the World, Unite!

"A specter is haunting Europe"—this isn't a warning from the latest issue of the *New York Times* or any other important newspaper of the world, although it might have been in view of the current financial and political crisis.

It is, in fact, the very first sentence in *The Communist Manifesto* by Karl Marx and Friedrich Engels, published in 1872.

The specter that was haunting Europe at the time was communism. What followed, in the new century, confirmed that the specter was more than specter. In 1917, the Russian Revolution installed the "proletarian dictatorship" and started the great project of building a communist society, freed from the cruel "exploitation of man by man." At the end of World War II the East European countries occupied by the Red Army were also pushed into the communist paradise, soon to be joined by China, revitalized by her own Revolution and those of other Asian countries. In 1989, the entire system crumbled from within on account of economic failure, the too-strong connection between utopia and terror, and the decay of a closed, rigid society, corrupt and demagogical. It became obvious to everybody that exploitation of man by man isn't worse than exploitation of man by the state, that only freedom and free competition can provide social progress.

The inflamed appeal, "Proletarians of the world, unite!" which concludes the famous *Manifesto* proved at the end of the twentieth century to be an empty slogan, only good for parades and party meetings.

Today, the specter that is haunting Europe, and not only Europe, is no longer the ghostly communist danger, but the last and harsh crisis of capitalism, the global capitalism of the global modern society. Together with the ever active and ubiquitous specter of terrorism, the monetary crisis is at the center of everyone's anxiety.

Indeed, the difference between rich and poor, between the richest rich and the poorest poor is growing scandalously by the day, as is the difference between developed and underdeveloped countries. The promise of a more harmonious society seems outdated, and the political rhetoric is offering clichés rather than solutions. The entire world sometimes seems ungovernable. Although the rebellious impulse isn't yet in an explosive phase, the underlying resentment is bubbling up on numerous private Facebook pages, tweets, and cell phones, sharing angry and confused messages to nowhere.

The prediction by Marx that the concentration of capital will, in the end, weaken the state has proved to be true, even if the cure for it is not found in his revolutionary ideal and instructions. Financial crisis is shaking the stability of our free-market society and our free illusions about that society. Has the crisis to be solved by the same people who grasped and used for their own benefit the volatile and complex rules of the capitalist dynamics? What the leading banker Lafitte said in 1830—"now the bankers will rule"—is the reality of today and a not very enjoyable one. Labor is now not the only source of value; the money game itself is creating wealth, and it's not at all certain, in our global and interconnected, metanational world, whether the enlightened liberal and democratic state, or communities of states, are able to push the powerful capitalists to disgorge part of their wealth, as Keynes had hoped and predicted they would. The world Marx was scrutinizing was a primitive capitalism, just beginning, as was his rationale. We may still want to ask ourselves if, in our evolved capitalism dominated by the power of the corporation, what he saw then as "constant revolutionizing of production, everlasting uncertainty and agitation" are not also valid observations in our complex, refined, populist, and worldly capitalism of today. For now, as then, "the need of a constantly expanding market for its product chases . . . Over the whole surface of the globe" with the need "to nestle everywhere, settle everywhere, establish connections everywhere." In every country there is the "cosmopolitan character to production and consumption."

Fortunately, we may still have reason not to see that "all that is solid melts into air, all that is holy is profaned."

We no longer expect and hope for a Marxist "abolition of private property" as the *Manifesto* proclaimed. Nor do we believe that the history of all hitherto existing society is only "the history of class struggles," or that any social class is better than another. We already know too well where such a vision might take us, what terrible consequences such a narrow-minded and oppressive project had. History has forced us to accept the imperfection of human beings. Resigned to accept reality and to wait no longer for idealistic, utopian theories for bettering the world, we have to accept the sometimes brutal pragmatism of our time.

We have to look to the new principal actors in the current crisis, to trust and scrutinize their knowledge, their lucidity and their own motives to solve the impasse. The rich own the world. They are the sponsors of our hospitals, stadiums, museums, monuments, and universities, the board members of the most important economic, cultural, and social institutions. They seem to possess the means for implementing drastic change or catastrophe.

The corporate mentality dominates the main sectors of society and we may wonder when exactly the post or public transportation, the Army and police—and even the White House—will be "privatized" in order to work efficiently and in accordance with the capitalist canon.

The class of the wealthy isn't a homogenous class and doesn't necessarily have the rebellious urge of those whom Marx called the proletarians. They turned out to be far from admirable in their role as icons of a new age just as the nouveau riche or even the old rich of today have failed to embody perfection. And I don't just have Mr. Madoff in mind.

"Capitalism with a human face" may be the latest echo of the enlightened Prague Spring of 1968 that announced the call-up of socialism with or without a human face. We should not forget the lessons of yesterday, nor should we forget that one class of humans is no better than another.

Should a *Manifesto of Capitalist Impasse* call for unity of all the rich people of the world? Should we emphasize the dark specter of chaos, and the urgent need for a solution? Perhaps our skepticism should be overcome by pragmatism. We might learn some lessons from the "dictatorship of the proletariat," a warning for the behind-the-scenes dictatorship of the privileged rich.

September 2011

THE DADA CAPITAL OF EXILES

I am looking down on Central Park and recall from half a century ago in a small town in northern Romania a tall, white-haired man proclaiming his poem, "The Colors Red and Black." Gazing over the park, I remember those Stalinist-era verses:

In New York, everything is beautiful.
Heroes come, heroes go.
Children, born for Sing Sing,
Cover the streets like pellagra.
Yellow karate-blood
Pulses through each building.
In the harbor the Statue of Liberty!
Behind her elevated falsehood
Yankee ghosts howl at the moon
Tormented as if from pellagra
By the colors red and black.

The red of the Revolution, of course, and the black of the oppressed race. Cliché was the common currency of all communist dictator-ships, but they had the opposite effect to what the regime intended, for they cast an aura of forbidden fruit around the slandered New World metropolis, making it seem a glowing Olympus of modernity, an urban Everest of adventure.

The few trips I was allowed to take as a citizen of socialist Ro-mania did, of course, have moments of rapture for me, novice that I was. Yet New York remained a dream, so foreign and distant that I never imagined I would have the chance to compare illusion with reality. My eventual escape to New York had nothing to do with tourism. Sudden terror before this omnipresent, all-devouring monster was soon overtaken by fascination.

The critic Irving Howe, a New Yorker of long standing, tried to temper my enthusiasm. "To enjoy this city you need a good apartment and a certain salary." I was living in a miserable hotel in a rundown neighborhood, consumed with a newcomer's neurotic insecurity. Yet I found everything irresistible: the city's rhythms and colors, its contrasts and surprises. That Walt Whitman and Mark Twain, Herman Melville, Henry James, and John Dos Passos had lived here, that Enescu, Brancusi, or Eugen Ionescu had been successful here in no way raised my hopes.

Life in and with this city was hypnotic as a drug. Over the last seventeen years this addiction was established through daily negotiations with life's routine. New York's metabolism filled me with its energy and its toxins.

Although I felt that I, an exile in the land of exiles, belonged even more to a world to which no one can really be said to belong, on September 11, 2001, I was finally able to proclaim, "I am a New Yorker," just as President Kennedy had declared himself a Berliner when that former National Socialist capital was in danger of being invaded by militant communists.

The Old Testament tells how work on the tower in Shinar, in ancient Babylon, was disrupted because man aspired to reach the heavens and divinity. Suddenly the builders could no longer understand each other. Different languages divided them. In present-day Babylon in Chinatown, in Little Italy, in Russian Brighton Beach, and in the alleys and byways of New York, all the world's languages are spoken. The builders of the Twin Towers, whatever their native tongues, wanted to be Americans, citizens of the New World, the towers they built symbolizing the stature of freedom.

The attack on the towers of Babel was unexpected but not unpredictable insofar as it represented the hatred of Allah's fanatical followers for the symbols of modernity. In the World Trade Center, human creativity and collaboration were universally codified. Of course, the building lacked poetry. Yet the towers could still have been a symbol of worldwide poetry, not commerce. As the Surrealist poet André Breton said, "It is above all our differences that unite us."

Surprisingly, for such an extensive, cynically efficient cluster of humanity, the city displayed surprising civility and solidarity during and after the attacks. It immediately regained its strength, its sense of humor, and its industriousness. After September 11, 2001, skyscrapers, clubs, and restaurants of all kinds sprang up like mushrooms, with almost more vitality than before. Moreover, the city refused to give its votes to a president who exploited its disaster for political gain.

Romania is often called the Land of Dada, not because one of its sons, Tristan Tzara, was a founder of Surrealism, but because of the absurdity and paradoxes of its daily life, particularly in its politics. In exile, I immediately identified with another capital of Dada, the "cosmic republic, that speaks all languages in a universal dialect," as Johannes Baader put it. Here, the old and the new are accomplices in celebrating life "in all its incomprehensibility"—exactly the subversiveness that the Dadaists loved.

A famous map painted by my friend and compatriot Saul Steinberg depicts the global village as seen from Manhattan: The distance from the Hudson River to the Pacific Ocean is the same as the distance from Ninth to Tenth Avenue on the Upper West Side, and somewhere beyond the calm ocean float Russia, China, and Japan. Saul's other maps evoke his past: Milan, the city of his youth; Zurich, where Dada got its explosive start; and the Romanian city Buzău, where he was born. (See "Made in Romania," above, pp. 176–86, for my essay on Saul Steinberg.)

A map of my own fate would encompass Bukovina as my native

land, the Transnistrian concentration camp of my childhood, the communist labor camp Periprava, where my father's identity was altered, the Bucharest of my student years and my adulthood, Berlin, my exile's starting point, and finally New York, where my exile found its residence. This fate is its own "Babel," a confused mixture of memories and places.

Here on the Upper West Side, in the middle of a triangle formed by Central Park, Lincoln Center, and the Hudson River, I was once in the habit of beginning each day with an exotic act of devotion, a ritual of humility. I now had a good apartment and a certain salary, so Irving Howe's conditions for life in the city were fulfilled. From my window, I washed the Rubbish Gangster: shaven head, bull neck, and swollen nose, from which dangled mucus-encrusted strands of hair, his short arms bursting with criminal power. Every day, at the same hour, he appeared with his metal trunk stuffed with all that he had collected from street-corner garbage cans; it was as if he wanted to ensnare me with his street sorcery so that I could see the city's unfathomable contrasts.

The writer, caught up in the shelter of solitude, does not have much time to wander about. His neighborhood is his world, the geography of his calendar. Luckily, the streets of New York offer extraordinary spectacles wherever one is. In the Bronx or in SoHo, in Washington Square or Times Square, in front of the New York Public Library or near a hot-dog stand, across all the planets' races, the banal vies with the exceptional for one's attention. All faces, ages, and events, sooner or later, can be found here.

Routine increases banality and thoughtlessness; the personal disappears. You pursue your business here as only New Yorkers can, but every once in a while you look up and wonder, "How did I get here?" Or, rather, "How on earth did mankind come so far?"

I often look at New York's architecture as if looking at an art book. On my way home from Bard College, in Annandale, where I teach,

I am greeted by the George Washington Bridge majestically suspended over the Hudson River. It is a glorious welcome, even in fog.

The same is true of the skyline. Approach the city and you see the urban center of the world—a hard and harried place, marked by social contrasts as dizzying as its skyscrapers and with a sense of transience as elevated as its buildings. Its workforce labors round the clock and its inventiveness, energy, and diversity counter provincialism with scorn. Like America itself, although so utterly different, New York can only be comprehended "synthetically." This festively incoherent capital of Dada is a spectacular fusion of freedom and pragmatism. Misery and magnificence, seduction and neurosis create and recreate the dynamic, unmistakable spectrum of New York life.

In this city you learn to limit yourself. It is impossible to take in all at once the innumerable symphonic or jazz concerts, or parades celebrating ethnic or sexual minorities. You can't attend all the lectures, panel discussions, and auctions where everyday dramas and dreams are bartered. You can't sit in all the taxis driven by these loquacious ambassadors from India and Russia and Haiti, from Pakistan and Ghana and Guatemala. At best you can grab a mere crumb of this frenetic global kaleidoscope. In the end, in New York you own nothing more than the instant, the now, the right now.

Again, I look over Central Park. "Dada covers things with an artificial tenderness," wrote Tzara. "It is snowing butterflies that have escaped from a prophet's head."

Translated from the German by Tess Lewis, 2005

Part III

THE FIFTH IMPOSSIBILITY

Like Kafka's own life, his works explore both an individuality, and simultaneously, the essential territory belonging to no one. To no one, and to anyone, and to each one, but above all, and after all, they explore the territory belonging to Kafka himself: the vast territory of uncertainty and of questioning. This space–time of existence and of writing becomes increasingly dramatic as it comes to be claimed by the obsession and by the sign . . . of the impossible. The geography, the psychology, the therapy, even the theology of the impossible?

Kafka was greatly concerned with the impossible. He considered himself a product of the impossible, which became his native soil and sky, and which he recreated ceaselessly as poetry—meaning, as life—with a magical and austere fixation.

In Kafkaesque terms, both the possible and the impossible are linked to the essential, seen as a monster of mutually inseparable halves: love and literature.

When he speaks about the fulfillment of love, Kafka refers to "impossibilities," almost in the same way as when he describes the manner of his writing: "And so, despite all, you want to bear the cross. To attempt the impossible?" Not waiting for an answer, Kafka hurries to sketch the premise: "There can be only three possible answers: 'it is impossible, and so I don't want to,' 'it is impossible, so I don't want to right now,' or 'it is impossible, so I want to.'"[1]

To forestall any remaining traces of confusion, he takes care to repeat what he has said before, on numerous occasions: "In an absurd way, I am terrified of the future and of the unhappiness that can result from my temperament and my deficiencies in our life together, which profoundly, and in the first place, will affect you, given that I am a cold, egotistical, unforgiving being, despite the weakness which conceals rather than tames these traits."

Many years after his inability to stay together with Felice Bauer had been confirmed, Kafka mentioned the situation of the Jewish writer writing in the German language to Max Brod. Again three impossibilities ("the impossibility of not writing," "the impossibility of writing in German," "the impossibility of writing differently"). Not surprisingly, he added a fourth impossibility: the "impossibility of writing."

Kafka will succeed in assuming, defeating, and reversing this "impossibility." He will succeed in making it nourishing (if we can use such a term) and creative, difficulty having become devotion and destiny ("I don't feel anything besides literature, and I can't and I don't want to be anything else"). He will do so only after understanding the personal impossibility of love, an impossibility which he will not cease to invoke, from whose trauma he will persist in extracting the aphrodisiacs of future failures. ("Impossible to live with F. Intolerable to live with anyone. I don't regret this; I regret the impossibility of living alone.") Only after he accepts and overcomes this "impossibility," only after he makes it nourishing, will it become devotion and destiny: "I am nothing but literature and I cannot and do not want to be anything else."

Walter Benjamin writes: "From the very moment he is certain of failure, everything seems to go without a hitch, like a dream. There is nothing more memorable than the fervor with which Kafka underlined his failure."

As much as it is sought and reclaimed, the possible cannot compete with the seduction and the complicities of the impossible. One might say that the possible and the impossible exist in a continuous and paradoxical complicity, as if they contained, singly and together, codified and replaceable parts of failure. The real seems to become substantial, meaningful, only when it is filled with the stigma and the significance of the impossible; the extreme individualization makes the real denser and more obscure, modifying its consistency, its colors, and its integrity through a sort of instantaneous, dark alchemy.

The impossible is not only the simplistic, irrevocable negation of the possible; it is also its sumptuous, enriching wound, which validates the sickly, nocturnal augmentation of unexplored availabilities through contrast and complicity.

Seen in this manner, as part of, and relative to, the possible, the impossible becomes a sort of revenge of the possible's deficiency transformed into proximity, an intense leap into nothingness.

Thirsty for the possible's domestic empire, the writer completed his true existential and literary apprenticeship by testing his inadequacy against the all too accessible reality of other individuals. The impossible resulted—imposing its surprising connections through the ambiguous ravishing of the possible—as a fecund and protean "unreality," whose enigmas the writer will explore, whose topography and topoi he will trace, and which will remain, in the end, the incomparable "K. Archipelago."

Herman Hesse was right when he said that Kafka's texts must be considered neither religious, nor metaphysical, nor moral, only poetic. Nevertheless, since Kafka remains the most Kafkaesque character of his own literary creation, his nocturnal existence as well as his intensely codified works cannot be purged of his unsettling questioning. The poetic relationship between the possible, the probable, and the impossible allows for a reading that repudiates limits, even the limits of poetry itself.

In the life and writing of Franz Kafka, uncertainty migrates, imposing its grip; it explodes even at the heart of the real, gaining in this manner an unexpected conspicuousness.

As much as he might have been attracted by the real and the possible, Kafka remained fixated on the pendulum and in the pendulations of the impossible, always interested in the mysterious game of the probabilities that destabilize reality, a reality which constantly fascinated him and for which he was always hungry, a reality which humiliated him and reconfirmed his alienation. Scrutinizing and experimenting with the one-on-one relationship between the possible and the impossible, between the real and the unreal, he did not hesitate to place the immediate and the expected chances of the real's success under continuous interrogation.

Kafka often referred to the two enemies which made up and destroyed his being, which defined themselves through this exhausting antagonism, enemies which could not be stopped:

> Among those at war within me, from whose confrontation I am primarily made—with the exception of a minuscule, tormented part—one is the good, the other one evil. From time to time, they change roles, which heightens the confusion of their already confounding confrontation. Until very recently, I could still imagine that the improbable would happen, a radiant perspective, the probable perspective being perpetual war. Suddenly, it seems that the loss of blood is too great. When the evil one will not find—possibly or probably—a decisive new defense weapon on his own, the good one will offer him precisely this. I thought that the war could last, but it can't. The blood doesn't come from the lungs, but from one of the combatants' decisive blows . . . it is not the type of tuberculosis with which one sits on a daybed and is nursed back to health, but a

weapon that continues to be of the utmost necessity as long as I continue living. And they [the combatants] cannot both live.

Kafka's secret hope of failing in his efforts to adjudicate the possible, his hope of being a man like any other, is made possible and simultaneously denied by the obstinacy with which he tests the password that would grant him access to the impossible. The impossible appeals to him again and again, seeking complicity and concupiscence. At last, the impossibility of being in the world imposes a solution, which is nothing more than a trick, like the mathematical abstraction *ad nihilum*, but which nevertheless becomes the regimen of survival: living in impossibility, as one of the paradoxically animate forms of life.

"See how many impossibilities are in our letters. Impossibilities on all sides!" writes Kafka to Felice Bauer in one of the numerous letters addressed to the unknown—which is invoked and asked to assume a name and a face—rather than to the being who had caught his attention. "To write letters, to undress in front of the greedy ghosts that wait precisely for this," the sender would note carefully.

When he mentioned the difference between "minor" and "major" impossibilities, Kafka still seemed willing to believe that his addressee was part of the latter category, justifying in this manner his epistolary fervor: "we must not bow down before minor impossibilities, otherwise the major impossibilities will no longer allow themselves to be perceived."

With each new step on the unstable terrain of the underground, between the two types of impossibilities, Kafka underwent his true apprenticeship, not only the sentimental but the literary, coming to know and to embody himself. Felice Bauer, the fiancée whom he left and to whom he became close again only in order to break up with her definitively, is indeed the genuine embodiment of the "possible," of the normality which Kafka had convinced himself he desired as a sort of salvation, but which he discovered to be foreign, annihilating, and inaccessible, a normality which, with all his efforts at "destabilization," he did not succeed in toppling from its solid enjambment in the real. "For almost 5 years I have kept striking at her, or if you prefer, at myself," Kafka will later confess. "Happily, she was unbreakable, that strong, invincible Jewish–Prussian mix. I wasn't as strong; after all, she was only suffering, while I struck *and* suffered."

At the tail end of many delays, the letter to Carl Bauer in which Kafka asked for his daughter's hand in fact transcribes a last desperate attempt—not to transform the impossible into the possible but to place a definitive tombstone over the possibility of marriage. It is at this moment that the fiancée also receives the sentence of freedom, through which the marriage betrays its essence: "the mistake is precisely in this general impossibility," the Kafkaesque verdict decrees.

We thus understand how exactly impossibility—a "major" impossibility, certainly not the banal chance of marriage—tempted the writer with masochistic predispositions toward self-blame; we understand why the "suitor" prolonged his game, with its damned black beads. "The union we have all wished for has now been recognized as impossible by each," stands the conclusion of the experiment, after the breaking off of the first engagement, at the beginning of the long travail before the second engagement, which will lead to the inevitable: a last decisive breakup with Felice, by means of a letter in which the sender describes himself in an uncompassionate and unjust way in order to have the desired disastrous effect on the fiancée's parents.

In the vast Kafkaesque underground of selfhood, the ambiguous interaction of the possible/probable/impossible proves more ample and more significant than reality itself. The dynamics of this disquieting turn also mark the Kafkaesque opus. The arrival at *The Castle*, a possibility seemingly on hand, though always put off, heightens its mystery not necessarily by means of its inaccessibility, but by means of the suggestion that the act of entering demands unexplored, or still unknown, solutions, which cannot and must not be differentiated from the traps in which they hide and with which they identify.

The Trial begins—seemingly without motive and without warning—from the vast caprices of the possible and gradually configures its own epic (which even becomes a motivation), in which the absurd, in the double role of cause and effect, plays the humble yet arrogant role of intermediary between more and more obscure trapdoors of implication—of culpability.

As a type of perfection, "the possibility" of being "A Hunger Artist," who perfects his skill to its final consequence, meaning death, is in fact an impossibility which sets in motion the ambiguity of the role as a whole. In the Kafkaesque manner, the anthropomorphizing process enriches the canon of literary fable, as can be seen in "Investigations of a Dog" and "Josephine the Singer, or the Mouse Folk," as well as in a text like "The New Advocate," which begins thus:

> We have a new advocate. Dr. Bucephalus. There is little in his appearance to remind you that he was once Alexander of Macedon's battle charger. Of course, if you know his story, you are aware of something. But even a simple usher whom I saw the other day on the front steps of the Law Courts, a man with the professional appraisal of the regular small punter in a racecourse, was running an admiring eye over the advocate as he mounted the marble steps with the high action that made them ring beneath his feet.[2]

Paradoxically, in *The Metamorphosis*, the impossible is born and domesticated by the miraculous into a theater of complicities. The revelation of the impossible is not estranged from the revelation of the dangerous potentialities of an inoffensive possible. The border between the two states is frequently undermined, forcing the possible to offer up its disquieting unreality in the form of oneiric visions and bringing the impossible into the most banal and phantasmal proximity to the possible. Only when he becomes an insect does Gregor, in fact, become what he had always been but had understood only rarely. Only then does his true "place" in the family and in the world start to become clear. The interiority that had always been ignored can no longer be concealed, the questions that had been put off for so long become urgent.

The Samsa family reveals itself as well through the self-consuming tragedy. Only after the most devoted member of the family, more and more estranged, suspect precisely because of his excessive devotion, is forced to exhibit his "dissociation," and is no longer able to repress the secret, does the "normalized" family rediscover its cohesion and its responsibilities, its enterprising spirit and its hopes.

The metamorphosis seems scandalous because of the drastic and ultimatum-giving manner in which it acts on the real, but it exhausts its function not in the realm of the fantastic or in that of the impossible, in the unreal, as might be expected, but in the most modest routine of the quotidian. The metamorphosis imperiously demands to be considered and thus eliminated as a form of reality, as simple reality, not as shock or nightmare. Everything then reenters the sphere of fantastic normality. What else could we call the disappearance without a trace of the unfamiliar family member who had been, until the previous day, an inseparable part of the Samsa quartet? Gregor was not capable of defining himself outside the perimeters of the family, and perhaps it is because of this that he is at last forced to define himself outside the perimeters of the world. Only in this manner, incarcerated in his old self and in his new insect self, does his humanity breathe free, intensely, painfully, suicidally: the insect with a human soul proves to be more "human" than those around it, more human than they can bear to think.

When Kafka refers to the Jewish question, and related to this, to the problem of the Jewish writer's language, the problem of his homeland, he is referring again to the impossible. To him—from his point of view, which to him *is* the central point of view—the Jewish question seems negated, forbidden, impossible. "You have your homeland and you can relinquish it, which is perhaps the best thing one can do with one's homeland, especially since you don't relinquish the unrelinquishable part of it. But he doesn't have a homeland, he doesn't have what is to be relinquished, and he must always think to seek it out, to build it up, even when he doffs his hat or when he lies in the sun or learns to write a book which you won't translate . . . yes, Max must always think about this, even when he writes a letter to you," Kafka writes to Milena, speaking of Max Brod, but no less of himself. "Writing a book which you won't translate . . . even writing a letter to you" . . . Not only the question of belonging, but the question of language is already suggested with discretion and patience.

Kafka defines himself to his Czech lover and friend as "the most typical of occidental Jews. This means, with slight exaggerations, that I haven't been given even one second of peace, everything had to be won, not only the present and future, but even the past—that which every human being has inherited, even this had to be won."

We understand why, in a letter addressed to Max Brod and in his conversation with Janouch, Kafka maintains that the Jewish question or "the despair related to it" has, in fact, unified the inspiration of Jewish-German writers. A thematic full of "impossibilities," Kafka explains . . . because this problem expresses itself in a (German) literature which seems to be a fitting destination only on the surface. In reality, however, given that there exists no rational reason for accepting this transfer ("since the problem is not really a German one"), the writers who assume such an undertaking are confronted with three impossibilities, which Kafka lists and analyzes. These impossibilities apparently refer only to the problem of language, but naturally they go on to overstep it. For Kafka, as for any writer and more than for any writer, the word is itself the essence of being, the deepest of all depths and the center of selfhood. In this sense, as in many others, Kafka pushes Jewish tradition to the extreme, pushes meaning to its true premise: "Language has been an issue of life and death for Jews ever since the nomadic tribe destroyed the idols and stood in their place the word as God. To live and to die as a member of this tribe means strictly following the *word* of God having become *Law*," Ernst Pawel, Kafka's biographer, accurately points out.

The first impossibility to which Kafka refers is "the impossibility of not writing."

"I could have built the pyramids with the effort needed to keep me alive and to keep me rational," he wrote to Felice Bauer on April 13, 1913. We understand what it means "to keep alive." He himself admits it in another letter to Felice, just a week later: "I am awake only among my imaginary characters" (April 20, 1913). He will repeat it in his August 14 epistle: "I do not have literary interests, I am made of literature. I am nothing else and I cannot be anything else." He repeats it even more drastically in a letter to Felice's father of August 28, 1913: "my entire being is bent towards literature." For Kafka, this is what it means "to keep alive." "My entire existence is bent towards literature . . . the second I abandon it, I cease living. Everything I am and am not is a consequence of this."

And, in another letter, on June 26, 1913: "My attitude towards writing and towards people cannot be changed; it is a part of my nature and not circumstance . . . just as the dead should not be and cannot be pulled from their graves, just so I cannot pull myself from my table at night . . ." "I cannot write and consequently live," he notes seemingly in passing, tracing the indissoluble relation between writing and "keeping alive," in an epistle sent less than two months before the one cited above, in April 1913: "I cannot write and consequently live except in this systematic, continuous, strict way . . . I have always been afraid of the world, not of the world itself, properly speaking, but of its intrusion into my feeble existence." Lastly, an expected affirmation in a letter of August 20 of the same year: "In my view, the spoken word eliminates the importance and the seriousness from everything I say. Writing is the only form of expression that suits me."

"To travel the night with my writing, this is all that I wish for. And so to die or to lose my mind, this is, also, what I wish for, given that it is the inevitable and the long anticipated consequence." Such a profession of faith needs no commentaries. Kafka is nothing but literature not because literature is something different from life, but precisely because it is the most bizarre and most complete embodiment of life, more alive than life itself, and, at the same time, its posthumous quintessence. "The infinite feeling continues to be unlimited in words, as it was in the heart," he writes.

In Kafka's case, more than in anyone else's, the impossibility of not writing equals not living, no longer being able to keep alive. "I am nothing else but literature and I cannot and I do not want to be anything else."

Kafka formulates the second impossibility as "the impossibility of writing in German." He sees a tragic estrangement and a vulgar usurpation in the use of the German language: "Openly present or masked, or perhaps a self-tormented usurpation of a foreign property . . . which remains in the possession of an Other, even if not one linguistic mistake can be pointed out." The estrangement appears as a consequence of the ambiguity of an Other, a fissured, hunted being, in search of a "coming into possession" which would legitimize and justify it. Kafka seems to consider the acquisition and the use of the German language as a betrayal of identity, even as an act of piracy, imagined as the snatching of a foreign babe from its cradle and one's abusive acquisition of it.

In a letter to Max Brod, of June 1921, Kafka reminds him that "most of those who have begun to write in German wanted to distance themselves from their Jewishness, usually with the vague approval of the father—the vagueness was precisely what made the approval scandalous. They wanted to distance themselves, but their hind legs held on to their father's Jewishness, while the front ones met with no firm ground. And the despair which resulted served them as inspiration." The Other appears as a grotesque figure gifted with four legs, but grotesquely unstable, the hind legs rooted in the old paternal soil, while the front ones flail in the void above the precipice.

Just as the delivery of one's own identity—negotiable through the command of the real—becomes a form of treason, similarly trading one's identity for another implies a usurpation. Kafka expresses himself categorically in relation to the act of usurpation of a foreign "possession" (language) belonging to another, even when not one single linguistic error can be found in the writing of the Other. (Is one speaking strictly of an "ethnic" possession? Kafka and so many other writers and linguists have brilliantly proven in their works what G. Calinescu pointed out in relation to the great Romanian linguists of Jewish origin, in his *History of Romanian Literature*, which had appeared during the difficult period of the nationalist dictatorship: the intellectual character of language.) Today, in our centrifugal modernity, it would seem that intense "migration" accelerates the impurity and the mobility of all languages seized from their native cradle, and that the "foreign" child participates in the same hurried immersion in the hybrid language of the epoch, this language having become a global home. The premise from which Kafka begins, contradicted both yesterday and today by the writing of other master craftsmen like himself, as well as by an ever expanding world of the exiled, in fact speaks revealingly only about Kafka's own suffering.

The linguistic "piracy" of the foreigner? . . . The severe and exaggerated accusation rather allows one to detect Franz Kafka's own suffering, brought about by his contact with the real, his persistent suspicion with regard to the real. When he refers to the uncertain position of the Jew in the world, we might think today of the growing and diversifying population of all sorts of exiles, "uncertain"—as Kafka writes in a letter to Milena—"in themselves, and in the midst of humanity . . . urged to believe that only tangible possessions give them the right to survive."

The impossibility of writing in German also means the impossibility of living authentically, with full accreditation, in German. Of course, we remember the famous episode of Kafka's conversation with some fellow guests during a vacation, when his interlocutors, German officers, after a few of Kafka's replies, probably intrigued by subtle and bizarre phonetic differences, inquired about the "real" place of his origin:

> Today, when I entered the dining room, the colonel invited me so cordially to their table that I had to give in. So everything followed its course. After the first few words, it was made clear that I was from Prague. Both of us, the general, who was in front of me, and the colonel, were familiar with Prague. So I am Czech? Well. Try to explain to these veritable German officers what you are in fact. Someone suggested "German from Bohemia," and someone else "from a small neighborhood." Then the subject was dropped and the lunch began, but the general, with his acute linguistic sensitivity, schooled in the Austrian army, was not satisfied. After we finished the meal, he began again to marvel at the sound of my German, perhaps more disturbed by what he saw than what he heard. At this point, I tried to explain that I am Jewish. Certainly, his scientific curiosity was then satisfied, but not his human feelings. In that moment, probably simply by chance—since the others could not hear our conversation, even if a certain connection existed—the entire group got up to leave, even though yester-

day they had stayed on quite a while after lunch. The general too was very anxious to go, even though, ever so politely, he had brought our small chat to a sort of conclusion, before hurrying, with great big steps, towards the exit. This didn't really satisfy my human feelings either: why should I be a thorn in their side? To have to remain alone, without exploding in a ridiculous fashion, lest they then invent some disciplinary measure against me.

At a certain point, Kafka confesses in his *Journal* that even his love for his mother seems derailed by the alienation of German expression.

What about the fear and the horror, the attachment and the repulsion, the compassion and the awkwardness provoked by his love–hate relationship with his father? How would the famous *Letter to My Father* have sounded if it had initially been written in Czech or, let us say, in Yiddish? What would have become of Kafka's feelings and resentments?

The third impossibility with which the Jewish-German writer is confronted while trying to follow his inspiration (meaning his despair) is "the impossibility of writing differently." Does differently mean "in another language?"

In a letter to Milena, Kafka confesses: "I have never lived among the Germans, German is my mother tongue, my natural tongue, but Czech is closer to my heart." This is not only an indirect declaration of love for his young Czech translator, with whom he would maintain close relations, but also a declaration of love for other virtualities of the impossible, a reiteration of his incurable suspicions regarding the "attainable," regarding the deceitful and corrupting hospitality of the possible. Yiddish, he thinks, could instill "a belief in himself which would overcome fear." Kafka would reaffirm this intuition—also aspiration—above all in his correspondence with Max Brod. His relationship to Hebrew is vague, from afar, but its invocation seems no less intense. Again, it is a sort of *impossible*, essential, and last rediscovery, a language which he would hear frequently on his deathbed thanks to the young Dora Diamant, a rabbi's daughter, who not only brightened his last days on earth but initiated her moribund lover in the sacred language before he died. Nothing, however, could resolve the unsolvable. Kafka had been born in the German language, he had formed and deformed himself in the language of his writing. His servitude to the mother tongue? More than anyone else, as much as he might like to do so, the writer cannot give up the placenta. The borders of the mother tongue are both circumscribing and limitless. The writer himself makes possible the depths of the "possibility" in which he in fact lives. In Kafka's case, to speculate regarding another way of writing would be a vulgar innocence and an impertinence.

As the American writer Cynthia Ozick accurately observes, Kafka's fear was not that the German language didn't belong to him— he possessed it brilliantly—but that he did not . . . deserve it. Is it "the wish and the crisis of the split of the psyche from the articulation of expression," as Cynthia Ozick thinks? In fact, Kafka insinuates that it is impossible to be Kafka when he writes that "every day at least one line must be aimed at myself. I try constantly to communicate the incommunicable. After all, it is nothing else but fear . . . fear radiating over everything, a small and great fear, the paralyzing fear of uttering a word, even though this fear could also be the aspiration towards something greater than any fear."

To the three assumed negations, Kafka adds a fourth, namely "the impossibility of writing" pure and simple: "since despair was not something that could be tamed by writing."

A sort of contradiction in terms, since the desperation to which he had referred from the very beginning had become for him, as for other German-Jewish writers, and perhaps for more than them, as he had himself observed, a source of . . . inspiration, a stimulus for writing.

His suffering could only partially be abated by writing and could not be abated even by writing. As for language, Paul Celan had affirmed even after the Holocaust that *language is the homeland of the writer even when the language is German and the writer a Jew.* The despair to which Kafka refers becomes—as he confesses—"an enemy" of life itself, and so an enemy of writing, a sort of suicidal "moratorium," the last wish and testament before suicide: "writing was, in this case, only a moratorium, as for someone who writes his last wish and Testament, before hanging himself."

Only in his epistolary writings would Kafka use the word "Jew" to describe his despair; never in his literary works. "You ask me if I am Jewish," he writes to Milena Jasenska at the beginning of their relationship. "Perhaps what you are really asking is whether I am one of those anxious Jews"—meaning those Jews who do not resemble Milena's not at all anxious Jewish husband but rather are tormented, as Kafka himself, by their identity.

Kafka's relationship with his coreligionists is none other than the relationship with his writing: inevitability and insupportability, an equivocal relationship exhausted by stimulation and handicap. If we remind ourselves of his relationship with his writing and of his wish that his manuscripts be burned, we understand better, perhaps, Kafka's tortured and heroic acceptance even of this "impossible" premise, under which he continued to write and so to live. "What do I have in common with the Jews?" he asks in his diary in 1914. The possibility even when it is already an unshakeable reality might instantly become a typical Kafkaesque doubt and impossibility: "I have hardly anything in common with myself and should stand very quietly in a corner, content that I can breathe"—is a Kafkaesque Jewish answer to the Kafkaesque Jewish question.

The acuteness with which Kafka felt his "estrangement," his inadequacy in the face of existence as a premise of his life and writing, is clearly revealed by the four "impossibilities" he names. To these impossibilities I would add a fifth, surprisingly omitted by Kafka. It is an impossibility that, in a certain manner, includes all of the others, giving them potential and, paradoxically, precisely in this manner, also minimizing them, if not wholly neutralizing them; more precisely, it lessens their importance. We could name this impossibility "the translation," or "the radicalization," or "the carnivalizing of impossibility": exile. The exile before and after exile, the alienation at home and that of the ever-after through the expulsion of the foreigner, with his stolen language; this, in a truly foreign medium—linguistically, geographically, historically, and socially.

At last, the preceding three, even four, impossibilities become under threat of annihilation, Kafka's most precious property. Both a terrible and a privileged trauma, as I have often said. The interior and the anterior exile are transformed only now, in an extreme situation, one that cannot be escaped: *exile* itself. Exile from a language "stolen" and made one's own to the point of self-identification; exile from the country that had been the Homeland. To someone for whom it had always been a contested issue, the simplicity and the force of the notion of "Homeland" is reaffirmed at the very moment it is abolished. Let us remember again Celan's words after the Holocaust: *language is the homeland of the writer even when the language is German and the writer a Jew.*

The possibility of expatriation was not only just one more demonic variation of the impossible which tempted Kafka, whose seeker and slave he acknowledged himself to be. It was also a command, sometimes concrete and immediate, coming both from the ancient past of the tribe that had been driven off, and from a tangible immediacy, from the proximity of the environment he inhabited. "I have spent all afternoon out on the streets, bathed in Jew hatred"—he had once written to Milena. "*Prasive plemeno* [Czech expression for 'filthy brood'] is what I heard them call the Jews. Isn't it only natural to leave a place where one is so bitterly hated? . . . I've just looked out the window: mounted police, a riot squad ready for a bayonet charge, the screaming mob dispersing, and up here at the window, the ugly shame of always having to live under protection."[3]

The Homeland, the place where he is wished dead . . . a revealing truth regarding a certain Homeland . . . but also regarding a larger and more heterogeneous family: "the Homeland" as the place of birth, not only a linguistic locus but a geographical, historical, and national locus, and, by extension, a family of nations. From this point of view, the text of *The Metamorphosis* can be seen as one of the most terrible literary portraits of the impending Holocaust, symbolizing not only the individual's but also a collective destiny of rejection and annihilation.

The German-Jewish writer lived and survived in his "Homeland" through the contradictory and creative convergence of three, even four impossibilities. Should he abandon them in favor of a more severe, a more complete, contradiction, one even less inhabitable? Translated with the other four impossibilities into a radical and opaque fifth impossibility, that of total estrangement, the exile is now faced not only with a *reductio ad absurdum*, frequent in mathematical problems without an immediate solution, but also with the extrapolating annihilation of the absurd. This he inhabits and allows it to inhabit him, in the fullness of absurdity and intensified estrangement from himself.

Exile itself, the reiterated and radicalized exile, transforms him into the most expressive symbol of impossibility. Given the proportions of the estrangement, the impossibilities—having become *the impossibility*—become an almost comic "negation of the negations," providing the tragic with its depth, taking it to its limit, and freeing it simply by offering it the energy of the carnivalesque, the acute conscience of the farce of being in the world.

Further than ever before from the sedentary normality of those hosted by a Homeland, a language, a community, an illusion of stability and of meaning, only now does the many-times-over exile embody the true human condition, valid always and everywhere, the inevitable condition of any mortal, called—so that all may understand—the vanity of vanities.

In its tragicomic extremism, this global "impossibility" continues to become more and more global today, in our cosmopolitan, postmodern, centrifugal world, a world that is both post- and intensely Kafkaesque, a world in which—whether it be New York, Mexico City, or Mumbai—the writer who writes in German, or Russian, or Spanish personifies exactly the unforeseeable potentialities of the fifth, the most encompassing, impossibility, that which has become the emblem of our time: an age which has been called the age of "all possibilities" and not only by the ironists.

It seems surprising that Franz Kafka did not mention this fifth impossibility, the most Kafkaesque of all, though he thought about it more than once. "I am here, at the General Society of Insurance, and still I hope to be in faraway countries, at a window above sugar-cane plantations, or looking out towards Muslim cemeteries." The exile of his family, of love and profession, the exile par excellence, any time and anywhere, did not necessarily have to meditate on the hypothesis of expatriation. We see this hypothesis in "The Hunter Gracchus," in "Jackals and Arabs," or in a shorter text like "The Wish to Be A Red Indian," which one should cite in full: "If one were only an Indian, instantly alert, and on a racing horse, leaning against the wind, kept on quivering jerkily over the quivering ground, until one shed one's spurs, for there needed no spurs, threw away the reins, for there needed no reins, and hardly saw that the land before one was smoothly shorn heath when horse's neck and head would be already gone."[4]

We see it also in "The Great Wall of China," as an opposition, but also as an unfinished and unfinishable preparation for a new

Tower of Babel. A horizontally sprawling construction, a solid, infinite "foundation" which the collapsed Tower had never had (having been in too great a hurry to reach the heights). Built to protect against an enemy that no one had ever seen but which was thought to be human, certainly not divine, the Wall, in fact, defends the Authority; the construction of "portions," whose meeting point is unknown, is at last divided into parcels and given to each individual citizen, who in turn comes to be identified with his or her parcel, whose existence is occupied and symbolized by a portion of the Wall. The force of the edifice is based on the weakness of each of its builders, all of whom are incapable of overthrowing the Authority, which resides in the enigmatic and far-off Center, by pulling this Authority towards them and so undoing it. This weakness fulfills the "unity of the people" and is the "earth" on which this population lives; its condemnation would mean the "shattering" not only of conscience but, even worse, of "the earth under one's feet."

The text, of a hallucinatory precision and stylistic aridity, perfectly adequate for a "report," scrutinizes the illusion of total and totalitarian coherence, the never-reached "fulfillment" of the utopian Project. Life itself is home to estrangement and indifference, meaning exile, consumed in ephemeral "portions" of destiny without destiny.

One could name exile, the fifth impossibility—fulfilling an interrogatory function for all the other impossibilities—as the impossibility of the operetta, to borrow E.M. Cioran's words, according to whom it is better to write operettas than to write in a foreign language.

Perhaps, it would also be suggestive to name it "the impossibility of the snail." Meaning, the impossibility of continuing to write in exile, even when the writer takes his language with him. The shell allows for refuge anywhere the snail may happen to go, but how utterly endangered it is, through its relocation; the life of its inhabitant is glimpsed as soon as he imprudently raises his antennae, antennae unprepared for the new earth, new sky, and new creatures, or for the appealing or hostile sounds of their languages. The shipwreck of the snail in the torrid and tormented desert of the dynamic, modern Babel more than once destroys his chances of survival.

Such an extreme situation seems drawn from the Kafkaesque premise itself, and our forerunner K could not but be un-attracted by such an extravagant hypothesis of self-destruction. Meaning, salvation through self-destruction: "The idea that Tibet is far away from Vienna seems silly to me," Kafka writes to Milena. "I am reading a book about Tibet; at a description of a settlement close to the Tibetan frontier, in the mountains, my heart grows suddenly heavy; this village seems so empty, so far away from Vienna. That which I call silly is the idea that Tibet is far away from Vienna. Is it really so far?" he asks her, asking himself, knowing all too well that the emptiness is not really far off at all, but dangerously close to Vienna, to Prague, to the house of his family, to the General Society of Insurance, to the room of his solitude. The sugarcane plantations had not really been far off either, nor the Islamic cemeteries, nor the Great Wall. It is not necessary to imagine Kafka in Saudi Arabia, or in communist China, or in Brazil, where the very un-Kafkaesque Viennese Jew, Stefan Zweig, would later, in exile, kill himself in order to authenticate one of the most expressive and most frequent Kafkaesque situations of the new millennium, hurrying to shatter memories and hopes. Similarly, it is not necessary to imagine Kafka in the New York of his protagonist, Karl Rosmann, in the city of exiles par excellence, or to imagine him nearby, in Newark, "in the room in the house of an elderly Jewish lady, on the shabby lower stretch of Avon Avenue," as in *Looking at Kafka*, by Philip Roth.

In any case, in the nocturnal room of his Prague exile, Kafka had been in these and in many other places far away and nowhere at all. Like many of Kafka's other premonitions, this "impossibility"—unstated, but nevertheless lived and expressed with the same anxiety and force—would surprisingly go on to fertilize the topoi of contemporary reality.

Kafkaesque posterity has extended the condition of the Jew to many other categories of exiles, without, however, nullifying the Jewish "impossibility." Primo Levi saved himself at Auschwitz through the German language. After the Holocaust, Paul Celan continued, despite Adorno's warning, to write not only poems but *poetry* in the language of his mother's butchers. To the end, the homeland of Mandelstam remained the Russian language, the language in which Stalin had signed his death warrant.

The generalized exile of postmodern global society has extended possibilities while trivializing the impossibilities of the exiled text, and all in a period which euphemistically calls its deviations and incoherence "mobility."

Joyce, Musil, and Thomas Mann, Conrad and Nabokov, Gombrowicz and Bashevis Singer, Beckett and Ionescu, Brodsky, Cortázar, and Danilo Kiš have conferred a new legitimacy on expatriation, along with everything that the keeping or abandoning of the maternal language in exile means. They are the forerunners of the world of vast interferences in which we live. It is difficult to imagine Kafka in the New World of today and even more difficult to see him in the clownish role of telegenic prompter of his own Works, as the computerized entertainment corporation of the Planetary Circus demands. The manner in which the solitary Franz Kafka surpassed the impossibilities he faced without truly surpassing them, surviving in the German language of his estrangement, reminds our memoryless epoch of the hope without hope contained in his unrepeatable model.

If, in our fight against the world, we must, in the end, take the part of the world against ourselves, as Kafka advised us to do, the lay prayer of writing remains a last refuge for refusal, as well as for resignation. After all, the suspect who prays through writing doesn't only exist as a mythic creation of profane letters spinning around the anagrammatic mystery of the world, still seeking his place in the repertoire of curiosities of so many derisory Homelands, but is real in his exile, and in his exiled reality embodies all of the impossibilities of his existence.

Translated by Carla Baricz, 2011

Notes

1. Here and throughout this essay, quotes from Kafka's letters are from Franz Kafka, *Letters to Felice*, trans. by James Stern and Elisabeth Duckworth (New York: Schocken Books, 1973).

2. Franz Kafka, *The Metamorphosis, In the Penal Colony, and Other Stories*, trans. Joachim Neugroschel (New York: Touchstone, 2000), 135.

3. Ernst Pawel, *The Nightmare of Reason* (New York: Farrar, Straus, Giroux, 1984), 408–9.

4. Franz Kafka, *The Complete Short Stories*, trans. Willa and Edwin Muir, ed. Nahum N. Glatzer (London: Vintage Books, 2005), 390.

INDEX